THE NEW STATE

AMS PRESS
New York

THE NEW STATE

by VICTOR PRADERA: *translated from the Spanish by* BERNARD MALLEY: *with a foreword by His Royal Highness* THE PRINCE OF ASTURIAS

LONDON

SANDS & CO.

(PUBLISHERS LTD.)

15 KING STREET, COVENT GARDEN, W.C.2

And at 76 Cambridge Street, Glasgow

Library of Congress Cataloging in Publication Data

Pradera, Víctor, 1872-
    The new state.

    Translation of El estado nuevo.
    Reprint of the 1939 ed.
    1. Church and state--Catholic Church.
2. State, The. I. Title.
JC271.P72 1974   261.7   79-180421
ISBN 0-404-56196-9

Reprinted from the edition of 1939, London
First AMS edition published in 1974
Manufactured in the United States of America

AMS PRESS INC.
NEW YORK, N.Y. 10003

FOREWORD

IT is with a certain diffidence that I have agreed to write the preface to this book. I greatly regret that the privilege of fighting for my country was denied me, first when acting under the impulse of my feelings, I went to Spain at the beginning of the war, and later by Generalissimo Franco himself when I asked him to let me have a place in the Navy. I feel that I should have had more hope of acquitting myself with credit in this simpler form of controversy than in dialectical argument. Nevertheless, perhaps one who is half English may be allowed to say a few words to help Englishmen to understand Spain when presenting them with the English version of the last work of Victor Pradera. He was one of Spain's greatest modern thinkers, and he died for the ideals for which he lived and for which he had worked.

My mother is a granddaughter of Queen Victoria, and my uncle, Prince Maurice of Battenberg, was killed serving as a second lieutenant in the 60th Rifles in October, 1914. I myself served for five exceptionally happy years in the British Navy, and it is therefore very sad for me to find that my own countrymen are troubled and perplexed by the British attitude, and that the British do not understand the issues in Spain.

I personally am convinced, and am always telling my Spanish friends, that the British have an ingrained sense of fair play, and that their misconceptions of the Spanish war are due to the fact that they have not been properly informed. There is a homely English proverb, "What is sauce for the goose is sauce for the gander." Let me try and apply it to recent events in Spain.

1. *So-called Rebellion.* In 1934, when Russia subsidized an armed rebellion in Asturias, the very people who in England to-day are denouncing Franco for rising against the legal Government, applauded the rebels and denounced the Government for suppressing the rebellion.

2. *Foreign Intervention.* Russia intervened in 1934, two years before an Italian or a German landed in Spain. In August, 1936, whilst the French "Front Populaire" was busily engaged in sending troops and ammunition into Spain, Franco was carrying on without any help.

3. *Air Bombardment.* Great Britain was greatly stirred by the air bombardment of the military objectives in Barcelona and Valencia. Admittedly the whole question of how far one is entitled to bomb a military objective, knowing that civilians will probably be killed, is a difficult one. As one who is half English, I can quote from the official *The War in the Air*:

> "The policy intended to be followed is to attack the important German towns systematically. . . . It is intended to concentrate on one town for successive days, and then to pass to several other towns, returning to the first town until the target is thoroughly destroyed, or at any rate, the morale of the workmen is so shaken that the output is seriously interfered with.
>
> "Long-distance bombing will produce its maximum moral effect only if the visits are constantly repeated at short intervals, so as to produce in each area bombed a sustained anxiety. It is this recurrent bombing, as opposed to isolated spasmodic attacks, which interrupts industrial production and undermines public confidence" (Appendix 6, Vol. VI).

Mr. Winston Churchill on civil casualties (Appendix IV):

". . . our air offensive should consistently be directed at striking at the bases and communications upon whose structure the fighting power of his armies and his fleets of the sea and of the air depends. Any injury which comes to the civil population from this process of attack must be regarded as incidental and inevitable" (October 21st, 1917).

May I be forgiven for pointing out that in the earlier period in the war, when the Republicans had supremacy in the air and systematically bombed open towns with no military objectives in Nationalist territory, there were no protests from England or from English ecclesiastics.

May I, in this connection, deal with the traditional British view that, so far as atrocities are concerned, it is "six of one and half a dozen of the other." Surely there is a universe of difference between accidentally killing civilians while attacking military objectives, and deliberately murdering men, women and children in cold blood. The Badajoz and Guernica myths have been analysed and refuted in Mr. Robert Sencourt's admirable book, *Spain's Ordeal*. I need deal no further with those points. It is important to insist that the atrocities on the Republican side are not a question of opinion, but of admitted fact, since the Spanish Embassy in London did not deny the Burgos Report, and, indeed, explicitly admitted that the Report was correct. Their defence was that they could not control these excesses; and yet the people who back this Government, which on its own admission has been unable to prevent the massacre of hundreds of thousands of civilians, men, women and children, claims the sympathy of Britain as a representative, democratic Government. Fortunately the truth is beginning to prevail. The simple device of labelling Communists, Socialists, or even Liberals, has succeeded for some considerable time, but English people are beginning to discover that Spanish Socialists are different from English Conservative Trade-unionists who describe themselves as Socialists. Mr. Attlee and Mr. Lansbury would certainly not feel at home if they stayed longer than a few days in Red Spain!

The Times, which throughout the war has scrupulously refrained from reproving either side, has maintained its high reputation for objectivity in its news services, and has summed up the situation in a memorable leading article which appeared on May 3rd, 1938:

> "Loudly as the Barcelona Government may denounce the unprovoked aggression of General Franco's rebels, their mentors in Moscow have already claimed the instigation of the Civil War as a triumph of their own subversive diplomacy. For this is one of the essential stages of the desired revolution, which must, it is dogmatically asserted, follow the same course in every country. These steps to the compulsory millenium are four in number: The first is the 'united front,' the second, strikes and disorders, the third, civil war, and the fourth, Soviet government."

The verdict of *The Times* was confirmed from an unsuspected source. Mr. John McGovern, M.P., representing the Independent Labour Party, an honest and convinced opponent of our cause, paid a special visit to Barcelona, and confirmed the view that the controlling power in Red Spain is the Russian Cheka.

The so-called "Black Legend," which has done so much to harm our cause in England, is composed of three factors: the Spanish Inquisition, bull-fighting, and the Conquistadores. As to the Spanish Inquisition, on the evidence of Llorente, a bitter opponent and ex-secretary of the Inquisition, it put to death 32,000 people in three centuries. On the evidence of the *Manchester Guardian*, a paper which has been favourable to the Reds, 40,000 people were killed in Madrid in the first three months of the war. Therefore, the Red Terror was a thousand times more destructive of life than that much-hated institution, the Spanish Inquisition.

As to the Conquistadores, I, as a Spaniard, am proud to feel that the spirit of a Cortés or a Pizarro, who conquered a Continent with a handful of men, has been reborn in those young leaders who are fighting to-day for the true and everlasting Spain. Nationalist Spain, as *The Times* now fully admits, is fighting the battle of Christian civilisation against Communism, and deserves the support of all fair-minded Englishmen.

It is therefore my pleasure and privilege to sponsor this publication. The "Old" State for which Victor Pradera died is now revealed to us in all its truth as the New State which, under God, will be the salvation of Spain after the most terrible experience that can befall a nation.

JUAN DE BORBÓN.

Rome.
December 1938.

TABLE OF CONTENTS

THIRD PART: THE GOVERNMENT OF SOCIETIES

A MEMOIR

I AM honoured by the request of a few lines for the new edition of *The New State*, Pradera's last book. It is an easy, yet, at the same time, a difficult task. It is a simple matter to give oneself up to the tender memory of a friend who can never be forgotten, a martyr for Spain and for the Catholic cause; but it is beyond my powers to attempt to dissert upon his great work as a thinker and as an apostle. So I devote myself to the first of these duties.

Victor Pradera was one of the men who exercised most influence in the development of my modest political life. He was some years older than I, a sufficient reason for looking upon him as a master, not only in the order of merits, but because he was far advanced in the matter of public service and political history; yet this difference in age was not such as to prevent whole-hearted confidence and intimate friendship between us. Pradera was a national figure, an outstanding national figure, but his influence was greatest in Navarre and the Basque Provinces; and Revolution, which never forgives, chose him, the noblest of victims, to be sacrificed in his homeland, in the Basque country he had so often moved with his fiery Hispanic eloquence, scourging those who would prostitute the consciences and the traditional sentiments of the people with the morbid creations of that wrongly-styled Basque Nationalism, the insolent conception of minds a hundred times accursed, which in Pradera found its most efficacious adversary.

13

When I was an undergraduate, Pradera, still quite young yet fully qualified as a civil engineer and as a barrister, was member of the Cortes for Tolosa. The Carlist students of that epoch were formed in the spirit of the Basque deputy who often upheld alone, with the tenacity that always characterized him, the traditionalist principles at a time when the world was engulfed in Liberalism; very different from the period comprising the last few years, when Traditionalism almost became the fashion because the premises of Liberalism had borne the natural fruit of their consequences.

Basque Nationalism had not yet made its appearance in the form of an active and extensive Party. The poisonous seed was still dormant in the mind of Sabino Arana[1] and a few followers; and Pradera's campaigns, when I commenced to fight by his side, were vehemently directed against political and anti-clerical Liberalism which the leadership of Canalejas[2] superimposed upon the government of Spain.

Pradera was then the guide of traditionalist youth. I do not say of Catholic youth, because, in those days of confusion, Catholics were often divided by heated disputes about the *thesis* and the *hypothesis*, and even by differences concerning the interpretation of documents of authority.

Unlike most of us, Pradera's forbears were not of traditionalist stock. As he so often related to me, he came to Traditionalism through conviction, through reading, by the imperative of that formidable logic which was his chief characteristic. His Traditionalism was the result of unshakable persuasion. He

[1] Sabino Arana y Goiri (1865-1903). Founder of the Basque Separatist Party.
[2] José Canalejas y Méndez (1854-1912). Liberal Prime Minister under King Alphonso XIII. (Translator's notes.)

acquired it as a child and it remained with him until death. One of his most prominent features was his legitimist conviction. He was never a monarchist out of fancy or personal attachment. Monarchy, in its abstract sense, was for him the highest form of government by reason of the harmony and unity it gives to the functions of authority. With the realities of Spain always in mind, it was the régime suited to her historic tradition and to her internal Constitution. Within the monarchy, legitimacy of origin conjointly with that of administration and office, was the only sovereign power that Victor Pradera esteemed adequate. He would often say that, when hearing the cry "Long live the King!", he always thought of the magnificent doctrinal content of this aspect of our motto.

When the present century was in its eleventh year, the faltering condescensions of Liberal governments and their lack of understanding and appreciation of the sound regionalist solutions always advocated by Spanish Traditionalism, caused the separatist virus to spread through the Basque country with corrosive intensity. Pradera, then living at San Sebastian, aloof from parliamentary affairs, was the most resolute champion, the most courageous warrior who, like a knight of old taking the field on behalf of his lady, came forward in defence of Spain. He was definitely regionalist, substantively regionalist, and consequently anti-nationalist in the secessional aspect. His speeches and lectures, his continuous struggle for the vindication of the tradition and of the profound Spanish sentiment of the Basque people, fill a period that must remain indelible in the minds of those who lived through it, and brought an accumulation of incontrovertible doctrines and conceptions.

Navarre, "the eldest sister of the Basque Provinces," as Pradera used to say, was spared the nationalist pestilence. The formidable political sense always proverbial in that ancient kingdom, and the uprightness and clear vision of the men of Navarre, presented a powerful barrier to Nationalism. In 1918, the moment chosen for the initiation of separatist alienations, Navarre returned Pradera as its representative in Parliament. It was the culmination of his work. Rarely has the parliamentary tribune reached greater brilliance or produced deeper emotion. A spiritless but sectarian Basque minority, reinforced by the numerous and well prepared Catalonian representation, was advancing in a process of denationalizing Spain. The Liberal government and its majority in the Chamber did not resist the attack, although many of its constituents were adverse to it. The traditionalist minority, small in number but backed by the will and incomparable eloquence of Pradera, was the sole political representation to maintain the true thought of Spain.

Pradera did not oppose the separatist Utopias with the easy declarations of centralizing Liberalism. His solid, traditionalist formation sprang from deep philosophical roots, and his historical culture caused him to feel strongly the regional autarchies which, far from impairing the intangible unity of the nation, would actually enhance its vigour. Nobody, like Pradera, could define and delimit the national and regional ends without any possible confusion. Cambó, accustomed to easy passages in the parliamentary medium, open to every kind of compromise, encountered for the first time a redoubtable adversary. The other deputies not wanting in patriotic feeling welcomed, with praise and cordiality, the ardent orations of Pradera; and so, in a Chamber that, in one way or another, was hostile to him, he became the pivot of that parliamentary epoch. His oratory was uncommon and unmistakable; it was characterized by energy rather than by eloquence. The words left his lips like sharply cut stones from a catapult. It was the manner that became his logical and decisive mind.

The dictatorship set up by General Primo de Rivera in 1923 made use of Pradera's services more in an advisory and informative capacity than in public office, towards which, as one formed in the ranks of the opposition, he felt little inclination. Moreover the independence of his character, and even his impetuous temperament, constituted noble impediments rather than qualities propitious to the exercise of official functions. The only nomination he accepted was that of member of the Consultative Assembly, and even this, towards the close of the dictatorial régime, he resigned because certain legislative resolutions were not in concordance with his principles.

The revolutionary outburst of 1931 marks the initial point of Pradera's highest political and cultural action. To a man of such intense patriotism and of such deep-rooted convictions, the spiritual upheaval entailed by the anti-Catholic and Socialist Republic was bound to be enormous. Yet those years of recent, unhappy memory provided a wide field for the development of the activity of one who was the soul of valour with the qualities of a born fighter. Pradera was the standard bearer of the thought and action of the counter-revolution.

With Maeztu, with Pemán, with Sainz Rodriguez and other leading figures of anti-revolutionary intellectuality, he lived through the five execrable years

B—n

with no other yearning than the salvation of Spain. Inspired by unconquerable faith in this ideal, his work as writer and lecturer in *Acción Española*, the association of greatest traditionalist efficacy in the cultural order, was inexhaustible. The same is to be said of his apostolate in the cities, towns and country-side of Spain, notable after the constitution of the *Bloque Nacional*, the political organization of which he and another martyr for Spain, the deeply-lamented and never-to-be-forgotten Calvo Sotelo, were the master-minds.

In his crowning book, *The New State*, Pradera placed the entire fruit of his great political, historical and philosophical learning at the service of his patriotic preoccupation. The New State, new because it is so old, was, to his mind, the Catholic and Monarchic Spanish State, the historic and traditional State adjusted to present-day realities. This book of Pradera and *La Hispanidad* of Maeztu constitute the most accurate concretion of Spanish political thought, and are the clearest exponents of the counter-revolution in the intellectual plane. Pradera in Spain, like Maurras in France, was a torch illuminating the altar of the fatherland.

In these dramatic days that are nevertheless a time full of hope in the reconstruction of our country, the pages of *The New State* offer a more lively interest. The redeeming perspective of the rise of the regenerat-ing State is to be found luminous and complete in its conceptions.

God has not willed that its author, a scholar and a patriot, should enjoy the spectacle which to him would be unsurpassed, of this magnificent spiritual reaction that is preparing the sure national regeneration, and has deprived us of his precious co-operation. In their cruelty and hatred, "reds" and separatists destroyed so noble a life when the country he loved deeply needed him most. His fate was shared by Calvo Sotelo, Maeztu, Honorio Maura, Beunza and many more, whose deaths, in higher or lower proportion, must be counted irreparable losses to the future of Spain.

Providence, ever inscrutable in its purposes, has perhaps not decreed that the salvation of Spain be due to those in whom the firmest hopes were centred. But who can perceive the ways of God? Yet the sacrifice of their lives, and their work as precursors crowned by martyrdom, have an inestimable virtue.

So the memory of Pradera and of his work extends over the future like a luminous projection.

EL CONDE DE RODEZNO.

(Minister of Justice in the Spanish National Government).

PROLOGUE

FEW men, like Victor Pradera, have accomplished
wholly and completely the function to which they
seemed destined in life. Undoubtedly, God had committed to him and, indeed, to the entire traditionalist
community of Spain, the duty of preserving and of
translating the treasure of national tradition in times
of desertion and oblivion. With Nocedal, Menéndez
y Pelayo, Aparisi and Mella, he may be likened to
those firm stepping-stones that afford safety to
travellers crossing a river. Their steadfastness and
loyalty enabled tradition to pass over the revolutionary waters and to reach the bourn where it is
now restored and rejuvenated.

Victor Pradera fitted his spirit in a full and sub-
missive way to this mission which, being one of preservation and safe keeping with a view not to momen-
tary but to future efficaciousness, required inflexible
integrities and not accommodation and temporiza-
tion. For the achievement of this mission, it was
enough for Victor Pradera to devote all his zeal and
ardour to integral, plenary and undeviating truth
without the least reduction or modification. As
he did not anticipate adjusting it, for the moment, to
the conventionalism of ordinary active life, he had no
reason to think of expedients of adaptation. As he
conceived truth, he adored it in all its magnitude. It
was perfectly consonant in the region of pure thought,
the only place where, as in a tabernacle, he kept it,
awaiting the cleansing and purifying of the altar of
the fatherland which would thus be rendered worthy
to receive it.

To the mind of Victor Pradera, only one form of mental honesty, of intellectual rectitude, existed; and that was logic. He rendered to logic a *cultus* similar to that accorded to honour. To defy it, to distort it or even to palliate it, he considered mental treason. I remember him at a banquet of *Acción Española*, in San Sebastian, at the height of the ruthless persecution under the republican régime. The representative of authority had, before the commencement of the banquet, begged the speakers to exercise moderation and prudence. In all good faith, Pradera had promised to do so. Afterwards, when the time came, he rose to propose a toast, as only he knew how, building up in Cyclopean fashion, as it were, an inflexible concatenation of ideas that naturally concentrated upon Catholic unity, the King, and the *coup de force*. He was at the culminating part of his oration, with features strained and flushed, the vein of his forehead standing out, when the telephone bells began to ring, and the delegate, by order of the civil governor, attempted to suspend the speeches. I recall the almost ingenuous amazement with which Pradera received the order, and the almost child-like seriousness with which he answered the delegate: "But, surely, all I was saying was logical?"

To him, that meant everything. His honest passion for truth made him unable to realize the explosive and detonating effect it causes when, without alloy or mixture, it is flung into the midst of a society and a State set up precisely upon falsehood. He could not conceive how a great love could be, for the State in which he lived, a great crime that one day was to bring about his death.

His chief office in life was that which I have stated: to guard and to declare the whole truth; to point the way to the final goal, to the supreme ideal that must ever be kept in sight, if the endeavour and advance of each day are to be rightly directed. The spirit of Pradera was a maximum thermometer, stationary at the highest temperature of the passion for truth and for Spain. Others, more astute, would say how much could be done in a day. He, more discerning and more fervent, would calmly enounce the final irrevocable purpose; and when very near to it, as one having carried out his trust, he died on the very borders of the promised land. . . .

Years ago, after the coming of the republic, his duty of continuous recollection and indication of the supreme finality became more vehement as he found himself faced by a convulsive succession of events with unsuspected possibilities of realization. Rapidly, the road to the great integral ideals began to be shortened. Every day, goodly sections were traversed as if in the hurry of making up for the slow march of so many years. Suddenly, theory took on the appearance of a manifesto and of an actual programme. The faithful and the die-hards began to be looked upon as actuating possibilities in daily public life. Mella's speeches left their setting of pure doctrine where many had placed them as in a hazy remoteness, and sprang into the middle of life with the renewed vitality of the eloquence of a moment, of the tidings of a day. The red berets[1] also leapt from the old romantic prints of the Carlist wars, and appeared in the corridors of Madrid cinemas, keeping order in crowded meetings, inspired by the intense feeling of the hour. The recovery of the intransigents, the theorists and the philosophers could not be more complete.

[1] The red beret or *boina* was worn by the old Carlists or Traditionalists. To-day it is worn by large numbers of General Franco's army and by civilians. (Translator's note.)

58803

Pradera felt no need to move from where he stood. Serene in the position he had always occupied, he found himself in the guerillas of the vanguard. He had no call to place himself in front; the others ranged themselves behind him. Then came those years, swift and epileptic, when Pradera was guide, herald and captain. No change of tone could suggest itself to him; his discourses of yesterday, of themselves alone, were transformed into the oratory of a political platform. His passion for integral truth became converted, nowise varied, into a passion for the unique and immediate salvation of Spain.

It was then that Pradera daily attended the coterie of *Acción Española*, love of his loves, where his Beatrice and his Laura—his truth ever intact—passed from a remote dream to a living reality. There, among those young men who listened to him with respect, among those friends who followed him with devotion, among those soldiers who offered themselves to him with saintly valour, lay all his enjoyment, all the compensation of a life of ascetic renunciation and of chaste expectation. One could almost touch the promised land with one's hand. The time of sowing and portending was being closed. His long mission of guardianship and pronouncement of truth was being consummated and terminated. It was there, very near. No more preaching was needed. There was nothing to do save to die for it.

He died for it when triumph was dawning so that his life of total renunciation and immolation should not pass one step beyond its exact and austere mission. Few lives had consorted more perfectly, never exceeding nor wanting, with the fulfilment of a unique mission. This was so much the substance and the sustenance of his life that when the mission was ended, life ended too. He was, at each instant, what his mission intended him to be: a herald, at first, a warrior afterwards, a martyr, in the end. The passion for logic which ruled his mind also presided over his life, which closed without a sigh, always in a perfect course drawn along exemplary heights.

So, shortly before death, a martyr for God and for Spain, he was able, with the joy of youth, to entitle his last book *The New State*. It was, at once, the same book of his whole life: the compendium and summary of his immovable truth, the praises of which he, like Mella, had sung so impressively. But life had gone round, and now that *old* State, upon its adamantine Thomistic foundations, had become *new*. . . . So, by conjugating the old with the new, the work of the herald and the guardian of the immutable principles was consummated and attained. He was free to go joyfully to contemplate it from the regions of eternal peace.

JOSE MARIA PEMÁN.

Pinto. *February* 1937.

INTRODUCTION

THE world, afflicted with every kind of woe, amid glimmers of hope, manifests this aspiration: a new State must be raised. In its wake, the distressful generations endeavour to shake off their prostration and to begin to move.

Humanity has ever been the victim of chimera. Even in the rare epochs of its existence when enjoying peace and quiet, it felt the urge of a change of posture. There is nothing unique in the instance of a whole people, as if possessed of madness, abandoning the broad paths of its felicity and persisting along the uneven, sinuous and checkered ways of its tribulation.

The new State could hardly be anything worse than the present State; but that it might be so is not metaphysically impossible. It is not enough, then, to cry out for a new State and to march blindly in gregarious aggregations towards where we are told it is to be set up. It cannot be disputed that we shall emerge from where we now are; but before setting out, we should duly take our bearings, and in the course of our journey, we cannot disregard the indications of the compass. The constitution of the State does not depend upon our tastes, our inclinations or our fancies. God, creator of man and of society, made him subject to laws, and if in His respect for human liberty, He has willed that laws dictated by Him, as universal legislator, shall be carried out by men in some form of order, that does not mean that the

27

fulfilment or non-fulfilment of the obligations created by those laws is left to our choice.

Another State, yes; but why a new State? Has humanity, perchance, always lived under the same? Has it ever known a good State? Can it be seriously maintained that juridical-social culture, indispensable in speculations of a political order, is to-day superior to that of past times? A new State! A moment ago, I hinted at the State we need. It is not the *new* State; it is the *good* State. This is because the State affects moral relations guided by reason to which nothing is new or old, but either true or false, just as conscience considers not *newness* but *goodness*.

This tremendous paradox, then, might occur: that the note of goodness being essential in the State, if, before everything else, we set it before us in the pursuance of our investigations, the result might be that the *new* State we seek would appear confused with some *old* State of centuries ago in the history of our land. Why not? Have we so little faith in Spanish thought? Can we claim a right, *a priori*, to doubt its powerful range and to take for granted that it did not exhaust all that, in the political order, lies within reach of human endeavour? A new State or an old State, what does it matter to us? Let us seek the State suited to the fulfilment of national aims; everything else will be added unto us. If what we find turns out to be old, so much the better; for experience will bring with it the seal of efficacy.

To investigate which shall be the State to supersede the present, carries with it the supposition that reason is charged with its discovery. There could be no greater folly than to waste cerebral effort in an undertaking devoid of finality. But to affirm that reason may arrive at the certain knowledge of the proper requisites of the State, implies the postulate of the existence of a political science which, in turn, demands the perception of cardinal principles investing knowledge with a scientific character. Moreover, whenever reason is appealed to in a question as to whether certain knowledge constitutes a science or not, man finds himself the centre of a vicious circle. This circle can be broken only by one or more truths which, being principles of the investigation undertaken, are proposed to reason by a higher science, postulated with axiomatic characters or with some aspect of evidence, and under reservation of subsequent confirmation in what they do not present. All are contained in political science and may be summarized in this proposition: political matters affect man in his life of relation with his fellows as a proper note of his nature. If this, like every other, is subject to eternal laws that form the tissue of science, it must be concluded, even *a priori*, that a *political science* exists.

It will not be irrelevant to remark here that one who considers himself a representative of philosophy has, without the least restriction, denied the existence of this science. The author of the following words is D. José Ortega y Gasset:[1] "I do not admit that one is a republican as the saying goes 'on principle.' I have always held that what are called principles have no

[1] Professor of Metaphysics in the University of Madrid. Author of *Invertebrate Spain*, *Meditations of Don Quixote*, and other works. He was a member of the group of writers and scholars known as "Al servicio de la República" ("in the service of the Republic") which aspired to form the intellectual background of the successful republican movement of 1931. The anti-democratic procedure of the new régime, and above all, the policy of a proletarian dictatorship eventually established under the presidency of Señor Azaña, brought a disclaimer from Ortega y Gasset whose republican ardour soon became appreciably less. Ortega y Gasset, in a notable newspaper article, exclaimed: "This is not what we wanted." His two prominent colleagues in the republican intellectual group, Señor Pérez de Ayala, late Ambassador to the Republic in London, and Dr. Gregorio Marañón, have both proclaimed their wholehearted support of General Franco, as also did the late Professor Unamuno very soon after the civil war began in July, 1936. (Translator's note.)

existence in politics.   Principles are things for geometry.   In politics there are only historical circumstances, and they define what must be done."[1]

The thesis of a philosopher could not be more
audacious or more depressing for the science he
cultivates, not because geometry, in order to function,
needs the support of a postulate that cannot properly
be catalogued among the "principles," but because,
being the science of extension, it must be provided
with this quality by another body of knowledge, the
inferior category of which cannot easily be admitted
in view of a loan of such quality.   But, further,
political practice without principles is something inconceivable; it would imply the inexistence of every
rational standard regulating human life and the
natural movements of man.   That which is the
foundation of the harmony of physical nature would be
entirely absent from man.   If philosophy led to such a
plight—thank God, only pseudo-philosophy can cause
it—one would have to exclaim with Charles Marx:
"The wretchedness of philosophy!"

The same Ortega y Gasset, immediately afterwards,
forgetful of what he had just said, and introducing
"principles" into political affairs with the intention of
disclaiming responsibility contracted through his in-
accurate vision, lays down that: *"only by means of it"*
(the republic) *"can Spaniards hope to become nationalized,
that is, to feel themselves a nation;"* that the republic
"is the only régime which automatically corrects itself and,
in consequence, does not tolerate its own falsification;"
that "the monarchies, on the other hand, are gradually
dying and rotting internally," and that Spain "can
only be reborn from a political discipline which should

[1] Article published under the heading "Long live the Republic" in the
Madrid newspaper *El Sol.*   Dec. 3, 1933.

commence by being a moral system, exasperatingly and exactingly moral, *reclaiming the whole man and saturating him, removing from him all baseness, all depravity, all uncouthness, all vulgarity and incapacity for noble undertakings, which he harbours within him.*[1]

If the republic is the only form of government by means of which "Spaniards can hope to become nationalized, that is, to feel themselves a nation," and the practice of government means that, and I would say, that alone, how did Ortega y Gasset venture to hold that there were no principles in it? This unblushing conclusion, were it true, entails a necessary logical deduction of evident or rationally demonstrated propositions. How did he affirm emphatically, dogmatically, that "the republic is the only régime which automatically corrects itself and, in consequence, does not tolerate its own falsification," if assertions of this kind do not affect circumstances, but that which is absolute in things, and what is absolute is their nature, and consequently the principles whereby knowledge of them is procured? How can he demand any political discipline "which should commence by being a moral system . . . reclaiming the whole man and saturating him, removing from him all baseness, depravity, uncouthness, vulgarity and incapacity for noble undertakings, which he harbours within him," if through lack of rigid and inflexible principles, morality does not exist, and if the work government is asked to do is nothing less than the transformation of the common man into a standard type of man according to an ethical pattern supplied by the interpretation of those principles? How does he so lightly dismiss monarchy from the art and practice of government, making a law of its dissocia-

[1] Article previously quoted.

tion from the people, and going so far as to convert it
into its own vessel of putrefaction?

Let it be noted that those who call themselves
intellectuals and representatives of modern philosophy
are responsible for much idle talk when they rush in
to discuss political matters. Only the schools repudiated as old and reactionary watch over the
prestige of the art of government and maintain it in
its rank. Thank God, it is a science. What a grievous
misfortune would be added to those humanity already
suffers, if it were not! The supporters of action in the
order of the government of peoples should not consider themselves defrauded on this account. Action
without guiding principles is epileptic agitation,
sterile and harmful. If Goethe said that "in the
beginning was action," St. John proclaimed that "in
the beginning was the Word." The world is led by
ideas: to prosperity, if they are true; to catastrophe,
if they are false.

Three most important consequences follow from
the scientific condition of what is known as the art or
practice of government. The first is that man cannot
be indifferent to its conclusions. The second is that
historical circumstances, great as their influence may
be—we shall see later that this is indeed so—have no
pre-eminence over principles. The third is that
government moves within its own orbit, where it is
independent of the other intellectual speculations.

If political science actually, as has been said, rests
upon certain principles because it is a product of
elaboration of another higher science, or upon
postulates offering evident aspects, the conclusions
drawn with logical exactitude from the application of one and another to real facts, will be in
agreement with human nature in its life of relation

which, by definition, is affected by the principles. For while the understanding does not show itself indifferent to the presence of a mathematical truth, modest and ordinary though it may appear to be, nor even before a physical phenomenon however bereft of greatness it may manifest itself, but assents to one and to the other as it might assent to the legitimate result of the most elevated speculation, it likewise accepts as true that which political science shows as befitting sociable man, and rejects everything that may oppose his condition of sociability. A confusion of terms that might be criminal were it intentional, has caused the world, or a part of it, to proclaim a systematic indifference in face of the consideration that there are other nobler subjects in the scientific hierarchy than that with which political science is concerned. It is true that the religious life, for example, is superior to, and therefore must rank above political life, a life of relation, so claiming its homage which, if it is to be worthy, demands a perfect knowledge and due appreciation of the subject matter involved. But not even this is the problem. The problem is that reason was given to us by God for the discovery of truth; that by the divine will, man lives in society subject to laws imposed by that will; that man being bound to cooperate in their fulfilment, it would be hazardous to regard them with formal indifference; that if they do not regulate what is highest in man, they govern one of his noblest aspects; and that God, being legislator of the natural and of the supernatural, the one contingent upon the other, it is of much importance, even for the purposes of the supernatural order, that error should not defile our conceptions of the natural order.

There can be no indifference either on account of

matter or by reason of *accidentality*. The meaning of
this term has, in the political sphere, been denaturalized in bastard fashion. That certain forms or
institutions therein may be accidental to man, does
not in any way authorize their elimination from all
resolution nor warrant their entire neglect nor the
affirmation of their insignificance in the life of relation
of man. There is nothing more accidental, in the
philosophical sense of the word, than wickedness or
goodness, than ignorance or wisdom. Specifically,
the saint is as much a man as the criminal, and the
same applies to the unlettered and the learned. Yet
no one would say that it is the same thing for man to
feel the aspirations of sanctity as to feel the base
passions of the delinquent, and to act according to
them, nor that to live a life of imbecility is the same
as to live a life of knowledge. But what nobody says
of man considered in himself, is, by one of those
aberrations inconceivable as they are current, asserted
of him so soon as he is studied in his life of relation. It
is not *accidental* (in the ordinary sense of the word) that
individually considered, man may be good or bad,
ignorant or enlightened. The political forms and
institutions whose destiny is precisely to provide man
with *social conditions* in order that he may rise with the
spirit and not sink with the matter, are considered
by many to be accidental. Neither before political
science nor before common sense can there be any
recognition of vacuities that enjoy the vouchsafement
of the evil arts of the government of peoples and of a
distorted perception of reality.

The first step taken by the promoters of the fallacy
was to put under lock and key the libraries in which
the texts of Christian philosophy, venerated in other
times, were kept. The substance or essence of beings

is one thing; the accident, another. But the accident is not, as the supporters of accidentality in institutions and forms of government imagine, something futile and unimportant whose concurrence, or that of its contrary, amount to the same. "To deny that accidents," says the great Mercier, "*truly add a reality* to the substance affected by them, is to condemn oneself to sustain one of these three propositions: that all changes produced in beings are substantial, that there is no change in Nature, or that the contradictory are identical."[1] What vital words are enclosed in this noble sentence, a consummate eulogy of the *accident* with which the great rebel prepared to sweep away the nonsense which ignorance was to thrust into circulation with pretensions of metaphysical profundity!

Furthermore—as will be seen at once—man does not live in a universal society subject only to abstract laws, but in the bosom of concrete societies, the institutions of which are the result of the consolidation in historical realities, of exclusively scientific social principles. It follows that political forms or institutions not only must be efficacious in attaining the temporal end, in so far as concerns the purely doctrinal order, but also inasmuch as it is demanded by the circumstances which, while concreting society, have individualized it. Not the man but the citizen is a member of society, because no universal human society exists. This now carries us to a conclusion which nobody can deem reckless after the reflections made. For the citizen, that is, for the human being who providentially must reach his temporal destiny in a determined particular society, there cannot be absolute indifference towards the principles animating its political institutions and the forms they may adopt

[1] Mercier: *General Metaphysics*, No. 159.

through strict observance of the conclusions of political science. Nor can those principles be disdained by reason of their accidentality both in the philosophical and in the ordinary sense of the word, if they fail to lead man to his temporal destiny. Nor, finally, can they be set at naught in relation to the concrete order, should they lack efficacy within the same. I beg the reader to pardon my excessive insistence upon what in a moderately philosophical atmosphere would be reputed commonplace, for unhappily the total ignorance of philosophy in those who proclaim it, has triumphed for the moment in that corrupting and corrupted medium.

What has been said points the way to the exact determination of the influence of historical circumstances—which are also accidents—upon political principles. Like all other circumstances, they may qualify,[1] but not invalidate nor substitute those principles. That principles, in their application, must bear circumstances in mind, cannot be placed in doubt. The suggestion that only the latter enter into political life is refuted by the philosophical conception of their condition as accidents, and even by the etymology of the term. To affirm that in political life there are only historical circumstances which define what is to be done, is to reproduce in the twentieth century the anti-philosophical error with which Demosthenes reproached the barbarians, entreating the Athenians to avoid it. With this doctrine, man falls beneath animals which, in instinct, have a guide in the midst of circumstances. Man must *direct* events and not play second fiddle to them. Moreover, circumstances cannot give any *rule* of conduct which is imposed by the connection, morally

[1] St. Thomas Aquinas: *Summa Theologica*, I^a-II^{ae}, Qu. xviii, art. 3.

necessary, between the human act and the end to
which it is directed. But as before remarked, they
can *qualify* that rule. So arise the *concrete* political
institutions that are governed by scientific principles
embodied in determined facts and circumstances,
transcending in time and space.

One name comprehends them all: tradition.
Nothing need be said concerning what it stands for
in the life of peoples, for the people themselves are
tradition. As Mella said, they constitute "not a
simultaneous whole but a successive whole." With all
the content and significance of tradition, it is no more
than the support or material foundation of political
principles at a given moment, and their vehicle, not
their main-spring, in the course of time. Political
science which, as such, originates in an abstraction,
does not stop at setting forth reasons, ways and means
for the government of the human life of relation, but
goes on to aspire to govern a determined society.
Hence doctrinal foundations do not present themselves
in the Spanish political thought elaborated during
centuries, merely forming a system, but animating
living realities. It could be said that in the Spanish
traditional policy, principles and facts are joined in
hypostasis, of which the former are the spirit, and the
latter the matter, the composition being the concretion of a universal political doctrine applied to a
particular society. The foregoing emphasizes that
tradition is not all the past. What is opposed to the
principles derived from the nature and life of relation
of man cannot be traditional, since, as already
remarked, tradition must be animated by them. Nor
can a merely eventual past be traditional. Tradition
is the past that *qualifies* sufficiently the doctrinal
foundations of the human life of relation considered

in the abstract; it is, in other words, the past that survives and has the virtue to make itself future.

So in the traditional Spanish political doctrine, satisfaction is given to the three consequences we are examining, inasmuch as it takes up the study of man politically, just as he is in his own nature, and not imaginatively, with his life of relation as conatural to him, and accepting the corollaries derived therefrom. It distinguishes historical circumstances from principles but defends the adaptation of the latter to the former; and when making a composition of both—definitely different for each people—it advocates the substantivity of the political order.

There are two ways of estimating the independence of a science: either absolutely, or in that which affects its own orbit. The first argues the independence of reason and the inexistence of scientific hierarchy in human knowledge. The second entails the subordination of science according to the order of the objects of knowledge, and the distinction or separation among these. Obviously, the first sense of scientific independence is heterodox, both in the religious sphere and in that of Nature; as much in the realm of faith as in that of reason. The second, indisputably evident, responds to the very nature of things and of the human understanding. In this sense—and in this alone—political science is independent of the other human speculations.

It is now clear that political science is subordinate to those sciences superior to it by reason of their formal objects: to theology, to philosophy and to ethics. Nobody but St. Thomas has voiced this double aspect of subordination and independence respecting the human sciences, and nobody is likely to do so in the future. Referring to the sacred science and to the natural sciences, the rational foundation being applicable to the latter in regard to the diverse objects they investigate, he said: "What characterizes the sacred science is that its knowledge comes from Revelation and not from reason. So it is not called upon to prove the principles of the other sciences, but *must only judge them;* because anything which in the other sciences is found to be *inconsistent with the truth* of the sacred science, is condemned as false."[1] Extending this argument, it may be said and must be said that the sciences superior to political science *judge* its conclusions, which they condemn as false in so far as they may be opposed to their own principles and conclusions.

The method of the present study cannot be authoritative or dogmatic, but rational, contrasting with reality. It is not a case of a speculation taking its principles from a science that could only be known by a Revelation. We should then have to accept those principles by reason of the authority which deigns to communicate them to us. It is a question of things which the understanding knows by means of its own powers, and in their investigation, authority, according to St. Thomas, is a very feeble means of demonstration.[2]

But neither does reason suffice by itself. In the endeavour to obtain the principles of political science, abstracting them from reality, the results must be contrasted with the same. Through a defective abstractive operation which lack of demonstration caused to be concealed, the world feels it is dying, and cries out for a new State. We shall not fall into the same error while we have at hand that opulent

[1] St. Thomas Aquinas: *Summa Theologica*, I*, Qu. i, art. 6.
[2] St. Thomas Aquinas: *Summa Theologica*, I*, Qu. i, art. 8.

Spanish tradition, a hypostatic union, as was said, of science and history.

As, in the end, political science concerns the government of man in his life of relation, its study may be divided into three parts: First, man considered in himself; second, his life of relation, or society; third, the government of societies.

FIRST PART

MAN

CHAPTER I

THE HUMAN BEING

It has been said that man is a microcosm. While the content of the phrase is true, it is very possible that those who utter it may not fully realize the breadth of its meaning. Vegetative, sensitive and intellective are the terms which in perfect distinctiveness describe the three lives that manifestly abide in man. Like a vegetable he grows as he is nourished, like an animal he feels, and like an angel he thinks. Minerals being the object of assimilation by animals and vegetables, the whole of the created world is concentrated in man in whom careful study will reveal the foundations of animated nature.

But this is not all. Man is the image and likeness of his own Creator. Through his spiritual soul, his thought and his will, he offers a distant resemblance of the divine Trinity; through the personal composition formed in him by animal and rational existence, he traces the hypostatic union of the divine and human natures in Jesus Christ, his Redeemer. In the sphere of knowledge, it is quite natural that the mysteries of the Blessed Trinity and the Incarnation

41

of the Word should lie beyond our comprehension. Nor do animals understand the truths emanating from mathematical or ethical sources, or from the issues of natural religion that to us may be evident. The acceptance of the fact that animals have *knowledge* of things although their mode of knowing them may be different from that possessed by man, would amount not only to an absurdity but would become mere nonsense, if after admitting the existence of truths outside the range of purely animal cognisance, the possibility of a kind of super-human knowledge were to be denied. But such folly would be intensified on reflecting that in man, the soul, the intelligence and the will, while psychologically distinct, are but one spiritual being; and that while animal and rational characteristics constitute different natures, in man jointly they form one person.

It is indeed true that our psychological conscience, amid so much variety, shows the unity of our being. In vain has psychology demonstrated that periodically —in comparatively brief periods—human bodies undergo complete transmutation of their material elements; for, in childhood, in youth, in adolescence, in the prime of life and in old age, man feels himself the same throughout. When he perceives distinctly these modifications as they are experienced, he also detects, with very singular features, the background of permanence and unity upon which these successive changes take place. Conscience, distinguishing as it does in all clearness the acts proper to the three lives seen in man, nevertheless realizes that these are not produced in isolation or in separation. The manifestations of intellective life are always accompanied by others of the sensitive life; man is considered at once as a corporal being and as a principle of spiritual operations. Even Descartes, who set up an insurmountable barrier between body and soul, could not but write these words: "Nature teaches me through feelings of pain, of hunger, of thirst, etc., that my relation to my body is not that of a navigator to his ship; rather am I so closely united, bound up and confused with it as to form one single whole."[1] How is the intimate interdependence between the sensitive and intellective orders to be explained? How can body and soul form the unity acknowledged in the words of Descartes?

Enlightenment can come only through the existence in man of a unique internal principle of his diverse operations all ordered to an appropriate end; or, in other words, granted the principle of the operation of a being is called *nature*, through the formation of spirit and matter into one sole nature which, requiring one sole substance, demands a corresponding substantial unity of soul and body. So, of necessity, the former acts in the human compound as the substantial form of the latter,[2] and is the exclusive principle of the operations of three lives, intellective, sensitive and vegetative.[3] Not otherwise can the *unity* of the human being, as recognized by the psychological conscience, be explained. Only thus may it be said in all propriety that *a human nature* exists: that which we feel palpitating within us. In this way alone may it be laid down that animality and rationality belong to one *sole person*.

This being, so complex and at the same time endowed with such perfect unity, was placed by its Creator in the midst of that Nature which it comprehended in its person, and there its activity was exercised without hindrance under a twofold aspect. In

[1] Descartes: *Sixth Meditation.*
[2] St. Thomas Aquinas: *Summa Theologica,* Iᵃ, Qu. clxxvi, art. 1.
[3] St. Thomas Aquinas: *Summa Theologica,* Iᵃ, Qu. clxxvi, art. 3.

the interior, by means of immanent acts of its understanding and will, which, in the act of reflecting and in the movement of mere volition, do not emerge from the domain of the spirit. In the exterior, by obeying an irresistible tendency that urges it to seek outside itself objects, the possession of which alone is capable of calming the disquiet caused by the inclination. Internal impulse, unrest, possession of an external object which man calls *his good*, a state of rest which possession brings with it, and which in ordinary terms, in a major or minor degree, is called *happiness*, constitute the various stages of the process of human activity.

In simultaneous and successive reproduction, it is a matter of daily experience caused by diverse and even contrary urges aiming at objects differing as much among themselves as the original impulses. This is due to the complicated make-up of the human entity previously dwelt upon; and within each of the substances, it is due also to the various faculties they respectively possess. Indeed, each faculty is defined by its own object which becomes its *end* or its *good*, and in this relative sense, man has before him as many ends as faculties of every kind. From what has been stated, it should be inferred that if, in these manifold processes, there did not exist a ratio of harmony and an order in the particular objects of the human faculties, man would never attain the condition of rest known as happiness, because of the variance and antagonism already mentioned. The ratio of agreement is suggested by the same consideration as that which led respectively to the conception of soul and body as a substantial form and as animated matter, that is, the unity of the human being which demands one nature incorporating the principle of the activity of all the faculties, and so regulating and subordinating partial tendencies to its own impulse. It thus becomes evident that the exclusive aims of the different faculties are directed to the end of Nature itself, the principle of the total activity of being. It is likewise plain that the objects of the faculties are not genuinely ends, in the absolute sense of the word, but *means* subordinated to the end of the human person considered as a whole. This end, in regard to which the pursuits of the various faculties have no other character save that of means, is, lastly, the true *good* of man.

Amongst all the objects, particular goods of the various faculties constituting their ends, a synthesis or combination of them all or realities of a degree superior one to another, in which is to be found the true good of man in the sense expounded, the good that is the sole end of his nature? Beyond dispute, it is widely known that the human being possesses a boundless capacity of aspiration to created objects that in any fashion may be termed *goods*. However great their quantity, however varied their nature, they are ever desired in larger number and in the most diversified conditions. To judge by universal experience, nothing in the created world embodies a sufficiency to satisfy the craving for good which is the torment of mankind; and reason succeeds in justifying the phenomenon to which experience points as something uninterrupted in the history of mankind. Neither wealth nor corporal goods can be the ultimate end of man, for both sustain human nature in which the conception of its own end must be contrary to what is naturally directed towards it as an end. Nor can honours, glory or power bear such an attribute, for honours and glory are a reflection of some possessed reality which, therefore, would itself be, in any event, the good that as an end had already been excluded; and power is nothing unless exercised on behalf of something that can be esteemed an end. It is obvious, too, that pleasure cannot occupy an ultimate category, for it is not properly a good but rather a consequence of the possession of a good.

Even any good of the soul must also be ruled out because, considered in itself, it is "as a potentially existing thing . . . and the power of performing exists for the act which is its complement."[1]

It is certain that man, like all beings, has an end. There is, indeed, *finality* in the universe, showing itself under a double aspect inasmuch as each substance possesses an internal principle by means of which it reaches a fitting end while drawing to the same the forces emanating from itself. In like manner, the mutual actions of beings, in pursuance of their respective purposes, adapt themselves to others of an extrinsic character and beget a general harmony not immediately sought by their agents. According to this teleological conception therefore, the agreement of the whole is a result of internal arrangements peculiar to the elements.[2]

The fact that substances have finality means, definitely, that the objects intended as ends should be, in some sense, real causes of the different operations of the substances themselves. Throughout the whole of Nature one observes this relation of causality which we shall call *final* in order to distinguish it from the *efficient*. Because the end is desired, the will determines, in rational natures, to bring about an act or a series of acts considered *necessary* or *useful* for the accomplishment of the end. Because a thing is

---

[1] St. Thomas Aquinas: *Summa Theologica*, Iᵃ-IIᵃᵉ, Qu. ii.
[2] Mercier: *General Metaphysics*, Nos. 237 and 238.

longed for, the movements of an animal are designed and ordered to its attainment, and because they lead to an issue *constantly* useful in the physical world, neither desiring sensitively nor willing rationally, a concert of numerous and varied operations is the result.

What is the purpose of man not found in any created thing yet pertaining solely to him because, as has been said, it must bear the same relation to *his nature*? Only outside creation can it be discovered; consequently it can be none other than *his Creator*. For the moment, it is irrelevant to inquire into the question as to how this may be; other branches of research deal with this matter. The scientific medium in which we are working will be justified by recording it, and by remarking that only an infinite Being, by reason of its attributes, is capable of satisfying the human yearnings, the modality of which has been already analysed.

Nevertheless it is clear that although the purpose of mankind may not be found in this life, the acts performed during its span cannot but be related to life itself. From this obvious consideration it become apparent, by induction, that the idea contained in the term "human end" would, in the present state, be persistence in the tendency or way which, in time, would lead mankind to his final purpose or object. Again, the end man may attain in the present life, that is his temporal end, will be of a *moral* character because it proceeds from the regulation of acts in a rightful direction, thus implying requisition which is pertinent to the faculty of the will.

From what has just been said there accrues one of the most transcendent consequences in the human order in general, and in the political order in particular. If the infinite Good alone is able to constitute the happiness of man because it is his final purpose, his propensity towards the same—unlimited by definition—would be contradictory if it were *necessarily* claimed by created objects. Moreover if the notion of *necessity* in his inclination towards them will not stand, one must conclude that the will, in everything not comprehending its final purpose, remains *free*. Human freedom, which has given rise to countless aberrations through arbitrary or erroneous conceptions, has no other foundation and no other justification than the existence of a final purpose for man different from and superior to all created things. Unless it be placed in God, the philosophical demonstration of its existence is precluded. There would remain, as a sole means of proof, the fact revealed by intimate sense confirming that the will, in respect of particular goods, while motives continue identical, may determine in a positive or negative sense; it may resolve or not resolve.

But the quality of freedom is not opposed to the existence of a necessary connection between an act of the will and the ultimate purpose, not by reason of the subject but by that of the relation. Assuming this, although man remain entirely free regarding the act, as previously stated, should he fail to perform it, he would not attain his purpose and for its achievement he would *have* to accomplish it *freely*; in other words, he *must* accomplish it. So is born in man the *moral duty* by virtue of his status as a free being, and in consideration of his final purpose and of the necessary connection between the same and a determined act. Furthermore, if man is destined to his end, and if in order to attain it he *must* perform certain acts, both his destiny and his action would be frustrated if besides *duty* or *obligation,* there did not arise a *moral power* permitting fulfilment. This *moral power* is *right,* the inevitable consequence of the existence of a necessary end and of the duty of procuring it.

From this reasoning, it will be seen that the supposition of the Rights of Man not having been proclaimed on earth until the French Revolution is one of the many falsehoods which have deranged the world. What the Revolution did affirm was a distorted caricature of its own, an expression of man's plenary independence. Theoretically, the revolutionary rights are boundless, and those originated by natural law are limited by the fulfilment of a duty. As a result, the former amount to a radical obstacle to social fellowship which will always be upset by the protest of citizens against the enactments of rulers who endeavour to make it possible by reduction; the latter agree with the sense of sociability which precisely urges men to fulfil their duties.

From all that has been expounded, it may be inferred that duty, in the logical order, is included in the category of relation, and essentially, in the moral order, it must occur among moral beings. As no moral being inferior to man exists, the generating relations of his duties must be reckoned within one of the following three classes: those which bind him to a Superior Being; those arising from association with his fellow creatures; and those pertinent to himself. The scheme of this work, as set out in the Introduction, prescribes that the relations contained in the second group be considered when the subject of society, to which they.refer, is dealt with. For this reason, those of the first and third groups are detailed here.

The contingency of man is a conspicuous condition of his being. He is born, he is subject to many

D—n

changes throughout life, and he dies. His existence does not belong to him by virtue of his essence. In other words, he does not live necessarily because he is man. If life is not his doing, neither are the changes that he experiences, which become reduced to revelations of life itself. This contingency evident, notorious, implies—within man's way of reasoning— the logical concept of cause. Indeed, the cause of a thing is that upon which a thing depends.[1]

One must conclude then that life has been given to man by another being: because, if this be denied, the inference is that he gave it to himself: an assertion contradictory to his birth, his changes and his death. Man has therefore a creative Cause, and it is scarcely needful to add that such a Cause must be uncreated, necessary, intelligent and personal; for anybody who does not acknowledge this will perforce accept, not only the difficulties of the thesis, but many more, and all the depraved aberrations which disbelief brings in its train, namely, that the Cause of man, intelligent and master of Nature, is irrational nature itself controlled by man. There is no other choice nor can anything more be said for those undiscerning in logic and unyielding in their folly.

Between man and his Creator there should, therefore, exist the relations which operate between effect and cause by reason of the definition of dependence. In the moral order, they must be accepted by man voluntarily as specified by volition itself. So *logical* relations become relations of voluntary *dependence*; they pass from the *natural* to the *moral* sphere. Now to every being, in accordance with its nature, two things are essential: to exist, and to act in conformity with that nature, and as the specifically human faculties are

---

[1] Mercier: *General Metaphysics*, No. 196.

the understanding and the will, the expression of moral dependency in regard to the first Cause must have a threefold manifestation in man: *adoration* relative to being; *submission* relative to the understanding; and *love* relative to the will. Also, as man is composed of soul and body and, in consequence, his internal acts are completed by the external acts, an indispensable part of *adoration* must consist of *public worship* (the first duty due to God); and being enabled to know the truth by means of authority and the exercise of reason, Revelation must be recognized, and the natural principles leading to knowledge of the Creator investigated (the second duty due to God); finally, since love demands the contribution of operations in harmony with Nature, acts will be accommodated to that imperative (the third duty owing to God).[1]

Three kinds of rights must correspond to these three duties. But if right implies power, and the relation of absolute dependence excludes it in the effect with respect to the cause, such rights will have to be exercised over moral beings distinct from the Creator, that is to say, over man's fellow beings, and so should be studied in the chapters devoted to the subject of society.

It would appear at first sight as if the human being had no duties towards himself, for bearing in mind that duty corresponds to the logical category of relation, the second term of this seems to be missing. Yet it should not be forgotten that through its psychological faculty of reflection, the human soul is at the same time the subject and object of the operation and that because of its freedom, its acts may have opposite meanings. When man dwells upon himself,

[1] Taparelli: *Theoretic Essay on Natural Law*, Vol. I, Bk. I, Ch. IX.

in so far as he does this, he is a different being from that upon which the reflection falls, and when he knows the rule by which he must adjust his conduct, and as an active subject in the knowledge of it, he is distinct from the passive subject to be regulated. Under this aspect, it may be said and it should be said that man, because his freedom is controlled by his end, has obligations in respect to himself. Wherefore the duties inherent to this group at once suggest themselves. If the relation generically constituting the duty of man towards himself involves, on the one side, a knowledge of the moral precept and on the other, the need of applying it, man, as an active subject of the relation, ought to perfect his understanding by removing the impediments standing in the way of knowledge, by strengthening his reason and by attaining his proper object. The first requisite enforces the correction of vices of the imagination that deceive the mind by presenting fancies from which ideas are formed, and the subduing of the passions that dim the intelligence. The second demands the endowment of the understanding with the quality of habit producing an extraordinary increase of natural energy. The third requires the intellectual practice to be of a character suitable to the promotion of knowledge of the end and of the means leading to the same, and not a mere instrument for training the intellective faculty. The enunciation of this is the enunciation of the rights correlative to the duties enumerated.[1]

But once the rule is known, it must be applied; and this application is a function proper to the will which is governed by conscience. Man's duty to himself is consequent then, upon obedience in every case to

[1] Taparelli: *Theoretic Essay on Natural Law*, Vol. I, Bk. I, Ch. X.

the bidding of an upright conscience through the production of moral virtues and the mastery of the sensitive part of human nature. To master it, nevertheless, does not presuppose its destruction. The preservation of being is natural to all creation, and as the human being is made up of soul and body and the latter may be destroyed by violence or annihilated by continuous action, it will be incumbent upon man not to attempt against its existence and to defend it against the causes working against it. The right to live is a consequence of this duty.[1]

Those rights derived from duties placed on evidence by the study of mankind and those that may be discovered as a result of the moral relations of sociability, are rights of Nature. They stand therefore, above, and cannot be ignored by any kind of positive legislation. They were not unrecognised by Spanish lore. In our regional *Fueros*,[2] every one is honoured with guarantees and sanctions so efficacious as to appear excessive to the modern mind. Yet none has a revolutionary character; none is the ferment of social anarchy nor the necessary cause of violent repression enforced by the condition of society. As the idea of duty inspired their consecration, the rights embraced by Spanish tradition as natural rights were a lifespring and not a death sentence. No, the Rights of Man and those of Citizenship were not born in the pools of blood stagnant beneath the guillotines of the most despotic, tyrannical and liberticidal of all revolutions. It was their pharisaical deformation that had such a beginning. If the Revolution was inexcusably criminal, it was still more distinguished by its arrant hypocrisy.

[1] Taparelli: Ibid.
[2] Fuero: A privilege, a liberty, a charter; ancient custom or practice of a place; from *Forum* where the Romans enacted laws and administered justice. (Translator's note.)

CHAPTER II

HUMAN NATURE

As seen in the previous chapter, the internal principle of human activity is called *Nature*. By its impulse man is directed to his end. So there can be nothing more interesting than to inquire into the conditions under which it is exercised, in other words, whether its operation is efficacious or not. The most far-reaching problems, as much in the general human order as in the particular political order, are thus placed ready for our consideration. For it must not be forgotten that political science, in the right sense of the word, not in that which gave it a monstrous perversion, affects man in his life of relation with his fellows as an essential feature of his being, and also that through this relation he is led to fulfil his purpose.

Actually, the matter to be pursued in our invesitgation will be contracted to the mode in which Nature acts. Three doctrinal systems offer us corresponding solutions: that of the natural goodness of mankind; that of the total corruption of Nature; and that of its enfeeblement with respect to the primitive forces for the attainment of good. The first is the Pelagian error restored by Jean Jacques Rousseau and accepted by Socialism; the second is the Protestant heresy; the third is taught by Catholicism. Let nobody be amazed at the unexpected appearance of a theological question on the very threshold of political science. Donoso Cortés long ago explained to us how natural it is. He says: "M. Proudhon has written in his *Confessions of a Revolutionary* these significant words: 'It is remarkable how we encounter theology in the course of all our political studies.' There is nothing to cause surprise except the astonishment of M. Proudhon. Theology, because it is the science of God, is the ocean that contains and comprehends all things."[1] Let not this quotation appear as a disavowal of our appreciation of the independence of political science, set down in the chapter serving as an introduction to the present work. There, the double meaning of the word "independence" was made clear, and in addition, it was pointed out that if theology was not responsible for *proving* the first principles of the other sciences, it certainly *passes judgment* and condemns as false whatever is found in them contrary to sacred truth. Under this aspect, theology contains and embraces the other sciences according to the words of Donoso Cortés. Indeed, it will be seen very soon that not a step can be taken in the study of political science without deciphering beforehand the actual condition of human nature; or, in other words, without accepting the Catholic dogma of original sin.

The contradiction that man holds within himself is nothing esoteric or mysterious. Its explanation may require something higher than natural talent; but the fact is within everybody's understanding. The poet of paganism has left it to us as a testament of ancient ethical science framed in brief and admirable verses: "*Video meliora—Proboque—Deteriora sequor*": "I see what is best; I give my approval; but I follow what is worst." A more finished likeness of human nature cannot be traced in fewer words. St. Paul, with no less vigour and conciseness, described the law he "saw

---

[1] Donoso Cortés: *Essay on Catholicism, Liberalism and Socialism*, Bk. I, Ch. I.

in his members" in these terms: "For the good which I will, I do not; but the evil which I will not, that I do."[1] Paganism and Catholicism coincide in the fact. How can it be explained so as to draw from it the standards of conduct to be observed by man in the superhuman undertaking of attaining his end?

Pelagius, a monk of the fifth century, is the panegyrist of the powers of human nature. To his mind, man is to-day what he was when he came from the hands of his Creator, unaffected by corruption and weakness from any cause whatever since that time. Through an all-powerful will, he fulfils his destiny both in this life and in the next without any superior aid. The goodness and beauty of Adam on being created are qualities that adorn all those who are born. Papini, portraying St. Augustine contending against the Pelagians, writes: "Replace Pelagius by Rousseau, and you will at once realize that the skirmishes and battles of Augustine are not cold relics of a defunct life, but actually something quite *up-to-date*, to use the idiom of to-day."[2]

Observe withal how the father of the Revolution expresses himself on this point: "It would be sad for us," he says, "to be obliged to recognize this distinctive and almost unlimited faculty (perfectibility) as the source of all the misfortunes of man; yet, in fact, it does withdraw him, in course of time, *from his original state* where, in quiet and innocence, he was wont to spend his days."[3] Later he adds: "Men are perverse; a sad and continuous experience provides the proof. Nevertheless, man is naturally good; I believe I have established this."[4] It has been shown that the fact

[1] St. Paul: *Epistle to the Romans*, Ch VII, v. 19.
[2] Papini: *St. Augustine*, Ch. XXVI.
[3] J. J. Rousseau: *Discourse on the Origin of Inequality among Men.*
[4] J. J. Rousseau: *Discourse on the Origin of Inequality among Men.*

of human perversity is admitted by Rousseau as it is admitted by Paganism and Catholicism. Rousseau affirms *"man is naturally good."* What is the purport of these words? They can only mean that human nature, being actually endowed with goodness, evil must reach it from outside. Let us listen again to his own words: "What," he proceeds, "can have perverted him unless it be the changes that have taken place in his constitution, the progress he has made, and the knowledge he has acquired? Human society may be admired to any degree, but it cannot lessen the certainty that *it necessarily leads men to hate one another* according as their interests run counter, and also to perform mutual service apparently, while *in reality doing one to another every conceivable damage.*"[3] Briefly, man is born with natural goodness, but society is the author of the evil observed in him.

A two-fold consequence—as I have remarked upon another occasion—arises from what has just been written. If human nature is good, everything spontaneously emanating from it will also be good; and if society is the cause of the evil, then besides being responsible for whatever evil be noticed in man, it must be considered his greatest enemy. For it is evident that if what is natural in man is good and the root of good, it would be wrong to characterize any passional movement as evil. Consequently, human education would have no other purpose save that of promoting the development of the passions, and of destroying all that the individual may have acquired socially as an adequate means of curbing them. Subversion, both ideological and verbal, cannot be more complete. Romanticism was the literary expression of so appalling a detrusion, which must needs pass

[3] Ibid. Note 9.

from the realm of thought and deed to that of law. According to Rousseau, the right of man in his state of Nature—that is, outside society—"is unlimited in everything he desires and may attain";[1] and the fundamental problem of social order is "to find a form of association that will defend and protect the person and property of each member against all common force, by virtue of which, each will obey no one but himself and remain as free as before."[2]

From the sentences quoted, there is derived not a right proceeding from a duty, not the submission which this imposes, but total emancipation in respect of others. The idea of duty, indeed, fades away and disappears. Moreover, it is evident that the subversion must also pass from the juridical order to the political. If the natural inclinations of man are good, there is no room for vice or crime. In any case, society, the sole producer of wickedness, rather than man, is responsible for these evils. For this reason, when repressive measures are ordered by social authorities in countries ruled by the doctrines of Rousseau, there always arises a morbid sentimentalism on behalf of the delinquents—with quick forgetfulness of the victims and not infrequently with reproaches to them—which excuses the former and turns deaf ears to the plaints of the latter. It even demands from society a strict account of the use of force while heedless of the most manifest infractions of the law. No proof whatever of this doctrine—condemned by the Catholic Church in the writings of the Pelagians— is put forward. It required a double demonstration: the first as to society which, like the asp, elaborates its own poison; and the second concerning the channels

---

[1] J. J. Rousseau: *Social Contract*, Bk. I, Ch. VIII.
[2] J. J. Rousseau: *Social Contract*, Bk. I, Ch. VI.

or avenues through which the virus approaches and penetrates the human heart. Rousseau takes for granted that man, outside society, "spent his days in quiet and innocence"; that it is society which "necessarily leads men to hate one another"; and having recorded these assertions, he calmly pursues his work of dissociation. Neither, however, is a matter above or beyond reason; both, were they true, would have proofs within our understanding. Rousseau treats as dogmatic that which belongs to the rational order, and once its certainty is affirmed, he enjoins as a rational truth that which he treated as a dogma. The Rousseau doctrine is definitely nothing but a *false dogma*.

Here is the teaching of the Catholic Church about the present state of human nature. Man was perfect when he came from the hands of his Creator; he could not be otherwise. By definition, frustrated action cannot be imputed to the Almighty. After man was made, one reads in *Genesis*: " . . . God saw all the things that He had made, and they were very good."[1] The idea of goodness is reiterated in the Book of Ecclesiastes by Solomon in these words: "Only this I have found, that God made man right."[2] What is meant by the goodness of Genesis and the righteousness of Ecclesiastes? If between God and man there are relations of causality, as established in the previous chapter; if reason is a characteristic faculty of the human being and the noblest of all; if in the hierarchy of natures, the spiritual is superior to the corporal, it is not difficult to conclude that the goodness or righteousness of man must consist of the submission of his reason to God, of the lower forces of his being to reason, and of his body to his soul.[3]

[1] Genesis: Ch. I, v. 31.
[2] Ecclesiastes: Ch. VII, v. 30.
[3] St. Thomas Aquinas: *Summa Theologica*, I^a, Qu. xcv, art. 1.

But it is notorious that in the actual state of humanity, neither is the body subordinated to the soul nor the lower forces to reason; and in face of the contradiction which a Creative and Omnipotent Being and the fact of imperfect creation imply, there is no other course than to admit that in created man, a fall which has lowered his status has occurred. Man of to-day is not what he was when he left the hands of the Lord. Could we, with the powers of our reason alone, continue along this path of such transcending research? The Catholic religion answers negatively; but it reveals to us what has happened. That loss of balance must have had a cause; and as Nature loses nothing intrinsic, it must be concluded that the perfect state of man, through the submission of his reason to God and the resulting subordination of lower forces to reason, and of body to soul, was due to a supernatural gift gratuitously added to human nature by God. As a punishment for a transgression affecting it totally, human nature was deprived of this supernatural gift, the cause of the deprivation being *original sin*, the state lost being that of *original justice*.[1]

The circumstance of the use of the same adjective qualifying justice and delinquency should not pass unremarked. As the justice was not intended for the first man, considered *personally*, that is, not an *accident of his person* but of human nature, so also the default did not injure Adam alone, but the entire Adamic nature, which is that of all men. Moreover, as something belongs to a person *per se* and something by gift of grace, in the same way, something may belong to Nature for its own sake, as issuing from its principles, and something by grace. So, original justice was a gift of grace divinely granted to human nature in the

[1] St. Thomas Aquinas: *Summa Theologica*, I*, Qu. xcv, art. 1.

first father, who forfeited it through the first sin.[1] Both justice and transgression refer then to *natural state*, not to persons or individuals. This is why Revelation proceeds to tell us that men who would have been born under the original justice assigned by God to their nature, on receiving it now from their parents, are born without that *accident* which was lost not by the person of Adam but by his nature. So original sin was called the sin of Nature.[2] It cannot be doubted that the importance of this loss is very great; but it will serve to make clear, for the second time, that when realities which are accidents are under-estimated, and attempts are made to justify certain doctrines under a plea of accidentality of things, people do not know what they are talking about.

This last point must be insisted upon in order duly to enter into the economy of this dogma which, in spite of its gloominess, is not devoid of a redemptive character. When through the guilt of the first man the boon of original justice was lost to mankind, it was not the dispossession of what was due to him as essential to his nature. Original justice was a grace, not a condition of humanity; and inasmuch as it is an accident of Nature and not of the person, its loss ought necessarily to affect all men. In his imposing style, Donoso Cortés writes thus on the subject: "The transmission of the consequences of the sin explains itself without any kind of contradiction or violence. The first man was born embellished with inestimable *privileges;* his flesh was subject to his will, his will to his understanding, which received its light from the divine understanding. . . . Falling into wretched rebellion, our first parents were justly bereft of all their *privileges*

---

[1] St. Thomas Aquinas: *Summa Theologica*, Ia-IIae, Qu. lxxxi, art. 2.
[2] St. Thomas Aquinas: *Summa Theologica*, Ia, Qu. c, art. 1.

. . . and human nature being in each individual, Adam, who is that same nature, lives perpetually in each man. . . . There is something in me that is not he, something that distinguishes me from him, something that constitutes my individual unity and renders me different from what I most resemble; and what makes me an individual variety in relation to the common unity, is what I have received and do possess from the father who begot me and from the mother who bore me. *They have not given me human nature* which came to me from God through Adam, but they have placed upon it the family stamp and likeness; *they have not given me being but the manner in which I am,* providing the lesser in the greater, namely that by which I am distinct from others, in that by which I resemble others; the particular in the common, the individual in the human. As what is human in him, causing resemblance to the others, is the *essential* in man, and what is individual and distinct is only an accident, it follows there is no man considered as a whole who does not resemble Adam more than his own father, because what he receives from God through Adam constitutes his essence, and what comes from God through his father makes his form." [1]

What were the effects of the default of our first parents, called original sin, in the natural order to which political science belongs? If man, as laid down in the previous chapter, ought to maintain himself free along the way leading to his final purpose—the object of his present life—striving by means of his understanding for knowledge of the acts connected with that purpose and the application of his will in their accomplishment, what influence has original sin exercised over these two human faculties?

[1] Donoso Cortés: *Essay on Catholicism, Liberalism and Socialism*, Bk. III, Ch. I.

Before replying to these questions, it is well to make an elucidatory comment. We are moving entirely on dogmatic ground. The Catholic Church warns everybody when considering these matters that they do not belong to the order of reason, but to another higher order: that of faith, which reason, by its own powers, cannot reach, just as rational truths are totally beyond the sensitive powers of animals. Adequate proofs for the full satisfaction of the understanding cannot therefore be demanded as in the case of Rousseau, for the philosopher of the Revolution invokes no order above the natural one in which he moved. Faith is not demonstrated; were it demonstrated, it would not be faith. Yet faith is not a thing utterly separated from reason. As it rests upon infallible truth, though it may not belong to the rational order, it cannot within this, be convinced of falsehood.[1] In other words, no proposition rationally invested with the necessary requisites so that logically and metaphysically it may be considered *true*, will be *contrary* to a truth of faith, which, after all, is a *rational* though indirect method of demonstration. Reason, then, has a vast field wherein to exercise its specific activities within the orbit of political science in relation to the dogma of original sin, contrasting it with scientific realities, and emphasizing the harmony existing between the one and the others. This is the challenge that faith makes to those who, refusing to accept it, invoke the rights of reason. Affirming a supernatural and consequently superior condition to that of human reason, it defies those who declare themselves devotees of the latter to set up a contradiction between faith and reason. The challenge is twenty centuries old, and down to the present, no

[1] St. Thomas Aquinas: *Summa Theologica*, I^a, Qu. i, art. 8.

conqueror has yet appeared in the lists. Momentarily, because of the noise and dust that was raised, some thought the veracity of faith had been defeated; but it never looked more radiant than at the end of these contests when the uproar became a melodious march of triumphant clarions, and the dust served to inter its adversaries. We are now witnessing one of those victories in the political order with the failure of the doctrine of Rousseau.

But it is not only in matters of faith that reason has the proper action just indicated. If it does not prove the principles because, according to what has been said, they are of a supernatural order, it may start from them—exactly as in human sciences—to demonstrate other truths or to make clear more than one point concerning faith. This, not only on account of the impossible antinomy between reason and faith previously proclaimed, but also because grace, far from destroying Nature, actually perfects it.[1] The connection between the one and the other seems even more intimate if it is borne in mind that the supernatural, according to the phrase just quoted from the *Summa,* must of necessity have a support in Nature. When the Catholic religion proclaims as truths the existence of God, the obligation on the part of man to worship Him, the immortality of the human soul, the difference between good and evil, and the eternal sanctions, which Weiss calls the five dogmas of natural religion, it proposes nothing that cannot be grasped by the powers proper to reason. But when, from the foundation of these truths, it reveals the intimate life of the Divinity, the creation of man in a state of grace, his fall, the Incarnation of one of the divine Persons in order to redeem him, the actual existence of grace and

[1] St. Thomas Aquinas: *Summa Theologica,* I^a, Qu. i, art. 8.

the elevation of all human beings, base though they may seem, from creatures to chidren of God, it teaches man truths of which his own intelligence would not convey the shadow of a shade.

Catholicism, then, links the worlds of reason and faith, or the natural and the supernatural, not merely placing them side by side but harmonizing them. Because it is evident, in the first place, that if man is not capable of conceiving even the intimate life of God, except by way of Revelation, the knowledge of the divine existence, which is discovered by reason, constitutes an antecedent to that acquirement; that if the fact of the infusion of grace can only reach his intelligence supernaturally, grace will act upon a spiritual soul that is studied rationally by man; that if Redemption is an eminent and profound mystery inaccessible to human understanding, through it man perceives in his being the traces of a contradiction disclosing his fall; and that if the Beatific Vision, his final destiny, is of a supernatural order, reason previously indicates it as a destiny natural to an infinite being. In the second place, the antecedent of a natural capacity for good inclinations is the antecedent of man's supernatural capacity to act under grace. "We Christians," says Cardinal Mercier, "know that reason and faith, science and dogma are made to live together. Reason prepares sincere souls and leads them to faith. . . . Grace destroys nothing, rather does it edify and exalt. . . . Christ came amongst us to regenerate Nature. . . . Let thinkers scrutinize the attributes of the transcendent Being, First Beginning and Supreme End of all that conscience reveals to us. . . . God has made the human heart and knows its fibres thoroughly; so when he deigns to enrich it with his sanctifying gifts, he alters nothing of his first

work.   Christianity is nothing but the divine sublimation of the most generous instincts of our nature."[1]

Nature is, then, the basis upon which grace acts;
and, in consequence, the natural truths themselves
are the object of sublimation by faith.   The Vatican
Council has consecrated dogmatically this truth
by proclaiming that *"recta ratio fidei fundamenta
demonstrat."*[2]

After this exposition, it is not to be wondered at that
the loss, by transgression, of an accident of the supernatural order should react upon the natural order
where matter influences the spirit although inferior to
it.   That reflection alone shows the need of inquiring
into this expressed influence before taking up the study
of the specifically political problem.

[1] Juan Zaragüeta: *The Catholic Concept of Life According to Cardinal Mercier.*
(Phrases taken from the same.)
[2] Vatican Council: Ch. IV.

CHAPTER III

THE HUMAN FACULTIES

THE connection of man with animals lies in the *proximate genus*; the *specific difference* renders him disparate from them. Animality likens man to animals, his rationality makes him different from them. The essential faculties of rationality are the understanding by means of which man knows things, and the will through which he commands the desire for them.

In order to act appropriately, an active being like man—as represented in Chapter I—must be somehow united to his object in the operation. This can occur through a double conception: by the object possessing a nature of its own, enabling it to unite with man and to be in his mind because of its likeness; or by the inclination of the mind itself towards the object. The first form of union is intellective, the second, volitive.[1]

How can man know things with intellective knowledge? Obviously through the presence in his mental operations, whatever they may be, of one circumstance: certitude. If he were not certain of something, he would never know anything. Happily, the existence of certitude is an indisputable fact to which we are subject as to an indeclinable necessity. Who asserts that he begins to philosophize by doubting, deceives himself heedlessly from the first moment by affirming with *immovable certainty* the existence of

[1] St. Thomas Aquinas: *Summa Theologica*, I^a, Qu. clxxviii, art. 1.

his doubt. The fact of certitude is prior to every philosophical system, without any of which, humanity has been certain in thought and will and also in the existence of an external world.[1]

We are, therefore, certain that we exist, that we think and that we do so through the medium of a power of the soul naturally adequate to the intellective operation. What then is the essential object of the understanding? It is a commonplace experience that only of sensible things does man become *immediately* cognisant, meaning those he perceives by means of the senses and the fancies they produce in the imagination as concrete, singular and individual things. But once they are so perceived, in the closest intimacy of the human being a transformation of that knowledge takes place by which the things apprehended, without ceasing to be what they are, lose their features of concretion, of simplicity and of individuation, and the knowledge is converted from concrete to abstract, from singular to general, from individual to universal. A tree perceived by the sense of sight is a perfectly determined thing. Subject to the psychic operation indicated, it constitutes a concept applicable to all the trees that have existed, exist and may exist in the world. Hence the proper object of the human intellective power is being, insomuch as it is abstract and universal, or its representation in the mind with these marks; in a word, the idea.[2]

So there is nothing in human intelligence that has not existed beforehand in the senses; but the scholastic adage expressing this thought—*nihil est in intellectu quod prius non fuerit in sensu*—should be completed

[1] Balmes: *Fundamental Philosophy*, Bk. I, Ch. II.
[2] St. Thomas Aquinas: *Summa Theologica*, I^a, Qu. lxxxiv to lxxxvi.

with this other proposition: *sed alio modo est in sensu, alio autem modo in intellectu*: (but in the senses in one way, and in the intelligence in another).[1]

Things sensible, which by the intellective operation of abstraction become the proper object of the understanding in so far as they present to the same their universal content, are correspondingly poles of attraction of our volitive faculties. Moreover, as in the order of knowledge, abstraction produced the due object of the understanding, so also is that of the will produced in the appetitive order. This means that a thing known and willed under its concrete forms is the proper object of the senses and of the sensitive appetite respectively: the universal is that which, as such, is known to the intelligence, and, as such, is desired by the will. The real will of man is, then, the act that has, as a formal object, abstract and universal good.[2]

How the will desires its proper object has been anticipated in Chapter I. It does not desire particular goods *of necessity*, and its attachment to the object will only be necessary when the latter is the perfect felicity, or the vision of God in His essence, which constitutes the final purpose of the will. This quality of willing or not willing while the motives of the acts remain constant, is what is termed freedom or free will.

To desire or not to desire one of two things is to choose; that is why the nature of free will should be fixed in election, which, not admissible in respect of the end of man, may yet affect the means of attaining the same. This is obvious because, although good is the proper object of the will, this, in particular,

---

[1] Mercier: *Psychology*, Vol. II, 170.
[2] St. Thomas Aquinas: *Summa Theologica*, I^a, Qu. lix, art. 1.

always shows itself to be limited, and under the two-fold aspect of the existing good and of the missing good, reason may assess things in relation as eligible or ineligible.[1]

The result of this exposition is that as freedom constitutes a quality of the will, the characteristic of which is the election of means to attain an end, its imperfection arises precisely from the possibility of choosing, not between two goods in relation to the end, but between good and evil, which term covers everything that deviates from good.[2] This imperfection has been raised to noble rank by the Revolution, and in its consecration as such, humanity has shed oceans of blood at the foot of the altar set up for its adoration. Further, if one remembers that right is the moral power that helps man to perform the acts leading to his end, it must be concluded that freedom, which is capable of turning him away from that destiny, is not right. Nobody disputes that freedom is a condition of man; that it is also a condition of crime is beyond doubt. If without freedom there is no right, neither is there delinquency without freedom. In other words: if right is confined to the field of freedom, all that lies within such bounds is not right. Outside the zone corresponding to it, is that pertaining to crime.

Freedom is, in consequence, qualified and limited in social life by right, the great restrictive element of its juridical orbit. It is plain that this restriction cannot be at the behest of an arbitrary individual judgment —the essence of despotism—but must be determined objectively by the social end. Without it, freedom, far from being the august condition of social life,

---

[1] St. Thomas Aquinas: *Summa Theologica*, I[a], Qu. lxxxiii, art. 3 and I[a]-II[ae], Qu. xiii, arts. 3 and 4.
[2] Donoso Cortés: *Essay on Catholicism, Liberalism and Socialism*, Bk. II, Ch. I.

would be the ferment that would corrupt it. In political science there are few things so clear, so speculatively unopposed and so practically unknown since the French Revolution, as this capital truth: "Right is the great controller of individual liberty."

But the investigation would be incomplete if we did not distinguish between moral and physical freedom. Interior freedom is one thing and exterior freedom another. There is a two-fold act of the will, one immediately belonging to, or—as it were—born of the will and, in the language of psychology, elicited by the will itself; another, commanded by the will and exercised through the medium of some other power, such as the act of moving, that is commanded by the will and exercised by means of the motive power. As regards the proper act of the will itself, no violence can be done it; but as regards the acts that are commanded by the will, the latter may suffer coercion by the exterior power concerned.[1] In other words, interiorly, man is always free; by coercion in the execution of the exterior act, he may not be. So the gulf separating the Catholic from the revolutionary doctrine becomes clear. The entire ethics of Christ are based upon *imputability* and *responsibility*, concepts that have passed into the juridical order produced by the civilization brought forth by Christian morality. Neither would responsibility exist nor would imputability have a logical foundation, if man did not possess interior freedom and if, in the exterior, he were forced to perform acts not willed by him, or if he were coercively prevented from performing those which he wills. But the concurrence of responsibility in the *elicited* acts is an unalterable doctrine of the Catholic Church.

[1] St. Thomas Aquinas: *Summa Theologica*, I^a,-II^{ae}, Qu. vi, art. 4.

Jean Jacques Rousseau, on the contrary, ignoring the fundamental distinction pointed out, proclaims the following: "Man was born free, yet everywhere we find him fettered. One may think himself master of others when truly he is but a slave like them. How has this change come about? I know not."[1] What is the sense of this logomachy? Does it mean perhaps that man *interiorly* has ceased to be free on account of acts subsequent to his birth? The supposition is utterly false. Did *his external life* perchance *depend* upon nobody at birth? There can be nothing more notoriously absurd. Man, by nature, depends upon his fellows to a greater degree during the first instants of his existence, for without that dependence he would die. Moreover, from that earliest time he is seen chained to the hardest shackles that can be conceived: those of pain and ignorance. Let us say with St. Thomas: Man is free in his *elicited* acts; he suffers coercion in the *commanded* acts. Is it not amazing that upon such crude amphibology, a political system has been constructed under which the whole world has been governed?

It is now time to return to the question already formulated in the previous chapter. What were the effects, in the natural order, of the loss of the supernatural gift called original justice, by our first parents? Or, in other words: did this loss cause any damage in what strictly corresponds to Nature? Here, in synthesis, are the two answers given to the question respectively by Protestantism and by the Catholic Church. The former asserts that through the effects of original sin, human nature became totally corrupt; the latter, that its forces were weakened without suffering any depreciation of principles. The sole

[1] J. J. Rousseau: *Social Contract*, Ch. I.

enunciation of these theses emphasizes their immense importance in the political order.

The three basic dogmas of Protestantism are as follows: first, the psychological doctrine of the total corruption of human nature, and of the negation of free will; second, the soteriological doctrine of the redemption of man solely through Jesus Christ, excluding all co-operation of our good works[1]; and third, the ecclesiological doctrine of the denial of papal authority in favour of the exclusive authority of the Scriptures individually interpreted by divine inspiration.[2] These dogmas appear explicitly proclaimed in the thirteen propositions with which Luther opposed Eck, and the answer he made to the Franciscans of Insterbourg in the following terms: "To deny that man sins in good, and that a venial sin is not so by nature, or that sin remains in a child after baptism; to deny this is to trample upon St. Paul and Jesus Christ together. . . . He who alleges that free will is master of his acts, good or bad, knows nought of contrition or of free will. The same judgment applies to one who believes man is not justified by the faith of the word alone, or that faith is not destroyed by each mortal sin." "Free will is nothing, because man cannot but do evil, he can never do anything good except by the grace of God. Consequently free will is not free, it is enslaved by sin." "That the Roman Church is constituted over all others is only proved by simple decrees of the Roman pontiffs issued during the last four hundred years." "Just as a ruined city or a crumbling house preserves the name and title it had before and will have in

[1] In making this reference to the soteriological foundation of the Redemption, the author considers it as part of Protestant doctrine when it is affirmed that its application is made solely through Jesus Christ. (Translator's note.)
[2] Mourret: *General History of the Church*, Vol. V, Part II, Ch. I.

future, yet is incapable of doing what it did before, so does it happen with free will."[1]

What is to be said of this doctrine in so far as it may affect the political order? When calmly examined, it is certainly a matter of profound astonishment that people who boasted of their love of liberty and pleaded for the independence of civil society, should have adopted such a standard. There is no teaching so ignobly degrading to the citizen as that of the Reformation. To deny that man is master of his actions by free will is to remove the foundation of civil life. To maintain that freedom can only do good with the assistance of grace, and that what proceeds from it is naturally evil, is to make impossible, on one side, the effect of grace itself, and on the other, civil life in its proper sphere. The supreme guarantee of freedom which Christ gave to this poor humanity in these words: "Render to God the things that are God's, and to Caesar the things that are Caesar's," is absolutely destroyed by Protestantism. Yet Protestantism begot Liberalism. What, in other times, might seem paradoxical, is not so to-day. Full individual independence, and not the defence of civil freedom, has ever been the object of Liberalism, in spite of avowal to the contrary.

In view of this, no effort will be required to understand that the consequences of the battle won by the Catholic Church over Protestantism would affect, not only religious issues, but would, of necessity, be extended to the civil order. The Church saved herself at Trent, but she also saved the State. That those poisoned by the Revolution should not desire to appreciate this, is no argument against the evident fact, just as the existence of light cannot be doubted

[1] Rohrbacher: *Universal History of the Catholic Church*, Vol. XII, pp. 37 to 42.

because the blind do not perceive it. An outline of the Catholic thesis according to the great Doctor of Aquinas, and the definitions of the Council of Trent, are sufficiently convincing.

In the previous chapter it was laid down that original justice, in which man was constituted by God and through which the body was subject to the soul, the lower forces of his being to reason, and reason to God, was a supernatural gift freely added to Nature. Punishment of the misdoing known as *original sin* caused the total loss of original justice and the equilibrium it had produced; man fell into the bondage of sin. His redemption could only be conceived by supernatural means—the merits of our Lord Jesus Christ—who as man merited for humanity, and as God merited infinitely. These merits are applied to every man by the Sacrament of baptism, by which he is supernaturally regenerated and becomes again a child of God, worthy of reaching the supernatural end to which he had been raised by original justice. Man's justification before God does not consist solely of the remission of sins, but also of the sanctification and renovation of the inner man by the voluntary reception of grace and of the gifts accompanying it. He does not attain this justification by his own works performed according to the lights of his nature or the precepts of law, but by divine grace. Nevertheless, it cannot be reached by faith alone; the co-operation of the will is essential.[1]

Having established in these terms the Catholic doctrine concerning the effects of original sin in relation to the supernatural gift of original justice, it may now be examined in connection with the effects caused in human nature. An exposition of the former

[1] Council of Trent: *Decrees on Original Sin and Justification.*

subject was indeed indispensable, not only for the purpose of avoiding confusion and undue application, but also as an antecedent of the latter. From what has been stated, one may infer in general terms the character of the true thesis. If original justice was a supernatural gift, an accident of human nature, it could not be held that its loss should adversely affect that nature either in the principles of its constitution, or in the properties caused by them.[1] Moreover as free choice is a natural quality of the will, to affirm that it is lost to man through sin, or reduced to an unreal name, a fiction or vain imagination, must be judged contrary to the most elementary foundations of logic, apart from being entirely opposed to human dignity, as already remarked when commenting upon this gross Protestant aberration. Equally untenable is the notion of man's property of free determination, moved and urged by God, co-operating in nothing towards its preparation and disposition for the grace of justification, incapable of refusing its consent, remaining like something inanimate in a purely passive state.[2] Neither was it possible, without scorning reason, to contend that after sin "man can do but evil," because the inclination to virtue is natural to man by the very fact of his being rational, for intuitively he knows certain principles both of the speculative and practical orders, that are germs of intellectual and moral virtues; and it has been seen that the proper object of the will is good, in the abstract and in the universal.[3]

Yet although the doctrine of Rousseau has been rejected, the origin of evil cannot be placed elsewhere than in man himself. How can original sin have been

[1] St. Thomas Aquinas: *Summa Theologica*, Iª-IIªe, Qu. lxxxv, art. 1.
[2] Council of Trent: *Decree on Justification.*
[3] St. Thomas Aquinas: *Summa Theologica*, Qu. lxxxv, art. 1.

the source of the evil of humanity when it has neither removed nor diminished the good of Nature in the principles constituting it, and in the properties caused by these principles? Did not St. Paul bring forward that contradiction which man holds within himself whereby "the good we desire, we do not; but the evil we desire not, that we do"?

One of the doctrinal points wherein the greatness of Catholicism is most intensely appreciated, is that which we are about to make the object of our inquiry in answer to the question recorded, and this, not only in the specifically religious, but also in the social and political aspect. The problem of evil fills almost entirely the area proper to society and government, both of which design institutions, conceive artifices, seek sanctions, that if they do not stamp out evil in the world, at least are instrumental in lowering its intensity or in attenuating its effects. To ignore its cause, therefore, is to render unfruitful and unavailing all that society and government endeavour to raise for the purpose of accomplishing their uninterrupted solicitude. Rousseau, reviving the doctrine of the natural goodness of man and applying it to the political order, failed signally. Revolution, seeking its inspiration in his predications and setting up the political systems that characterized the nineteenth century, has let loose torrents of blood in contrast with idyllic promises. Protestantism, which transferred to Revolution the supposed individual independence, made civil society impossible—as previously pointed out—with its psychological dogma of the total corruption of human nature and the denial of free choice. To proclaim the natural goodness of man and the total corruption of human nature, leads in one form or another to the same fact of the dissolution or negation of civil society. After what has been said, the anxiety with which the statesman turns to the Church for the solution of the enigma, can be understood. Will she not give mankind the key by which, while man and his nature remain free in the use of their faculties, the internal generation of evil may be explained, providing the indispensable condition for its extinction?

This has been done. The Church has revealed the dogma of the guilt of our first parents, and as its effects in the supernatural and natural orders have previously been shown, nothing remains but to draw the consequences in order to discover the origin of evil. We shall lay open the question with the greatest possible clearness, following, as heretofore, the saintly doctor and the Council of Trent.

One thing is that original sin has not removed or diminished the good of Nature in the principles constituting it and in the properties caused by these principles; but to say that it has not produced some efiect in the natural inclinations of the faculties, would be quite another matter. An illness, serious though it may be, nowise affects our nature, which continues to be the same in the order of its principles and the properties adorning it; but, on the other hand, the natural tendency of our faculties to their respective objects is notably diminished. The fact so obviously belongs to general experience that it is unnecessary to reinforce it with observations. It may be held, then, that although human nature has not been totally corrupted by original sin, it has been weakened; and it is this weakening effect that is first indicated by the Council of Trent as a consequence of original sin. "By this sin of dishonesty"—it defines—"all Adam, according to the body and to the soul, has suffered deterioration."[1] Further on, it continues:[2] "The Holy Council confesses and recognizes that concupiscence and inclination to sin remain in baptized persons."

Indeed it must be so, for, as St. Thomas discerns, once original justice was lost, man's activities were degraded from the due order through which they were directed to virtue. This debasement, besides inflicting injury upon Nature as a whole, striking at the very powers of the soul, brought about the detriment of the understanding by ignorance impeding its course to truth. The will, the irascible and concupiscible affections were likewise harmed, their respective orders to good, strength and pleasure moderated by reason, being impaired by evil, infirmity and concupiscence.[3]

There lies the origin of evil. Once it is disclosed, all that is sombre in the dogma seems to be dispersed by the light emitted from the solution. Man, after the Fall, has not been spiritually converted into something inanimate, nor has he been lost in the total corruption of his nature to the extent of being incapable of doing good. If his determination and will have been weakened, they have not been annulled. He may live in society which, with full authority, may repress the evil in man. If the origin of his present condition is the loss of a supernatural gift, the Redemption offers him means of restoration. In the former, the political order has an unshakable foundation; in the latter, it is given to all men to attain the supernatural end to which they have been destined. The nations which incorporated the legislation of the Council of Trent in their legal systems, endowed them with the corner stone which perhaps they lacked, while those

[1] Council of Trent: *Decree on Original Sin*, No. 1.
[2] Council of Trent: *Decree on Original Sin*, No. 5.
[3] St. Thomas Aquinas: *Summa Theologica*, I^a-II^{ae}, Qu. lxxxv, art. 3.

which repudiated it, knew not what they did or were ignorant of their own rights.

How Don Antonio Maura was partly wrong when he declared that "public law is neither Catholic nor Protestant," is now perfectly clear. Public law cannot be Protestant. In this, Señor Maura was right. But it must, of necessity, be Catholic, because the true conception of man, of his nature and of his faculties cannot be dispensed with. By upholding the contrary Señor Maura erred profoundly, not entirely corrupted by the evil yet not foreign to it. Not yet as Catholics but as politicians do we look up to the Council of Trent.

SECOND PART

SOCIETY

CHAPTER I

SOCIABILITY

It has been said that man was placed by his Creator in the midst of Nature which he comprehends in his person. But he did not remain there as the only specimen of his kind. A glance around will suffice to convince us of this elemental truth, and the fact of propagation—that is, the immediate origin of human beings not created by God out of nothing—makes clear that man is not alone, nor can he be alone The presence of man in life supposes the previous existence of other beings of the same species, who begot him, cared for him and protected him in his helplessness, guiding him in his first steps when he is quite incapable of action by himself. Without that previous existence of fellow beings and the ties it entails, the individual would not even come to life. Once alive, without the protection and assistance of his progenitors, he would inexorably die. This coexistence of human beings, begetters and begotten, permanent and constant by its very nature, is called society. It is therefore to be concluded that socialibility is a natural characteristic of man.

A more careful investigation confirms patently the

deduction which a first glimpse at the world of life suggests to our judgment. If the frailties and defects of human nature point to such an inference, the perception of its perfections likewise leads us there. The intelligence which requires for its progress other intelligences, the word of mouth that betrays the natural need of communication, demand imperatively the same conclusion. Speech would have no purpose if there were nobody with whom to communicate ; the intellective faculty with which man is endowed would lack nutrition and would decay if it could not exchange ideas. By the channel of communication that we observe in ourselves, by the necessity of the active and passive causes of our thoughts which presume continuous and permanent relations, we reach the same conclusion as that to which we were led by the contemplation of human weakness, that is to say: the natural necessity of society amongst men.

Long ago, ancient wisdom proclaimed so transcending a truth. Aristotle wrote this sentence: "It is seen, in an evident manner, why man is a sociable animal, even in a greater degree than bees or all other animals which live together. Nature, as we say, does nothing in vain. Amongst all animals, man alone has the use of speech." Later, drawing the final consequence from his judgment, he declares: "He who cannot live in society or he who needs nothing or nobody because he suffices in himself, does not form part of the State: he is a brute or he is a god."[1]

The maxim of the Greek philosopher was graciously taken up by St. Thomas Aquinas and christianized by him. When defending the solitary life as a means of obtaining spiritual perfection, the great doctor disapproves two forms of solitude: that which is the

[1] Aristotle: *Politica,* Bk. I, Ch. I.

product of a ferocity of spirit, and that aiming at a
total consecration to divine things which—says the
Saint—is *superior to man* because "he who does not
communicate with others is a beast or. God, that is to
to say, a divine man."[1]

One who in few questions brings his judgment into
agreement with true philosophy and Catholic doctrine, also bears positive testimony here. Marx, while
drawing erroneous conclusions from the assertion,
maintains the sociable character of man in the following terms: "Individuals produce in society; social
production, then, will be the starting point of our
investigation. . . . The farther we go back in history,
the individual . . . appears more clearly as forming
part of a greater whole; at first, still in an entirely
natural manner, of the family and of a tribe which is
the family extended; afterwards, of a community
under different forms, born of antagonism and of the
fusion of the tribe."[2]

The Catholic Church has held unswervingly the
doctrine of human sociability. Man being created—
she teaches—"the Lord God said: 'It is not good for
man to be alone; let us make him a help like unto
himself.' "[3] The divine word made man sociable; he
was not enabled to do so by choice of his will. Sociability is a condition of his nature, not the outcome of
his freedom. Leo XIII recalled this in his Encyclicals
Diuturnum illud and *Immortale Dei*.

It was Rousseau who, with his *social compact*,
attempted to destroy the immutable stability of
human society determined by the attribute of the
natural sociability of man. In the articles published in *Acción Española* which I devoted to the study

[1] St. Thomas Aquinas: *Summa Theologica*, II^a-II^{ae}, Qu. clxxxviii, art. 8
[2] Charles Marx: *Criticism of Political Economy*, p. 306.
[3] Genesis: Ch. II, v. 18.

of the false dogmas of Revolution, I fully exposed the Rousseauan fallacy about human society. For the purpose of fixing the foundations of the new State, it will be sufficient to recall that in the mind of the Genevan philosopher, the natural state of man is the savage in his greatest degree of savagery; that is to say, vagrant in the forests, speechless, with no kind of relation with his fellows. How he passed from this condition, supposed to be natural, to the social state diametrically opposite, was not easy to justify either with facts or by reason; and so, Rousseau appealed to his delirious imagination. He *supposes* a moment occurred when isolated man could not subsist in that state of Nature, because the obstacles detrimental to his preservation there became too powerful for the strength of which each individual can dispose in order to gain the ascendancy. Moreover, as men are not capable of creating new forces though they may, on occasion, unite and direct existing ones, those who lived in a savage state had no other means of preservation save that of forming, by aggregation, a sum of forces which, surmounting those of resistance, could prevail. Thus the social compact was solemnly agreed upon.

Only Revolution, ever forming a state of depression of human intelligence, could receive these deranged figments without resounding laughter. It seems as if Rousseau intended to accumulate in his doctrine as many absurdities as he found to hand. That man has lived in a savage state is indisputable. What Rousseau does not show nor even attempts to prove is that such should be the primitive state, and that savagery should have broken every social link. But that is perhaps least important. What is inconceivable is that he should *suppose* a fact as a foundation of the constitution of society; that he should confess his foundation is nothing more than *supposition*, and that, forthwith, he should proceed to draw consequences as if it were an undoubted and incontrovertible affirmation. There is no other example of a writer who has treated his readers with greater disdain and levity.

Why did Nature, all at once, increase in destructive forces which solitary man could not overcome? Why did man, on the contrary, not acquire new powers through the medium of habit which, by inheritance, would be transmitted to his children? How, if he knew not language, was he to propose the compact to his fellows? By what art, if they lacked the sense of justice, could they all discuss the proposal? Above all, how could men live, if at birth they did not have the help of their progenitors? If they had it, what was that manner of life if not *naturally social?* There are cases in which reason is ashamed of the fallacies to which mankind has assented. This is one of them. But it is not sufficient, once the social character of man as a distinguishing feature of his nature is established, to conclude that it is necessary for him to live in society. The mere statement does not solve the problem; it fixes the inception of the solution. Until now, the examination of man has led us to discover that he coexists with his fellows because coexistence is required by his defects and by his perfections. This coexistence has yet to be studied internally under the name "society" which we have given it.

The conception of "society," evidently, cannot be be regarded equally with that of multitude, not even a multitude of men. That the idea of assemblage is implicit in the conception of society is not to be questioned; but to contend they are identical is repellent to every moderately cultivated mind.

Neither can a multitude that to mere quantity adds a unitive reason, whatever it may consist in, be called society. People attending a spectacle form a gathering ephemerally united by the end which incidentally has brought them together; they do not make up society. Society, indeed, implies plurality but reduced to unity in a permanent and transcending manner. Where shall we find a sufficiently strong and lasting bond whereby the multitude, which of itself bespeaks numerosity, may be converted into unity?

If society, properly so called, only occurs among intelligent beings, the connecting force capable of uniting them must affect the two faculties which, as proper to the intellective life, we have studied in the previous chapter, namely, understanding and will. As truth is the object of understanding, and good the object of the will, social unity will require a knowledge of a truth the good of which men must be morally obliged to attain. Wherefore, in the society worthy of this name, there must be recognized unity of social end, harmony of intelligences towards the same, concordance of wills, and co-ordination of suitable means towards securing it. A society lacking any of these requisities cannot be called perfect in its kind; nor, according to good social principles, could the absence of any of the requisites mentioned be defended as an element of perfection. Nevertheless, the society vindicated by Revolution is of this type. Now, when we view it from a distance, there is nobody ready to cast a doubt upon it.

If society, properly so called, occurs only among intelligent beings; if the bond capable of connecting them is an end known and willed, and requires joint effort, two most fundamental consequences become imperative: the first, related to the extension of society, and the second, to the behaviour of those who form it. If Nature is identical in all men and its end the same for all, man's vocation is that of a universal human society. The instinct of sociability—fully demonstrated by the experience of centuries—has not encountered insurmountable barriers either in civilization, in races or in modes of life. A man lives in society with his fellows in spite of the fact of the differences of religion among them, the most dissociating fact even in mere civil life. As the human end is one, when an individual moves towards his end, the acts he may realize to that effect cannot cause others to deviate from theirs— should he bear relation to them—because, by definition, the end is the same for all. Rather, on the contrary, such individual action would lead others to the common end. In other words, man must carry out on behalf of his fellows those very acts which he was morally obliged to perform in order to attain his end. Man's duties towards his neighbour—the determination of which was postponed—are, then, analogous to those concerning himself, and they comprise co-operation in the fulfilment of the duties of every man to God. Hence reciprocal human rights arise. But in order to appreciate duly the conclusion arrived at, it must be borne very carefully in mind that until now we have been referring to men as *natures*, that is, *equal* to one another; that, therefore, equality in mutual obligations affects those described as natural, and that, finally, the rights that may, and should be reputed equal, are the rights *of Nature* or *of humanity*. But beside these special characteristics of Nature, there exist in the concrete individual—which is Nature's expression— others that diversify, distinguish and separate him from the rest. If the *natural* rights are the same in all men, and in all should be equally recognized and respected, the *personal* or *individual* rights accruing from the existence of differential features must be different. Equality regarding *natures*, inequality regarding *individuals*, is the great law of justice in every society.

As the duties that man has to himself affect the perfection of his understanding and of his will and the preservation of his life, those which he may have to his fellow creatures—thus forming reciprocal rights—will affect their understanding, their will and their life. The first duties will be contained within the term of *veracity;* the second, within that of *public morality*, and the third are those of respect for life and for the prerogative of others. The duties which are imposed upon all men, because they enjoin social co-operation in the fulfilment of obligations binding men to God, come under the word "religion."

The matter enclosed in the subjects of veracity and public morality is plainly and widely known; all that pertains to self-defence and the conditions in which it may be exercised are also common knowledge; and as the *positive* promotion of religious duties is attributed to another public society different from the civil body, which we shall consider at an opportune time, it seems fitting now to speak of *property* or *dominion* as a right created by the duty of self-preservation.

There can be no school which denies to man the power—in one condition or another—of availing himself of exterior Nature for the satisfaction of his bodily needs. If he lacked this power, man would disappear from the earth. Not even Marx, Henry George or Proudhon dares to deny it. Why do they not deny it? Is it perhaps because the labour by which man appropriates Nature is the product of his personal activity? But, even granted that nothing can oppose this supposition, are the roots extracted from the earth,

the fish obtained from the water or the beast hunted
and captured, the product of human activity? Without
possessing himself of those elements which are not his
personal production, of what use would it be to him to
proclaim his right to the mere form of his activity
which served to place those things at his disposal? If a
primary right of domination over labour can be discerned in man, there is not the least sign in him of a
similar right over exterior Nature. It may be concluded
then, that this right, being absolutely necessary to
mankind, which would perish without it, is not
originary.   So one is forced to ask this question:
"Who gave it?"

Though with blasphemy upon his lips, Proudhon
was once more bound to acknowledge that man's
power of maintaining his body by a vital union with
portions of physical Nature, which cannot be denied
him without causing his death, is, save for God,
devoid of all foundation.   He accepted the divine
existence as a hypothesis, as a necessary dialectical
instrument. Even in blasphemy, there can be homage
to the Divinity. It is seen in Proudhon in the sense of
confessing that the problem of property—even limited
by the strict terms in which it has hitherto been
expressed—imperiously demands a solution that God
alone can furnish. This is sufficient for us, it would
suffice even without Proudhon, to ensure that the eternal
word cannot be rejected. Revelation has made it known
to us in this way: "And He" (God) "said: 'Let us
make man to our image and likeness; and let him have
dominion over the fishes of the sea, and the fowls of the
air, and the beasts, and the whole earth, and every
creeping creature that moveth upon the earth.' "[1]
Man's right of property over exterior Nature *which he*

[1] Genesis: Ch. I, v. 26.

did not create, and which originally he lacked, was thus promulgated by Him who alone could promulgate it; by the Author and Creator of the things that were the object of the dominion. By donation made to him, man had the right to apply them to the sustenance of his life.

Evidently this dominion does not refer to the human individual but to the human race, to whom God gave the earth *without condition and in negative community* so that it should be possessed in the *state of grace* in which, as we have seen, mankind was constituted. But after the loss of original justice, the reiteration of the donation introduced a hardship: " . . . cursed is the earth in thy work, said the Lord; with labour and toil shalt thou eat thereof all the days of thy life. Thorns and thistles shall it bring forth to thee; and thou shalt eat the herbs of the earth. In the sweat of thy face shalt thou eat bread till thou return to the earth out of which thou wast taken. . . . "[1] Could the new manner of the exercise of the right of property, after the transgression, influence the régime of negative community distinctive of the state of grace? The entire subject of private property is covered by this question.

Obviously, from the moment the divine condemnation imposed sacrifice and toil upon man in his endeavours to detach the earth from its state of practical infecundity, not because its productive condition had been lost but because it was sparingly concealed in its bosom, human action became invested with a discriminative element from which it had been exempt before. Applied to this discriminative element, the principles of natural justice demanded that one man should not profit by the work that the sacrifice and pains of another had realized. Naturally,

[1] Genesis: Ch. III, vv. 17 to 19.

then, that exhausting effort with which the earth was wrested from its state of practical infecundity, took mankind out of the state of community in which it was placed. Nobody said, as Rousseau supposes: "This is mine";[1] but on converting a piece of barren earth into a fertile land, the man who had primarily worked that land had, with his labour, endowed it with the main condition of its destiny which it did not previously possess; wherefore it was no longer the earth given by God in negative community.

In view of this fact there was nothing save the following alternative: that the state of concrete fecundity should succeed the negative state of the land by which, no portion belonging to one more than to another, he who toiled, forfeited the hard-earned fruits of his exertion, nobody being able, in justice, to acquire it or to enjoy it; or that the soil, practically barren until then, should follow the condition of the hard fertilizing labour. The first solution entailed a profound, complete and irritating injustice. The second harmed no one. But apart from the fact that no substantial difference exists between shooting an animal in the forest and appropriating it—the right of property acknowledged by all schools—and transforming sterile into fertile land and calling it one's own, the solution of justice for the individual was a convenient one for society. If the effects of labour incorporated with the land are not attributed to him who accomplished them, they would be lost to mankind for, according to what has been noted, the human right in negative community only concerned unproductive land. In such a case, the land would have been the grave of man, not the element of his life.

Private property, after the fall of our first parents,

---

[1] *Discourse on the Origin of Inequality Among Men.* Part II.

had, therefore, a natural, just and becoming origin for human society. Neither covetousness, usurpation, nor violence created it. This is not to be taken as implying that rapacity does not figure in the *particular* origin of some concrete private property, nor that any specified case may not be due to unlawful encroachment, nor that violence may not have placed goods of all kinds in the hands of many. What is asserted in the face of these points which show common ignorance of the subject, is that the *primitive* human act which brought the land out of its state of negative community, as a natural effect of the change wrought in the condition of man and of the land, was not covetous nor usurping nor violent. When it took place, covetousness meant nothing to man because the whole earth was at his command. If any one usurped certain. property, it must have already existed in a way to make usurpation possible; and violence arrogated that same condition; besides, the prospect of one employing it against the whole of society is inexplicable.

But private property—arising from the most elementary principles of natural law, protected by social justice and enjoined for the convenience of society— never constituted and never can constitute an absolute right without limitations of a religious, moral and social character. Proprietorship, having originated in a divine donation destined to the satisfaction of human needs, its use will have to be rationally suited to that satisfaction if it is not to be illegitimate; and as all the goods of the earth have a social and not merely individual or private end, this proprietorship will be affected by a *social function* although, in itself, it *may not be such*. The corollary inferred from these two consequences is obvious: various tacit qualifying conditions govern private ownership. In the religious order, even if man could materially annihilate the substance and nature of the things possessed, the legitimate exercise of his right does not by any means go so far as to destroy the form of things without any higher finality, nor to use them irrationally or fancifully. In the moral order, though having the faculty of regulating his property and directing it to the satisfaction not only of his needs and those of his kin, "but also to the due decorum of his person in the manner fitting to his state,"[1] he is obliged, in charity, to assist his fellows in their needs. In the social order, private right cannot be an obstacle to public interest even in the case of extreme necessity, for when it stands in the way of public good, private property may be forcibly used for the benefit of the common welfare, or expropriated, and in the case of a life being in danger, the goods of others may be freely made use of.

Therefore, the foundations upon which the social edifice wherein the new State must be enthroned, are: society as an essential note of human nature for the attainment of the common destiny of men; their vocation for the constitution of one universal society; the conception of the human being inferred from his present condition; equality of natural rights; inequality of personal rights; and legitimacy and necessity of private property in the fallen state of mankind.

[1] Leo XIII. *Rerum Novarum.*

CHAPTER II

CHURCH AND NATION

THE fundamental social fact of the propagation of the species reveals that humanity, as it is constituted to-day, forming societies living in territorial extensions over which they exercise jurisdiction, does not retain the mode of its appearance on earth. The condition of its unity, withal, leads us to infer that its origin lies in a family. Whenever science feels the necessity of ascending as far as the sources of life, it finds in Revelation the explanation of the mystery or the confirmation of the truth discovered. "And God created man to His own image; to the image of God He created him. Male and female He created them. And God blessed them, saying: 'Increase and multiply, and fill the earth. . . .' "[1]

From that primitive family was humanity born, and later a universal fact was to influence what had gone before. There was a period in the history of the human race when it dwelt in dispersion over the earth to the extent that ties of relation between the different groups into which it had divided, were inexistent. Heterodoxy attempted to set up this reality in opposition to the biblical narration, inferring from it a multiple origin of humanity. The attempt was vain. Science, once more, coincided with Revelation against anti-religious fallacy. The unity of the human species being confirmed, its dispersion could not be due to

[1] Genesis: Ch. I, vv. 27 and 28.

94

any other cause than that betokened in the sacred books when explaining the variety of languages and individuals whose speech, until then, was one and the same.[1]

With humanity divided and dispersed throughout the world, the universal society that was to congregate all men was frustrated. Supreme difficulties were placed in the way of the efficacy of the united endeavours of all men towards their common destiny. They emanated from material distance and the obstacles that physically antagonized association, proceeding from seas, great rivers and mountains, the disjunctive effect of which was even greater in the beginnings of life. Of necessity, while the specifically human destiny subsisted and the sociable character of man was active, in the diverse fractions of humanity, particular societies, within which the members could realize their ultimate collective aim, came forth. The earth thus sustained not one universal society alone, but many concrete particular societies which apart from having, by their own state of being, a definite and specified end, were an eventual means—through the natural necessity of human sociability—of securing for their associates the destiny indicated by Nature for all men. The concrete societies were born, then, of a combination of the sociable character of human nature, which claims united action in a common purpose for the whole of the human race, with different realities circumscribing that nature to fragmentary groups of humanity. This conclusion, as will be seen in an opportune place, is of far-reaching importance.

But those primitive concrete societies formed immediately after the dispersion over the earth, did not

[1] Genesis: Ch. XI, vv. 1 to 9.

remain nor could remain isolated for an indefinite time. They constituted, it is true, not a natural proper state, but a mutilation of the universal society, maintained by the obstacles which the earth—where man was to attain his temporal destiny—opposed to the common endeavour. From the moment those obstacles disappeared—and they were bound to do so with the propagation of the species and man's striving to master the earth—the existence of a unique destiny superior to the exclusive destinies of particular societies was, under the natural impulse of sociability, bound to bring them into association, not only by the disappearance of the circumstances which, until then, had prevented it, but also because others of a cohesive character arose. There is no question that the common human destiny would be reached once the new society was set up, and that the law of association would be applied to the newly-formed bodies when connective realities, sufficiently important to enlarge the efficacy of human concurrence, were produced.

Indeed, after the tribes became settled, because the progress of agriculture and stock breeding made their nomadic life no longer necessary, from the municipalities came the municipal guilds. These have no other origin of legitimacy because family, tribe and township upon which they were founded, were societies wherein, during the respective stages of social evolution, the human destiny had been reached. Why should that historic law stop at the municipal guilds? Surely not on account of Nature, for within them the instinct of sociability continued naturally to throb; nor by reason of the destiny of man, which is one for humanity; nor through the absence of associating facts, for the obstacles that hindered association were greater, and the forces striving to remove them were less, in inferior civilizations. Therefore, there is not only no philosophical reason to consider the work of humanity in the ascendant sense towards universal society, as terminated with the municipal guilds; but there is certainly reason to affirm that in these, the tendency to their union would be even more lively than in lower societies.

So the nation, resplendent and magnificent, arose. It is, in consequence, the major, the concrete and the particular society within which man attains his temporal destiny, peculiar, by nature, to the universal human society. Its sole definition suggests three most important observations. The nation to which one belongs is not the public society in which one is born physiologically, although the etymology of the word appears to indicate it (from *nascor*, to be born); but that in which the human end is attained. The nation is the product of the sociable character of man which demands joint endeavour towards a destiny common to the entire human race, and of certain realities sufficiently transcending to reduce that endeavour to the terms of human aggregation. The nation, finally, supposes the existence of realities capable of social concretion, that is to say, of adding to the merely social features others which make a group of men into a certain people with the permanence and transcendence demanded by a collective personality, concrete and positive in time and space. They are the self-same facts[1] that, in their whole, make up tradition; and so, one must conclude by affirming, categorically and emphatically, that WITHOUT TRADITION THERE IS NO NATION.

But if physiological birth must be excluded as a fact capable, by itself, of binding a man to a nation,

[1] See the Introduction.

G—n

it should be stated that the latter morally creates him; for, if the nation does not always receive him in the cradle, it gives to him conditions of life accumulated and bequeathed by previous generations, moulds his character, guides him and perfects his mind. Because of this, a man is called the son of his nation, which, withal, puts him into relation with his ancestors who have gone before and his descendants yet to be; and the language of sentiment has found an effective word to describe this nation. One's nation is one's fatherland just as the woman who bore us is our mother. Likewise, the links between the nation and the citizen are tinged with filial love; and political science, applied to the fatherland, cannot be cold abstraction.

Nevertheless, one must not fall into the error of supposing that by their coalition in a larger body, the constituent societies lose their distinctive being by dissolution therein. Why should they lose it, if man preserves it intact in the family society, in the municipality and in the municipal guild? No; the nation does not consume its components, for personality and sovereignty are two different things, and the existence of personalities without sovereignty and subject to the supreme power of other personalities, is perfectly feasible. The standard personality, which is that of man, makes it clear. Being the most perfect—and the personalities of societies are nothing else than a reflection of human personality—it is subject, in every hypothesis except one, to the sovereignty of other personalities. That one hypothesis is the anarchist doctrine, which places sovereignty in every individual. Leaving the careful examination of this question to its fitting place, little need be added to what has already been said in order to establish in the nation the place of those societies which, by their natural alliance, compose it. These institutions, besides the end to which eventually they were to lead man—the common destiny—could have other particular ends for the accomplishment of which their subsistence is requisite. To put it more plainly, the nation is one great society of societies.

As already explained, besides a temporal end, man has another situated beyond this world. Hence he has two lives: a finite and an eternal life. It is not faith, but reason that dictates this. Faith confirms what reason, by its own powers, discovers. The immortality of the human soul, foundation of the eternal life after natural death, properly belongs, indeed, not to the order of faith, but to that of reason. Even had man not been raised to the supernatural order, and had Christ not founded his Church, in pure natural law two entirely distinct societies, the civil and religious, would exist for him: since being sociable by nature, besides the temporal end, properly so called, in society he would obtain the conditions that would lead him, in time, to the eternal by means of the fulfilment of the duties which, naturally, he has towards God.[1]

It is not, then, to be wondered at that in Christian civilization, besides the nation, there should exist another society called the Church; because it has been said[2] that Catholicism joined together the worlds of reason and faith, and sublimated the most generous instincts of our nature. Hence, as a natural religion,[3] it brings the entire human race to the knowledge of truths which, although capable of discovering by

[1] See Ch. I of Part I.
[2] See Ch. II of Part I.
[3] When the author speaks of Catholicism as a natural religion, this phrase should be understood in its certain and orthodox sense, namely, that Catholicism, as the only true religion, fulfils upon earth the destiny which would have been assigned to natural religion had such a thing existed. (Translator's note.)

itself, it had abandoned while led astray by error. Through its essential characteristic—the supernatural —it is a religious revolution, for natural religion can never become Christianity by evolution.

The natural religious end attainable by man through a natural religious society, would encounter, in regard to the universality of concurrence, the same obstacles as civil society encountered in the fulfilment of its own end; for while it is true that the latter, by the condition of its nature, becomes merged with temporal elements varying with man's stability on earth, and the eternal destiny, even if it be natural, is unaffected by such determinations, it is no less true that a universal religious society would require one supreme authority—as will be seen when we deal with this subject—and nobody on earth, save in very extraordinary cases, could hold that authority. Supposing the Catholic Church had not been founded, man would have directed his course to his natural eternal destiny through the medium of particular religious societies.

But participating in the authority that rules the Catholic Church, is a resolution by which God, author at the same time of a natural religious society and of a supernatural religious society, has instituted the Church, of His own will, for the two societies made one. Wherefore man, who recognizes that institution as an historic fact even without the inspirations of Revelation,[1] is bound to belong to the Church and to be a member of it by the special vocation of his nature, which no longer meets with the only obstacle that stood in the way of its full satisfaction; and every particular church, every sect is not only opposed to

[1] By affirming that man recognizes the Catholic Church without the inspirations of Revelation, it is not meant that the divine character of the Church can be recognized without Revelation. (Translator's note.)

the supernatural order, but is anti-human and anti-social. The supernatural note of the Catholic religion permits the due realization of the natural end. The Church is the only society that, being supernatural, satisfies, by its universality, the natural vocation of mankind.

Furthermore, not only has the supernatural in the Catholic Church perfected what is natural in man from the religious point of view, allowing him to constitute the universal religious society, but it has given civil society the supreme associating reality. The primitive civil societies were limited by the territory possessed by the cities. The true State—as Fustel de Coulanges proves[1]—did not exceed its territory because chiefly —as also noted by the learned historian—each society had its god; and although it has been said that difference of religion is not an insurmountable barrier for the instinct of sociability in the order of civil society,[2] it must be acknowledged that to the obstacles of a physical character with which the earth countered universal human concurrence, there was added a profoundly dissociating moral obstacle. Christianity, proclaiming one sole God, one sole heavenly fatherland and one sole family of divine adoption for all men, destroyed with its word one of the most active ferments of disgregation; and even from the human point of view, it has been the reality that has most stimulated the natural instinct of sociability. When Mella said that "the pagan world knew no nations," and that "the nation is a creation of Christianity,"[3] he was not the victim of excessive religious fervour; for if the Catholic religion did not create them

[1] Fustel de Coulanges: *La Cité Antique.*
[2] See previous Chapter.
[3] Juan Vázquez de Mella: *Discourse Delivered in Santander in August* 1908.

directly, it broke down the impediment which, in the greatest degree, opposed their constitution.

A State—and, therefore, the New State—will be unable to avoid, at the same time, the natural and supernatural reality of a religious society set up by its side and composed, besides, of an aggregation of men, which at once comprehends the whole or part of those composing civil society. This phenomenon should not pass unremarked by those who are bent upon the work of uprooting it.

Moreover, it is not a question of mere duplication. The aggregation of men is, in every society, *its material element* since the specific condition comes from the end pursued, and the human quality of being may aspire to various ends. Anti-clericalism—that doctrine which in the religious order is bound up with so much ineptitude—presupposes the entire submission of the Church to the State because the latter claims as citizens those faithful to the former, without even suspecting that the formal or qualifying element is the social end, and not the associated multitude, and that to determine the relations existing between civil and religious society, the respective condition of their ends must be examined. It likewise ignores the fact that rights inherent in a society by virtue of its nature proceed, beyond all doubt, from its end for the purpose of demanding from its members everything necessary, but nothing unnecessary, for the attainment of the end.[1]

If the same aggregation of men can be the material element of civil and religious society, and both are empowered to claim from their members all that is necessary to gain their respective ends, it is not

---

[1] In the author's work *Ferdinand the Catholic and the Counterfeiters of History*, this point is treated more fully.

difficult to presume the case in which the claim of both societies may be contrary or contradictory. Church and nation would then be found in a state of conflict. It is necessary, therefore, to set down the principles that would lead to its solution.

Consequently, what are the relations of the Catholic Church with civil societies constituted on earth? The answer is clear although it should be divided into two parts in view of the double aspect—natural and super-natural—characterizing it.

Because its doctrine comprises all the natural principles of religion and of ethics, the Catholic Church should maintain with those civil societies that order of relations corresponding to the natural religious society. As the purposes of all of them are different in kind, and as societies are qualified by the nature of their respective purposes, it is plain that there can be no relations of mutual dependence between them. The religious society cannot depend upon civil societies nor can civil societies depend upon the religious society. "In temporal things and in relation with the temporal end, the Church has no power in civil society; and even when composed of Catholics, a civil society is not subordinated to the Church in things concerning temporal affairs and its temporal end. On the contrary, it is perfectly independent."[1] Vitoria had said it in his usual energetic style: "The Pope is not the lord of the world. . . . Whence is seen the error of many lawyers like Sylvestre and others who think the Pope is lord of all the world *with his own power and that he has authority and temporal jurisdiction over all princes throughout the world.* I do not doubt that this is openly untrue, and if the

[1] Cardinal Tarquini: *The Principles of the Public Law of the Church*, pp. 79 and 80.

adversaries say it is manifestly true, *I believe it is a falsehood for the purpose of flattering and pleasing* the Pontiffs."[1] Finally Leo XIII, in his Encyclical *Immortale Dei*, expresses the same thought in this way: "From what has been said, one may see how God has made two powers co-participants in the government of the whole human race: the ecclesiastical power and the civil power, the one being set over the celestial and divine interests, the other over the earthly and human interests. Each is supreme in its own class, each has fixed limits within which it is contained, limits which are defined by the nature and special object of the province of each. The result is a *kind of double sphere of action* in which their peculiar rights and several attributions are circumscribed."

But mutual independence in one order does not mean absolute independence. Both civil and religious societies have the same *material* element, and their actions devolve upon the same *subject*. If what is claimed from the latter is contradictory, there must exist a formula to bring about, *in case of conflict*, the submission of one society to the other. The key to this cannot be found save in the nature of the social ends, for societies are judged by their ends. So the question is limited to the decision as to which end is to prevail by its more exalted quality. Does superiority correspond to the end pursued by the civil society or, on the contrary, does the purpose of the religious society manifest the advantage?

With its mere formulation, the problem offers the solution. The purpose of civil society is temporal happiness, the limits of its action being found on earth and in the purely exterior activity of man. Therefore, it only regulates an inconsiderable part of his whole

---

[1] Vitoria: *Question of the Power of the Church.*

life, and within that inconsiderable part, the least of his acts, for all immanent acts, even though they relate to temporal good, are outside the jurisdiction of civil society. On the other hand, the religious society provides the eternal happiness of man; the limits of its action, even in the purely natural purport, pass in their effects beyond time and space. They enter even into immortality for which religion prepares man; its searching look penetrates even the innermost recesses of conscience, for it controls not only external but the most intimate and internal acts. So it is evident that the superiority of the religious society over the civil society is as great as that of the immortal over the perishable. It follows that should these two societies enter into conflict, it is the mandate, the law, the rule prescribed by the religious society, which must prevail in man whose membership is common to both, even to the detriment of the mandate, the law, the rule enjoined by the civil society.[1]

In regard to this most interesting point, Leo XIII in the Encyclical previously quoted, thus expresses himself: "But as the subject on which both sovereign powers—religious and civil—devolve, is one and the same, and also as one thing is wont to appear, though under a different aspect, within one jurisdiction or the other, it is clear that God, most provident, did not set up those two sovereign powers without jointly constituting the order and procedure to be observed by them in their respective action. *'For the powers that are, are ordained of God.'* (Romans xiii, v. 1.)" He provides the means of arriving at a peaceful solution of the conflict in these words: "A regular coalescence between the two powers is necessary, an intimate

---

[1] See the author's work *Ferdinand the Catholic and the Counterfeiters of History.* Part II Section 4, II.

union resembling that of the soul and body of man, a not unreasonable comparison. The nature and scope of the connection can be determined only as we have laid down, by having regard to the nature of each power, and by taking account of the relative excellence and nobleness of their purpose. One of the two has for its proximate and principal object the care of the frail and fleeting interests of man; the whole purpose of the other is to procure for him the everlasting joys of heaven."

The supremacy of the Church over the civil society, in the case of conflict, being *rationally* established, it becomes expedient to realize its effects, recalling that the rights of every society have their source in the end of that society by virtue of which it may exact from its members all that is requisite for the achievement of the end, but nothing that is unnecessary thereto. The religious end has now been safeguarded in the conflict, but full consideration must be given to the due independence of the civil society in everything touching temporal affairs and the strictly temporal end. With a clear perception of the scope of the doctrine, it should be remarked that what has been said is derived from principles which govern every human society, whereby denial of the conclusions means denial of the very rights of civil society, considered in itself, and in a state of conflict with others inferior to it by reason of their particular ends (municipal guilds, municipalities and families). It has been truly said that "once these foundations are destroyed or enfeebled, the rights of the civil power will wane or become extinct, for civil society can have no other support."[1] If the nation disowns them before the Church, the municipal guilds will disown them before

[1] Tarquini: Op. cit. p. 53.

the nation, and the municipalities before the guilds. We already have painful experience of this.

After this there is little to add in fitting reply to the questions formulated from the supernatural point of view proper to the Church. The reasons binding Catholic nations to the recognition of her pre-eminence in case of conflict, are strengthened by the consideration that to the natural duties of men are added, in the Christian, the supernatural duties, the superiority of which, in respect of the former, need not be stressed further.

The great Vitoria sums up the relative position of Pope and princes in the following lines which may worthily close this chapter: "I do not say that it" (the civil power) "is not subject to the Pope; because it is true that all powers are subject to the Pope *by reason of the spiritual power* in so far as all men are sheep and he is their shepherd; but I say it is not subject to him *as a temporal lord* . . . which needs no proof, being evident of itself. But it can be confirmed. Because the temporal republic" (in the sense of nation) "is a perfect and integral republic, it is subject to nobody outside it; otherwise it would not be integral; and therefore, it may constitute itself as a ruling power *nowise subject to any other in things temporal.*"[1]

[1] Vitoria: *Question of the Power of the Church.*

CHAPTER III

LEGITIMATE AND SPURIOUS FORMS OF THE NATION

THE nation is a major society of societies, not of individuals. This was the final consequence resulting from the evolution of the natural instinct of sociability combined with the associating realities which go to make tradition. To afford the citizen the necessary means of attaining the temporal human destiny is the national end; to provide those conducive to the other particular ends is the exclusive object of the component societies of the nation.

Its organic composition, of singular elevation and majesty, was bound to overwhelm more than one frivolous or shallow understanding which, without penetrating beneath the surface of things, merely judged by appearances or claimed its view of conjunctive facts as the limit of social evolutional force. In this way were born the Democratic, Nationalist and Socialist systems, destroyers, in one form or another, of the organic concept of the nation. Thence arose, in modern times, various notions participating in greater or lesser degree in those systems, culminating on one side, in anarchic Syndicalism, and on the other, in the deification of the State or at least of the temporal end of man.

As always, it is Rousseau who first offers his usual contribution to error. The social compact, the absurdity of which has been made clear,[1] "produces immediately"—says this writer—"instead of the particular person of each contracting party, a moral and collective body composed of as many members as there are votes in the assembly, which from this very act receives its unity, its common *ego*, its life and its will. This public person, so formed from the union of all the others, in former times took the name of *city*, and now takes that of *republic* or *body politic* which, when it is passive, is called by its members *State*; *sovereign*, when it is active; *power*, when compared with its compeers. In regard to the associates, they are known collectively by the name of *people* and, in particular, they are called *citizens* in so much as they partake of sovereign authority, and *subjects* in so much as they are subject to the laws of the State."[2] So that "as the sovereign power is made up only of particular powers, there cannot be any interest contrary to its own."[3] Liberal Democracy was born when these words were written.

In the political order there can have been few more equivocal terms than "Nationalism." From France where, as in Spain, there are historical, linguistic and racial diversities, there have come to us echoes of Nationalism. Yet its cry is not of regional independence, but of national unity: "France for the French." French Nationalism is not dividing, but constructive; it is not against the fatherland, but against the foreigner. Invoking Nationalism, the three parts of Poland, separated by an act of force, have come together, so restoring the work of centuries. The undertaking was not inspired by an irritation of local pride, but by an exaltation of love of country

[1] See Ch. I of this Part.
[2] J. J. Rousseau: *Social Contract*, Ch. VI.
[3] J. J. Rousseau: *Social Contract*, Ch. VII.

and sense of unity. The Basque and Catalonian Nationalisms are something very different. With more or less crookedness in method, audacity or reservation in word, advances or retreats in action, they have one ultimate clear fina ity: to sever the ties, centuries old, which bind the Basque Provinces and Catalonia to Spain, and to set them up as nations by means of a criminal matricide.

So that there may be no doubt, let us present texts that cannot be challenged. Sabino Arana—the founder of Basque Nationalism—when interpreting the sacred Basque *Fueros*[1] with his stunted rural intelligence, claims in their name the independence of the Basque country, perverting their nature in order to justify his radically anti-Basque conception: "For the Basque people to rule themselves by their *Fueros* means to become again absolutely free and independent of Spain, with a government of their own, a legislative power of their own, and international frontiers."[2] An infamous book, a kind of Nationalist catechism, renders this thought of Sabino Arana thus: "What is Basque Nationalism? The political system which defends the rights of the Basque race to live independently of every other race."[3] His most conspicuous satellites explain it thus: "The being of the nation, that which is unique and necessary for its existence, is the race, the blood; a different blood or race from those of other human collectivities. . . . The quality of being of each race demands absolute freedom for its development."[4] "But what freedom is this to which it may and ought to aspire? Manifestly, to all freedom, to full independence."[5]

[1] See note on p. 53.
[2] Sabino Arana: *The Carlist Party and the Basque Fueros.*
[3] Iber: *Ami Vasco.*
[4] Kizkitza: *Guipuzkoarra, No.* 87.
[5] Engracio Aranzadi: *The Basque Nation.*

On his part, Prat de la Riba wrote and spread—
though it seems incredible he should have been
allowed to do so!—these blasphemies against the
fatherland: "Once for all, this monstrous bifurcation
of our soul had to be done away with; it had to be
recognized that we were Catalonians and that we
were nothing else but Catalonians; it had to be realized
what we were not, in order to know clearly, deeply,
what we were and what Catalonia was. This work,
the second phase of the process of Catalonian nationalization, was not brought about by love, like the first,
but by hatred. Nationality is a unity of culture, a
collective soul with its own sense, with its own thought
and with its own will."[1] Cambó, more tortuous,
said to the Basques when conveying to them the
Catalonian sense of Nationalism: "The conscience of
personality exists" (in the Basques) "and the desire
of perpetuating it is produced in you. . . . Your
Nationalist problem is now set forth in all frankness.
For others it is a question of a problem of good
government; but for us, Catalonians, and for you,
Basques, there is a problem of freedom."[2]

The national idea of the Socialists suffers from the
obscure confusions of its doctrine and the anti-
scientific aberrations constituting its foundations.
Here, with its notorious contradictions, is the Marxist
idea in regard to the nation: "Workers have no
country. . . . The proletariat will avail itself of its
political supremacy gradually to remove all capital
from the *bourgeoisie*, to centralize all the instruments
of production in the hands of the State, that is, of the
proletariat organized in a ruling class, and rapidly

[1] Prat De La Riba: *The Catalonian Nationality.*
[2] Francisco A. Cambó. Speech at San Sebastian, April 25, 1917.

Don Francisco A. Cambó (1876), leader of the Catalonian Regionalist
Party. (Translator's note.)

to increase the amount of productive forces. . . .
Once the antagonisms of class have disappeared in
the course of its development . . . public authority
will lose its political character. . . . In substitution
of the old bourgeois society with its classes and its
antagonisms of classes, there will arise an association
in which the free development of each will be the
condition of the free development of all."[1]

Let us examine the three heterodox theses[2] concerning the concept of nation. It would be sufficient
for the rejection of that of Rousseau to remember
that, much as the fruit falls from a tree, it proceeds
from the social compact, the existence of which has
not been proved. Moreover, its power of binding
those who take part in it would be null, and its
impossibility and absurdity would have been made
patent. Yet, in spite of this, it will not be unprofitable
to reflect a little upon the social product derived by
Rousseau from his false supposition; for, as already
remarked, under the denomination of Liberal Democracy it has enjoyed so much favour in later times and
has brought so many evils to humanity.

The author of the *Social Contract* does not tell us
why the *republic* or *body politic* issuing from the same
should be entitled to sovereignty. But leaving this
point for timely consideration, the distinction maintained between the particular components and the
moral collective body itself is quite evident. In
Rousseau's mind it is the *republic* or *body politic* that
possesses an *ego*, a life and a will; the multiplicity is
in the particular persons. The republic is, therefore,
a *personality* distinct from particular personalities, *mith*

[1] K. Marx and F. Engels: *Communist Manifesto*, Ch. II.
[2] The word "heterodox" is used in its political sense, as may be clearly
inferred from the antecedents stated, without extending the political heterodoxy
of Nationalism into the region of dogma. (Translator's note.)

special notes and characteristics. How, then, does Rousseau, after accepting it as evident, dare to assert that the interest of the republic is the interest of individuals because *it is composed of such*? How does he ascertain that the interest of individuals—isolated and not embodied—is one and the same?

The supposed uniformity of the interests of individuals, and their identity with the interest of the republic, leads us to the conclusion that there can never be discrepancy among citizens regarding their estimation. The interest of the republic would be only that unanimously determined as such by the individual members. It follows that either there must be unanimity in the ascertainment of what is the general interest in each case, or the general interest is non-existent, or at least it is unknown in the event of discrepancy. Democracy would then find itself reduced to immobility.

Rousseau could be little troubled by these impositions of harsh and intractable logic, knowing, as he did, that intolerance blurs the vision of the mind. But with a slight twist of the idea of the social compact the fraud was contrived. He writes: "So that the social compact may not be *an empty formula*"—he could see that this might be so—"it involves this provision: that only the covenant itself can give power to others, and that the whole body will *enforce obedience* on any one who refuses to conform to the general will. This means simply that *he will be compelled to be free*."[1] In this way was the foundation of Liberal Democracy laid. One-half plus one would be, hereafter, the fount of justice and freedom and the oracle of the general interest.

The dividing or destructive Nationalism, the separ-

[1] J. J. Rousseau: *Social Contract*, Bk. I, Ch. VII.

H—n

atist Nationalism preached in Catalonia and the
Basque country, is based, definitely, on the unity of
race—zoological Nationalism—or on the unity of
culture—intellectual Nationalism—as determining
principles of a national society. In the following
enunciation it will be understood in both forms. A
people of a race which is manifested by the existence
of a language, of a distinct personality, or of a unity
of culture, is a nation, and for these reasons it should
be independent of the peoples of another race, of
another personality and of another culture, and its
government given the note of sovereignty.

It would cost little—so insignificant are the foundations of Nationalism—to take for granted the basis
of the argument supporting its juridical doctrine.
Even acknowledging that race, unity of culture and
personality claim nationality, the Basque and Catalonian Nationalists would not have taken a step
forward along the road to the achievement of their
aspirations. To-day in Basconia there is no unity of
race, nor in Catalonia is there unity of culture;
neither Basconia nor Catalonia would exist if personality were the foundation of nationality. It is a
tragedy for Nationalism; but it is so. The Catalonian
and Basque movements have not even the principles
which their partisans assign to them. They preach
one thing and practise the opposite. Hence, in order
to carry out their criminal intentions, they never
appeal to reason but to uproar; never to calm discussion but to coercion and threats. That in Basconia
the race has not been preserved, and that inter-
marriage with alien races has modified it, is eloquently
stated by this fact. The "bosses" of Nationalism bear
these surnames showing the paternal and maternal
origin: Horn (Dutch) and Areilza (Basque); Campion

(contraction of the proximate primitive Campioni: Italian) and Jaimebon (French); Chalbaud (French) and Errazquin (Basque); López (central Castile) and Mendizábal (Basque); Leizaola (Basque) and Sánchez (from the province of Zamora, as is spitefully said); Landaburu (Basque) and Fernández (from either of the two Castiles); Monzón (Aragonese) and Ortiz de Urruela (Creole); Sota and Llano (the origin of these is clear). An unending list could be made in which the Basque blood has become hybrid, or does not appear at all in the standard bearers of Euzkadian Nationalism. There is no other example of anything like it. The absence of unity of culture in Catalonia is evident. Where lies the cultural resemblance of the inhabitants of the capital and the villages, of the territories of Levant and the West, of the North and the South, of the more educated classes and of the humbler classes? Why assume people are so credulous as to lend ears to such misrepresentations? But the absurdity is even greater. The Catalonian separatists aspire to form a nation with Rosellón, Valencia, the Balearic Islands and Alghero (in the island of Sardinia). Is anybody capable of discovering, not unity, but a common element of culture in all these utterly different peoples? If personality claims, of itself, national category, the Basque and Catalonian regions would not exist; and this is made clear by the simple consideration that these territories are groups of municipalities formed by families made up, in their turn, of individuals. Municipalities, families and individuals enjoy the note of personality, which is more perfect in individuals. Consequently, the latter would form isolated nations if personality were the foundation of nationality. Socialism being equally unsound in this direction, there is nothing more anti-scientific than Nationalism.

But apart from this, neither unity of race, nor of culture, nor of personality is the philosophical and social basis of the nation. Race, which is a reality, does not constitute a specific difference of humanity. Nor does its conception—as we have seen—enter into the formation of the primitive human societies proceeding from the universal society. Through mere variety it will affect, at most, the manner of being and not the specific being; and, in consequence, it might demand a peculiar mode of life, not a fundamentally distinct and separate life. But, in general, not even this occurs because, as races cannot always be subject to the cosmic influences that created them, the combination of the race with new ones acting diversely upon it, results in parts of the same race having different modes of being and life. Moreover, as the social and political institutions respond to these modes, there is no set relation between the race and its political organization, a supposition that would urge, under exceptional conditions, the independence of its government. The smallest race, the Basque race, is the most eloquent testimony of what has just been said. There is not the least resemblance among the traditional institutions and organizations of Alava, Guipúzcoa, Navarre and Vizcaya. What kind of structure would be suitable to the race?

What distinguishes a nation in the intellective order is not—as Prat de la Riba opines—*the superior unity of culture*. A nation, as we have said, is a major society of societies wherein the destiny appointed to the entire human race is fulfilled. As the subsistence of different societies was not an obstacle to its formation, neither does the existence of various cultures constitute a hindrance; and as the unity of those societies demanded a new social personality, the birth of the latter presupposes a culture higher than those already existent which, binding them together, gives a superior *unity of culture* to the nation. Even to suspect that Catalonian culture may be incompatible with Spanish culture would be to pay tribute to an unfounded dogmatism; to affirm such a thing after centuries of common life in which the cultural order has never been a cause of the slightest difference, would be irrational obstinacy that should be observed, pitied and removed. Catalonia, then, would not be a nation nor would it postulate its own State until it was proved never to have participated with other regional personalities in a culture superior to the peculiarly Catalonian culture, namely, that it had not shared with them *a national spirit* by which the human destiny had been achieved. Hence, if—as will be seen shortly—Catalonia, like the Basque provinces, like Aragon, like Castile, like Navarre, like the other natural regions of Spain, has the faculty of directing its collective conduct in what concerns its *particular* end, it has not that faculty in respect of the temporal human end which is proper to the nation of which all these regions are members, and in consequence *it cannot constitute itself a State*. Upon the clumsy confusion of the particular regional purpose with the human destiny, Catalonian Nationalism is based!

It was said in the previous chapter that personality and sovereignty are two different things and, therefore, that the existence of personalities without sovereignty and subject to the sovereignty of another personality, is quite feasible. There is nothing more obvious. Anticipating what is indisputably evident in this idea, sovereignty does not affect the essence of society; it arises from a *relation* which is a category of *accident.* The essential feature of an intelligent, free personality is the power of attaining its end by itself without being substituted by anybody in its action. This power is called *autarchy*, which means etymologically "self-government." A society is a collective moral personality of free and intelligent beings; therefore there can be none that does not enjoy *autarchy.* So the supreme power is not removed by the relations of dependency which, by reason of the end, may exist between various societies, and which are the foundation of sovereignty. As the free being does not act blindly, the said power must include the faculty of *foreseeing* the effect of its action, the faculty of *applying* it and the faculty of *connecting* its results with the end pursued and the established prevision. This is nothing else than the determination *of the law* of action; its application is the *execution* of acts; and the relation of these with the law and the end, is a *judgment.* Therefore every society, even that subject to dependency, can, *by reason of its end, establish rules, execute acts, and judge those accomplished*; or, in other terms, by virtue of its absolute power and *within the ambit traced* by its end, it possesses the *legislative, executive and judicial faculties.*

It will be seen from this that as sovereignty is a different thing from personality, so also it differs from the legislative, executive and judicial faculties. Sovereignty calls them sovereign, but does not create them. They are created by personality and so are enjoyed, *within the respective spheres of action appointed by their particular end,* by the family, the municipality and the region or municipal guild, all of which social elements, components of the nation by the subordination of their aims to the national end, are infra-sovereign societies. In any society that is not the primitive domestic one—and even in that, there would appear embryonically more than one difference —the existence of one sole legislation is absurd. In the actual degree of social evolution, four distinct legislations should rule every individual: the domestic, the municipal, the regional and the national. The admirable *Spanish "foral" régime*[1] consists, in substance, of the harmonic coexistence, of these precepts which here is not mere juxtaposition but internal and juridical agreement, that is, with unity and generality in each of the social orders.

If the region has the right of legislating, of judging and of executing, *through regional organisms in what concerns its particular end,* there is another personality *which legislates, judges and executes in and above the region* in what concerns *the national end* or common human destiny. It was the absolute power in the function of its particular end that attributed to the region the exercise of legislative, executive and judicial faculties. What determines the national competence is that, in respect of the common end, the region is an element of the nation just as in respect of the regional competence, the municipality is an element of the region. Here is the synthetic formula of this organization: *sovereignty*—supreme power which leads the associates to their common destiny—originates in the major society; *autarchy*, which is the government peculiar to the particular social ends, begins in each and all of the minor societies. This social conception is not a fanciful invention wrought outside experience; for the experience of centuries shows it to us in living form in Spain. It was not out of swollen vanity that the Kings of Spain, besides this title of the common

[1] Compilation of Statutes, Privileges, Uses and Customs constituting the Special Civil Law in Catalonia, Aragón, Navarre, Vizcaya and the Balearic Islands. (Translator's note).

fatherland, used those of King of Galicia and of Castile, of Aragón and of Navarre, of Guipúzcoa, of Alava and of Andalusia, Count of Barcelona and Lord of Vizcaya, but because each of these titles responded to different acts of the King of Spain. Under this title he was the supreme national authority; under the others he was the promoter of the inner life of each region.

The monarchy had made Spain to the likeness of man who was destined to dwell upon her soil. We have seen[1] that in him, there are three radically distinct modes of life, and that their diversity is reconciled to the indisputable unity of his psychological conscience through the existence of one sole vital principle, animating directly the various functions without the mediation of one particular law for each of them. The infusion into Spain of that undivided soul, the source of diverse modes of life, was the immortal work of Ferdinand and Isabella. Throughout the nation the King of Spain legislated, judged and executed with the regional organisms in what concerned the particular regional end. The concurrence, in the same *physical* person, of the Spanish Crown and the Crowns of the regional kingdoms, was the pledge of national unity. The coexistence of several organs of government was the guarantee of the diversity of legal forms and uses contained in the traditional "foral" régime.

As perfection in man arises from the harmonic development of the three distinct modes of life, so also the perfection of Spain sprang from that development of the regions under the organ of national unity. The austerity and idealism of Castile, the virility and courage of Aragón, the energy and industry of

---

[1] See the author's *Ferdinand the Catholic and the Counterfeiters of History.*

Catalonia, the fidelity of Basconia to her traditions, were the exponents of the greatness of Spain.[1] Let not those who feel the sorrow of Spain search for a new State. Let them return to tradition. There shall we find it, as we have found the true and legitimate national structure.

The national conception of Socialism is immediate absorption of individuals by the State, and remote free association of those who survive the dictatorship of the proletariat. The first part has been accomplished by Russia, and it is clear that the second part will never be reached. How could it be reached if the classes, as will be emphasized later, are natural elements of every society, and Socialism proposes to extirpate them? Socialism, through its destruction of what is natural, of what is spontaneously reborn, cannot establish that which it employs only as a slogan before the masses. Dictatorship of the proletariat: this is the reality. Association of individuals, in which the free development of each will be the condition of the free development of the rest, is the hoax, the logomachy, the bluff with which inferior intelligences are mocked. Either that free development has no limit in law or is regulated by it. Its results are only too well known. The first led to Protestantism in the religious order, to Individualism in the economic order. The second led to Catholicism, to organic society, to tradition, to the corporative and guild organizations. Socialism fundamentally rejects the whole of the latter. Actually it employs something which it loudly condemns, as a means of deception and as a pretext to seize power. It is this conquest, and not the betterment of the workers, which is its aim.

In this absorption of the individual by the State

[1] See the author's *Ferdinand the Catholic and the Counterfeiters of History.*

there is—indeed, there could not fail to be—an error touching the very essence of society which is not the end of man but a means of leading him to it; to the eternal end through the Church, to the temporal end through the nation. Society cannot, therefore, turn man away from his end nor replace him in his specific action towards its attainment. But as society is formed by men, and is a necessary medium for the human end, their co-operation cannot, by definition, be absent. Human personality, by reason of its destiny, appears as something superior to society; yet it is subordinated to the latter by reason of its activity. In other words: however wretched, ignorant and wicked a man may be, he is the centre of society in so far as society is the medium through which that man may reach his destiny. On the contrary, however exalted, wise, and holy he may seem, he only constitutes, by reason of his activity, a social element. The Catholic conception of man and of society removes the apparent antinomies which arise in the human order and, at the same time, it destroys the opposite errors of Individualism, Nationalism and Socialism.[1]

[1] Jacques Maritain: *Trois Réformateurs*, pp. 29 to 31.

CHAPTER IV

SOCIAL CLASSES AND BODIES

In the social evolution studied in foregoing chapters, only the subject of society was affected. The family developed into a tribe; when this became fixed, it became a city or a township; the associated towns constituted the region, the united regions made up the nation. But as man enters into the composition of all those partial societies which are his media, they, like him, must have some form of activity which, necessarily, would evolve with the respective subject. Because of this, it behoves us now to study these societies in their active sense so as to obtain a full conception of their organic composition. Knowledge of the social being in the subject reveals to us society in its static phase; perception of it in the evolution of its activity shows the dynamic aspect.

When examining the procedure of the family, the first suggestion is that, like every other society, it should be subject to the natural principle of sociability and to the vital laws immediately derived from the same. The primitive family covers in its meaning all those groups that remained isolated amongst themselves when mankind was dispersed; and there must have been· unity of purpose and diversity of means for the constituents of such a family. Because individual man is unable to satisfy all his needs, society— as we have seen—is precisely a condition natural to him. The division of labour, not in the restricted outlook of economy but in the broadest social sense, was perforce initiated in the family.

When the social entity reaches the municipal stage, it contains within itself persons whose individual activity, by virtue of the division of labour indicated in the family, has been directed, in a permanent manner, to the most diverse channels made requisite by the satisfaction of social needs; but, besides, the greater perfection with which this sufficiency is realized in the new society, reduces the simultaneous application of activities to fewer forms of use, thus originating clearer distinctions in those exercising a particular form, and producing a more accentuated and, at the same time, a more fundamental division of labour. Then there appear in society real categories of persons which, united in the same social interest, with their activity permanently regulated in an adequate sense, provide satisfaction to the different social needs. These categories of persons constitute *the classes*.

They come into existence in society in a spontaneous manner, like an expansion of domestic activity, responding to the diversity of the human faculties and to the sociable character presupposed by the impossibility for the individual to give satisfaction, by himself, to all the needs of the human being. A society without classes cannot, therefore, be even imagined. Their existence has such reality that "in order to prove it, one has only to deny it, and then see whether anything remains of the substance of the nation; deny them all, and the nation disappears. . . . Classes have always existed; they are founded upon human nature; the human faculties are their immediate causes, and the collective and social ends are their objectives. Those same organized classes are nothing but means;

and if I desired to give an exact and comprehensive definition of *civilization* and, therefore, of the ideal of progress which is none other than the course of social order and the ascent towards that civilization, I should say that it is the *equation between the human aptitudes and needs representing classes, and the objective ends towards which these classes tend.*"[1]

The fact is so widely known that even Socialists, enemies—as before remarked, of the social constitution in classes—have been forced to acknowledge it as natural. Engels admits the existence in the primitive communities "of certain common interests, the defence of which is necessarily entrusted to individuals though still under the sanction of the community: substantiation of disputes, restraint on the invasion of the rights of others, vigilance of waters, particularly in hot countries, and finally, in this entirely primitive savage period, functions of a religious character."[2]

The classes, then, are natural organs with which human society affords satisfaction to social needs; they emanate from society with the same spontaneity as the series of social personalities examined in previous chapters was seen to spring from the natural principle of sociability. As the fact does not concern solely human activity in the private but also in the public order, it must be concluded that some of the groups to which the members of a society naturally allot themselves for the exercise of their activity directed to the satisfaction of social needs, will have a specifically public character because their activity directly affects the organs of this order. For the due distinction of those not possessing this character,

[1] Juan Vázquez de Mella: *Complete Works*, Vol. VIII, pp. 154 et seq.
[2] F. Engels: *Philosophy*, Part I, Ch. VII.

they are called bodies of the nation and of the State; the generic denomination of social classes is reserved for the others.

Regarding the meaning of these classes, two errors must be avoided. In conformity with the modern fallacy, the members are classified according to their wealth; the erroneous conception, allied to primitive civilization, causes them to be inexorably ascribed to the class in which they were born. In the first case, the basis of the formation of the classes is not the end of human activity but a means (money). In the second, activity, which is free, becomes enslaved, and therefore, a human factor absolutely essential in everything affecting man is absent from this classification. The aggregations enunciated by the first error as classes, lack that permanence in the exercise of activity demanded by their condition, for wealth is one of the less stable circumstances of life; in the second misconception, the end of man is subordinated to that of the group. The division of human aggregations into upper, middle and popular classes conveys but a suggestion of posssssion that is of little interest to society; and when they are called *castes*, they reflect the false conception of the origin of social institutions without the slightest relation to their purpose.

From the point of view of social activity, every element of organization is to be found in the bodies and in the classes. But just as the natural principle of sociability is determined in various forms of particular societies, so also do the classes, by their disposition in relation to an object, give rise to institutions that establish a concordant alliance amongst them all. These institutions are called *corporations*. A class, then, is not a corporation, nor is a corporation a class. The class is an element of the corporation in so much as it refers to its specific object and likewise, the corporation contains only a part of the classes composing it. It can thus be said that class and corporation are elements of social organization in a horizontal and in a vertical sense respectively.

The corporation stands forth as a complement of the classes through the very character of human needs. Its origin, therefore, is entirely natural although it may require special action on the part of man in its constitution. For, while it is true that human needs are limited by human nature itself[1] and, consequently, the elasticity of the means to satisfy them is not indefinite, the objects with which they are satisfied, and the forms they adopt, may be extremely diversified and may demand the simultaneous concurrence of all classes in a permanent regulation. Apart from this, the work of the classes, by reason of its analytic aspect, may require the synthetic composition of isolated results.

Which are the classes of a nation, and which are the bodies and corporations belonging to the same?

In order to give an accurate reply to the question asked, let it be remembered that the idea of a nation assumes the existence of realities capable of social determination, that is, of adding to the purely social features others that constitute a group of men in one people, and not in another, with the permanence and transcendence demanded by a collective, concrete and unequivocal personality in time and space; and that these realities together make up tradition. If this be so, it will be impossible to determine *a priori* the importance and extension of the development of classes, bodies and corporations, for tradition varies

[1] St. Thomas Aquinas: *Summa Theologica*, Iᵃ-IIᵃᵉ, Qu. ii, art. I.

and is peculiar to each people. Yet in regard to classes and bodies, a minimum can be fixed without harbouring the slightest restrictive thought concerning corporations because, as we have said, the factor of their existence is human action and this, in general, requires a social atmosphere of relative progress.

If the faculties of man are the immediate cause of bodies and classes, a social need being the reason of the existence of these, there must be some sort of community or class for the furtherance of the paramount interests relating to the religious order and to the temporal order in which the two lives perceived in man are placed. If in the temporal order human activities participate in spirit and in matter, no political society can be without certain classes tending to promote the satisfaction of intellectual interest, and others with material interest as their specific object. If a people has a tradition, it should have a body to make it especially manifest. Finally, if the nation is a living personality, it should contain social elements to contribute to the prosperity of its life and for the purpose of its defence. Let us pass beyond the synthetic outline just traced.

It was said before that even had man not been raised to the supernatural order, even had Christ not founded His Church, in pure natural law two perfectly distinct societies, the civil and the religious, would exist for men. The intercommunication in the lives of both of these, through the identity of their members, is notorious. Moreover, if the elements of civil society are—by definition—given the character of *faithful* in religious society, those who foster this aspect of the whole human life, being members of civil society, would have characteristics distinguishing them from others, and would provide satisfaction of a need which, although belonging to a higher order than that of civil society, yet affected its subjects. In this sense, therefore, they would constitute a body within civil society. The said finality is attributed, in a Christian society, to the ministers of the Church who, under the condition of citizenship, form part of the nation. The clergy, therefore, are a social body arising from the first of the two concepts synthetically explained.

As man is a being composed of soul and body in substantial union, his activity proceeds from his single nature, and participates, of necessity, in things spiritual and things corporal. The absolute separation of the impulses, or the detachment of the respective interests is therefore inconceivable. Yet it is no less true that not all human activities share in an identical way in one or other principle of their nature, nor do their issues evince the same proportion of interest of one kind or the other. Granted this, it may be said that human activity can be conceived as perfecting the spiritual part in itself, or its application to the sphere of material accomplishment, thus creating in the nation, under a double concept, the class of the liberal professions and the working class. But both, besides directly satisfying certain social needs, furnish, with a third, the conditions wherewith to procure the satisfaction of economic needs; for these are the work of two factors acting in the social atmosphere: property (of natural elements, products or capital) and labour (intellectual and manual). The members of a society who, in a permanent manner, advance the first of these factors, constitute the class known by that name; and those who employ capital and labour, applying their personal activity to the cultivation of the soil, to the transformation of its

products, or to their adequate distribution, come
under the denominations of agriculture, industry and
commerce.

A nation, finally, has one life of relation and another
interior life which it develops within traditional
characteristics. Both should be protected and defended.
They are protected by justice, and defended by force
in the service of the law. These are functions exercised by means and modalities distinct from others,
causing the constitution of three bodies: magistracy,
diplomacy and the forces of land, sea, and air. A
fourth—aristocracy—not passive but active, with
proper functions of patronage, will express the traditional note.

Providing previous remarks concerning the composition of the political entity are kept in mind, everything that has been set forth may now be resumed in
an obvious classification. In every national society,
more or less prominent according to the significance
or import of the facts that make up its tradition,
there exist six social classes: agriculture, industry,
commerce, property, liberal professions and manual
work, and six State bodies: clergy, aristocracy, magistracy, diplomacy, army and navy, and territorial
regions. The national prospect is completed by
national bodies and corporations which, applying
property and intellectual and manual labour, or
one alone of these factors, to a certain object, promote respectively an aspect of a spiritual nature,
or further an agricultural, industrial or mercantile
interest while they may absorb the classes themselves
should the organic social progress extend so far.

When the votaries of the French Revolution hear
the word "interest" used in the matters that concern
public order, they receive it with a grimace of hypo-

critical repugnance. Yet, in the history of mankind there has never existed a less spiritual epoch than that instituted by the blood-soaked doctrines of the Revolution. During that time, all the materialistic frenzies of paganism were joyfully welcomed and elevated to a scientific category. Monism, Evolutionism, Positivism . . . are yet words of yesterday. "Concentration on things of this side," "the materialistic conception of history," "the social question is a question of the stomach," still resound as synthetic apothegms of revolutionary thought.

It must be said without any reluctance. Whoever preaches antagonism between interest and spirit doubtless feels unable to entertain any agreement between them; but this should invite a change of methods and not produce the perspective of a disjunction opposed to all reality as something fully accomplished. Reason, in the national order, does not deprecate interest; it only demands that, in some aspect, it may be of a public character. A political society which does not satisfy needs, denies itself because its *raison d'être* is none other than to satisfy them. In this satisfaction there is a double interest; in society, as a fulfilment of its purpose; in the associate, as the subject of the need.

Thus, *social class* does not mean only *interest*. A social class, naturally and spontaneously formed in a nation, tells its nationals that all citizens live by the specific application of its activity; that its sudden disappearance would be a national catastrophe; that, in consequence, the whole nation is interested in its subsistence. In other words, it is meant that the specific interest of the class is also, under a certain aspect, *the national interest*. It could not, indeed, be otherwise bearing in mind the origin of the classes and the form in which they are constituted. Hence, in regard to man who forms part of a social class, his own interest, in so far as it is the specific interest of the class, will always have a zone of agreement with the national interest. The allegation made by the revolutionary school that this social conception fosters class strife, falls to the ground by mere insinuation. Later, this point will be again considered when studying the institutions of government with which that conception is logically completed.

Although without the perfection given to the matter by the centuries since elapsed, ancient wisdom perceived, in all clearness, the organic composition of society and the essentiality of bodies and social classes. Here is an unambiguous text bearing witness to this: "It is expedient to examine," says Aristotle,[1] "how many things there are without which the city could not exist; among them we must needs find those held to be essential parts of a city. Let us see then, the number of such elements whereby this question may be rendered plain. Firstly, the means of subsistence; afterwards the arts, for many instruments and materials for the necessities of life are required. In the third place, come arms, because all those forming part of the association must be armed against the citizens who disobey constituted authority and against outside enemies who might attempt an unjust invasion. To the fourth place we allot the public treasury, which must cover the disbursement of war expenditure besides providing for its own needs. The care of divine things, called worship, occupies the fifth, though perhaps it should come first. Finally, in the sixth place, we have what is most essential: justice which looks after the the general interests of the republic and the reciprocal

[1] Aristotle: *Politica*, Bk. IV, Ch. VII.

rights of all citizens. Such are the things a city cannot dispense with; they are essential, for the city *is not a multitude of men* gathered together by chance. As we are saying, it is an agglomeration of people *sufficient in itself for all its needs.* If any of the expressed elements is missing, it is impossible, utterly impossible, for the association to be sufficient in itself." Later, he adds: "The discovery by political philosophy of the necessity of dividing the city into classes was certainly not made nowadays nor in any recent time."[1]

What political philosophy had discovered or rather inherited from common sense, was to be denied, naturally, by the antithesis of human wisdom: Revolution. Jean Jacques Rousseau unfolds without diffuseness the revolutionary teaching to which so many have merrily sacrificed rights in moments of insanity which defy all explanation. He writes: "In order to fix the enunciation of the general will, it is essential that no particular society shall exist in the State and that each citizen shall opine exclusively according to his own mind."[2] Not long afterwards, the French Revolution, taking up the meaning of the Rousseauan phrase, promulgated one of the most shameful, most unjust and most tyrannical laws recorded in the annals of the human race. It is dated June 14, 1791 and is known by the name of its author: Chapelier. It condemned as *unconstitutional and offensive to liberty and to the declaration of the rights of man,* all deliberations held and all conventions agreed upon by citizens of the same profession, craft or trade concerning the fixing of prices to the products of their industry or labour. Political society was thus torn and demolished.

But this was not the worst. Like every organism in

[1] Aristotle: *Politica*, Bk. IV, Ch. IX.
[2] J. J. Rousseau: *Social Contract*, Bk. I, Ch. III.

the course of putrefaction, the national fabric covers itself with others parasitically living upon its substance. These were the political parties. What is their true nature? Those who lived in them and by them will tell us. Count Romanones declares that "minorities constituting the strength of parties have no other ideals and principles than those of their leaders, who become real dictators."[1] Señor Cambó has written: "the interest of party and group was notoriously of higher import than the public interest." Azcárate acknowledges that "apart from other errors giving rise to *religious, local* and *class* groups which contradict the true purpose of political association, parties, as such, are affected with vices resulting from the inconsequence of politicians, from the predominance of party interest or of individual selfishness, from the coveting of power, and from a lamentable tendency to dictatorship, the sad bequest of three centuries of absolutism. The effect of all these causes brings flat contradiction between theory and practice, for what actually takes place is that instead of the country *availing itself* of the parties, and the parties of their leaders, these *make use* of the parties, and the parties *profit by the country.*"[2]

Similar testimony could be adduced interminably, but it should be noted that the texts quoted entirely agree on these three points: that parties lack *national* ideals; that they place their own interest before the general interest; and that the acquisition of power is their sole object. In face of this triple coincidence, the conformity in the despotic structural character of the

[1] Alvaro de Figueroa: *The Parliamentary Régime*, Ch. V.

Count Romanones (Don Alvaro de Figueroa) (1863), was the leader of one of the Parliamentary Liberal groups. He was Prime Minister several times, and was a member of King Alphonso's last Cabinet. (Translator's note.)

[2] Azcarate: *The Parliamentary Régime in Practice*, Ch. II.

Don Gumersindo de Azcárate (1840-1917), was perhaps the most highly respected Republican politician in Spain. (Translator's note.)

parties is less striking, unless it be to emphasize the failure of their supposed attempt to be instruments of freedom, and their constitutional incapacity of disengaging themselves from an assumed inheritance of the past. Such recognition entails the most ingenuous and unaffected—and therefore the most efficacious—condemnation of the system.

Azcárate offers no doubt whatever as to the existence of these defects in the political parties, but tries to excuse them as belonging to practice and not to theory; a dismal evasion showing the intellectual gloom produced in the noblest minds by revolutionary teaching! Are parties mere fruits of speculation or organisms for action in the reality of national life? What value can be attached to institutions that, in the functions for which they have been formed, never respond to the conditions imposed upon them?

The fact is that the exalted name "theory" is applied to what is nothing but a mortal revolutionary chimera. Theory is not an arbitrary composition of suppositions more or less strung together. Theory is the doctrine extracted *from reality* to which it applies evident principles or certain conclusions derived from higher sciences under the inflexible rules of logic. To employ the term "theory" in connection with the doctrinal medley compounded by Liberalism in the matter of political parties, can only be described as a kind of "confidence trick." Political parties can pretend to be nothing but what they are.

Furthermore, it has already been said that a nation is a concrete and not an abstract society, and because of this, it is governed not by mere abstract principles but by principles set in tradition. This is radically denied by the parties. Hence, their lack of *national* ideas is not a contradiction of the "theory," as Azcárate says, but a necessary consequence. How should we find in their function something not to be found in their formation? It may also be remarked that political parties cannot be, as Azcárate depicts them, servants of "the general ideas, tendencies and currents that go to make the common sentiment, the public opinion and the social will of peoples,"[1] because general ideas, tendencies and currents that embody a *common sentiment* cannot be discrepant as are those of the different parties, by definition; and there is no common sentiment, no true public opinion, no social will that is not wrought by a tradition which the parties repudiate by their very existence.

Can it now cause surprise that Count Romanones tells us that political parties have no more ideas and principles than those of their leaders; that Cambó affirms the interest of party and group to be more highly appraised than the public interest; that Azcárate admits parties are served by the country instead of the country being served by the parties, and that experience proves that the extinction of a party *not only does not cause damage to the nation,* like the disappearance of a class, but is actually a boon? It is logical, natural and even inevitable; the contrary would be inexplicable and exceptional. Let Democracy defend, if it so desires, its political parties now in a state of festering decay, despised and repudiated by all; but to attempt to distinguish in them the theoretical and practical sphere, is sheer humbug.

---

[1] Azcárate: *The Parliamentary Régime in Practice,* Ch. II.

CHAPTER V

NATIONAL SOVEREIGNTY

The nation has no superior in its kind; the evolution of the social personality has made this manifest. Its end is the temporal human destiny; this was palpably demonstrated. Sovereignty consists, precisely, in the concurrence of both notes: independence touching the person, and plenitude in the manner of the end. The doctrinal jumble which has been used in the attempt to enlighten the idea of independence, both by the German and French schools, has but led to total incomprehension and to confusion of the relations binding the nation to the State. Let us put away verbosity and get back to the lucidity of the old philosophy. If sovereignty is not an attribute of superiority and plenitude, there is no intellectual alchemy that can produce it. If the nation in the social order is not the sovereign body, it is wrong to apply such a term to that order. The nation, then, is supreme and, in consequence, national sovereignty exists.

Let nobody be surprised by these words set down by one who has all along emphasized the political error in Jean Jacques Rousseau. Besides the reality known philosophically by the denomination expressed, there is a myth to which the Revolution has given the same name. Many of its errors took root in the world because they were falsely made to circulate under old terms. Indeed, in Spain, the two words "national sovereignty" are an example of this. If the truth they contain were ever made a subject of dispute, it would surely never encounter anything but an atmosphere of light in our country. The genuinely Spanish philosophy and political science has always vindicated it. "No king or magistrate," says Suárez, "has or has had political sovereignty according to the ordinary law *immediately* received from God. This is a cardinal precept of theology and not a derisive phrase as alleged by King James. When properly understood, its truth is most striking, and it is superlatively necessary to understand the ends and to fix the limits of the civil power. This is nothing new nor is it an invention of Cardinal Belarmino, as the said monarch seems to have imagined; nor is it a doctrine taught solely by theologians but is also commonly defended by lawyers." Báñez writes:[1] "it must be noticed that the power held by the king is different from those offices held by the republic" (in the sense of a nation); "because the king has received his authority from the republic, and consequently with dependence upon the nation, conforming to certain laws so that he rules, not according to his will, but for the benefit of the said republic." "The royal power," says Molina, "descends from the human law of the republic." "The secular power," affirms Vitoria, "lies in all the republic and from it proceeds to the magistrates and to all the other powers. . . . The temporal republic is a perfect and integral republic, and so it is subject to nobody outside it; otherwise it would not be integral. Therefore it may constitute itself a ruling power in no way subject to any other in temporal things."

Vázquez de Mella, taking up the content of the teaching of Spanish philosophy and theology on this subject, stated his view in this admirable paragraph:

[1] Báñez: *De Justitia et Jure*, Qu. lxii, art. 2.

"With two exceptions in the Hebrew theocracy, the Church has recognized but two monarchies of divine right: the domestic monarchy of the father in the family, which is of natural divine right, and the monarchy of the Pontificate, which is of positive divine right. All other monarchies or polyarchies are considered as of *national or political* right, that is of human right. . . . The monarchy of divine right is a relic of the Divus Cæsar that appeared in the Middle Ages in the Ghibelline proclamations of the Fredericks; from Suavia it passed to the Protestant tyrants and was formulated by James of England against the doctrines of the great Spanish theologians, by Robert de Filmer in the 18th century and . . . by the Constitution of 1876 in the 19th."[1]

It was not the Constitution of 1812 which brought to Spain the principle affirming that sovereignty has its primary origin in the nation, and from it proceeds to become localized in the ruler. Not even by omission can such a thing be inferred from its text. On the contrary, the legislators of Cádiz, though with a defective vocabulary, acknowledge that in Spain this was the doctrine which pledged our internal Constitution. At all times the precise meaning of terms used should be determined, for it is well known—I have mentioned this in another place—that "in language there is also a form of truth resulting from the conformity of word and idea, and a cause of untruth is the disconformity between concept and term." This necessity becomes more pressing when the vocabulary habitually carries more than one meaning. Sovereignty in a limited being cannot be absolute. The notion of an absolute king is as absurd as that of an *absolute* nation. If the note of sovereignty in a king must

[1] Juan Vázquez de Mella: *Complete Works*, Vol. II, p. 129.

have a limit, that note in a nation must be equally limited. There is but one being who is absolutely supreme: he who can say of himself: "I am who I am." National supremacy, then, must be subordinated to a precept superior and anterior to it.

Vázquez de Mella has expressed this doctrine, inspired by good sense, in the following terms: "Absolutism does not consist, as some still believe, *in the unity of the political power* represented in monarchic or polyarchic form, but in the *juridical illimitation,* in the overflow of power that invades or distrains the prerogatives of individual or collective persons, subordinated in one respect, but not absorbed in that civil entity called State. From the moment when a power, whatever it may be, leaves its course, exceeds its due authority and enters into the jurisdiction of the other powers, possessing itself of a prerogative or faculty not belonging to it, absolutism, at least as a reality, is established. Hence we recognize that the royal power, and, in general, the political power of the State, whatever form it may take, must be limited by two great sovereignties; because we admit a trinity or *social trilogy* composed, in the first place, of the *superior spiritual power of the Church* which, having a purpose identified with the ultimate end of man, has the right to fix its relation with the State and *indirectly* to exercise influence within it. Next we recognize as inferior limits forming, in a certain manner, a social sovereignty, other subordinated hierarchies of social persons or bodies. These, apart from the individual person, whose natural rights we are the first to recognize as anterior and superior to every civil law, commence with the family, are prolonged in the municipality—an aggregation of families—and continue through the association of those municipalities into districts that later become united to form the region. All these powers, with other analogous corporations and with the classes connecting them, are those which limit, counteract and serve as an ORGANIC PREVENTION and not, like those useless powers you imagine, a MECHANICAL PREVENTION, against the abuses of political sovereignty, the third term circumscribed by spiritual and social sovereignty."[1]

The limitations of national sovereignty will appear plain after this exposition. By reason of the proper end of the nation, the fundamental limitation is found in the *natural law* whereby the action is made conditional on the end. Thus the sin of absolutism occurs when that action leaves the path made for it by the end. Whether the nation be affected by monarchic or republican, by aristocratic or democratic forms, is immaterial. By reason of the ends outside the province of the nation—the eternal destiny and temporal, non-national ends—the limitations lie in the autarchies corresponding to the respective societies exclusively and naturally appointed for the realization of those ends. In this conception of society, there are no guarantees written on paper; they are organic and natural, that is, automatic and efficacious. Against the abuses of the nation in the exercise of its sovereignty, the subject is defended above, by the only possible principle: the inspiration and deep sense of religion acting in the order of conscience; and below, by the alligation of sub-sovereign societies that oppose the abuse of national power, not with the isolated strength of one man, but with the potent forces of social autarchies. In turn, these are kept to their course by the State which, acting strictly according to law, claims independence in specifically national affairs.

[1] Vázquez de Mella: *Complete Works*, Vol. XI, pp. 17 to 19.

The instruments of the guarantees are, then, always ready for action; liberty does not roar in the streets, it emanates from order like a halo of light.

When pointing out[1] the illegitimate forms of the nation, we transcribed the text in which Rousseau describes the body politic which, in his judgment, was the product of the social contract, and to which he gave the quality of sovereignty while the contracting parties participated *in the sovereign authority*. The foundation whence the sovereignty and this participation proceed is not mentioned; but some idea of it may be gathered from the dogmatic assertion in the following terms: "The act of association involves a reciprocal pledge between the public and private individuals, each of whom contracts, as it were, with himself and becomes subject to a double relation: as a member of the sovereign body in respect to individuals, and as a member of the State in respect to the sovereign body."[2] The whole idea is definitely set out in the following example: "Let us assume the State to be composed of 10,000 citizens. The sovereign power can only be considered collectively and in a body; but each private person, as a subject, is accounted an individual. In this way, the ratio between the sovereign and the subject is ten thousand to one, which means that each member of the State *has, on his part, only a ten-thousandth part of the sovereign authority although he is completely subject to the latter*. If the people is composed of 100,000 persons, the condition of the subjects remains unchanged, each equally enduring the weight of the law while his suffrage, reduced to a hundred-thousandth, has ten times less influence in the concrete form of the resolution adopted. Consequently, while *the subject always remains one*, the relation

[1] Part II, Ch. III.   [2] J. J. Rousseau: *Social Contract*, Bk. III, Ch. I.

of the sovereign power increases in proportion to the number of citizens. It follows that the more the State increases, the more does liberty diminish."[1]

Without attempting to emphasize the assortment of contradictions in which the text abounds, enough has been transcribed to make it clear that to Rousseau's mind, in every society to which, without justification, he attributes sovereign power, each citizen has *a portion of sovereign authority* equal to the aliquot part which he represents in respect to the population. In other words, sovereignty is formed by the sum of equal fragments of it distributed among all the citizens composing the society. A principle of such eminence as sovereignty is to Revolution and to heterodox politics in general, is treated like the box of bricks given to a child for the purpose of reconstructing a picture. Neither human understanding, nor the credulity of men, nor their social sense could have sunk lower.

As the illegitimate conception of the nation, formulated by Rousseau in peremptory manner, was rejected by the refutation of the social contract whence it originated, the reproduction here of the same exception would suffice for the elimination of the equally spurious notion of sovereignty. But as in the former case, when we made no pretence of foregoing other opposing observations, we now also endeavour to make quite patent the absurdity and impossibility of the idea of the procedure of a sovereignty conceived in such terms.

There is nothing worse than to assimilate the spiritual order to the mathematical order. Either the natural rigidity of the latter is harmful to the former, or the substantial difference of the objects compared leads to real inconsistency and to monstrous irration-

[1] J. J. Rousseau: *Social Contract*, Bk. I, Ch. VII.

ality. Above all, when the person urging the analogy upon himself is entirely ignorant of both orders, farce begins to appear after tragedy. According to Rousseau, the more extensive the society, the less free the individual. This conclusion, already absurd, assumes sovereignty to be the same in a society heavily populated as in another of a smaller number of inhabitants.

But from his suppositions, not this consequence, but another even more crack-brained is drawn. Rousseau tells us that "the subject remains always one." Therefore, whether the subjects of a republic be 10,000 or 100,000, the subject will always be *the unit* and so equally free. Following mathematically this wild form of thinking, what varies is the *sovereignty of the society*, which in the State of 100,000 subjects will be *ten times greater* than in that of the 10,000. Sovereignty, then, will no longer be that spiritual note like reason, totally alien to the corpulence of the person in which it abides, but something rather like the weight of a basket of oranges which increases with the number it holds. Truly it is humiliating to realize that such jargon has, at times, exercised decisive influence over human society.

As a final consequence of these aberrations, we should have States with greater sovereignty than others which, definitely, would be to affirm the supremacy of the one counting the largest number of subjects, for in the idea of sovereignty there is included the sense of superiority in the order in which sovereignty is affirmed. Subconsciously, this point has actually been reached. What has been called "modern civilization" acts in practice as if minor States were peoples dependent upon major States. The misfortune of the revolutionary doctrine is that it is doomed to deny itself, whichever of the results reached from the equiponderance of the mathematical and social orders be accepted. If, as Rousseau says, "the more the State increases, the more does liberty diminish," the social contract has failed, for its finality was "to find a form of association that would defend and protect the person and the goods of each associate, by virtue of which, each one, united with all the others, would but obey himself and *would remain as free as before*." As growth is natural in human association, with it individual liberty would shrink; and if, as the equal maintenance of liberty demands, the sovereignty of society increases—this implies, as before remarked, the disappearance of every society save one—the social compact *would not create the sovereign power*. No sadder destiny for a political system than that of devouring itself can be conceived.

But, besides, even were so sinister a destiny not predetermined for Revolution, it would be condemned to juridical impotence, just as, previously, we observed it was condemned to immobility. In the expression of the innermost workings of its being, it boasts of power in the barbarous destruction that follows in its wake throughout the world. Nothing can be more clear. For the purpose of placing it on record, let us admit, for a moment, that each critizen has a portion of sovereign authority equal to the aliquot part which he represents in respect to the population. That authority could not be integrated except through transmission to the body politic by all the citizens, of every part of sovereign authority corresponding to them. In the example used by Rousseau himself, the constitution of sovereign authority would indispensably require the 10,000 citizens to convey their ten thousand fractions of that authority. The mere act of writing the words reveals the consequence with overwhelming clearness. In revolutionary demo-

K—□

cracies national sovereignty cannot possibly act, because it is morally and physically impossible for its resolutions to be supported by the unanimous acceptance of all the members of the body politic; wherefore sovereignty has not been integrated within it.

It had to be so; there can be no national sovereignty where there is no nation. It was seen[1] that the Rousseauan fallacy engendered a spurious national form, and it is but logical that only a false national sovereignty can be derived from such a source. Let us dwell further upon this consequence by reason of its immense importance in the constitution of the new State.

Setting aside the origin of human society as indicated by Rousseau, we will accept the reality he attributes to the compact: the production of a moral and collective body with its unit, its *ego*, its life and its will, to wit, a public person which is *the sovereign power*. Evidently, that moral and collective body is something different from the individuals who formed it and who continue to exist within it. Therefore, if that public person, distinct from the individual components, is—according to Rousseau's own admission—THE SOVEREIGN, the individuals cannot be such. This being so, it cannot be assumed that their assembling is the origin and cause of *the sovereign*. Admitting the production of the moral and collective body with sovereign personality by the social compact, sovereignty can only reside in that body, namely, in the nation. It is not *in the multitude*, a word used to describe the mere sum of individuals living within the nation.[2]

Shortly after affirming all that is antecedent to this irrefutable conclusion, Rousseau states, as we have seen, that each citizen has a portion of sovereign

[1] Part II, Ch. III.   [2] Part II, Ch. I.

authority equal "to the aliquot part which he represents in respect to the population"; and, almost
unnoticed for the moment, he gently gravitates from
the nation to the multitude, from the sovereign to the
subject. Thus is the multitude identified with the
nation. The rest is now child's play. The legerdemain,
accomplished with the aid of noisy music to distract
people's attention, passed unheeded. It is therefore
necessary to disclose the discreditable nature of the
sophism well worthy of revolutionary baseness. It
amounts to the same as comparing the dump of
materials with the building which is to result from
them, and attributing to them what can only pertain
to the finished work of the architect and builder.
Sovereignty is a note of the nation; but the nation is
not to be identified with the multitude. The exercise
of national sovereignty by the multitude as a specific
right, or through its attempted identification with the
nation, is, first a substitution of personality, then a
usurpation of power, and finally a metaphysical
impossibility.

The fact of substitution of personality stands out
with such evidence as to make people's lack of perception appear amazing. If the multitude, that is, the
sum of individual persons forming a nation, requires
for its constitution a common end and an organic
union under one direction and with one same spirit in
order to attain that end, the multitude will be only the
matter of the nation just as the diverse elements of
building are not the edifice itself. That it is a usurpation ensues from what has been stated, for the
multitude would exercise a right that does not belong
to it but to the nation. That there is a question of
metaphysical impossibility is shown by the fact that
the multitude is ever varying, not only in opinion but

even in composition. So it comes to one of two things: either those who at each moment become part of the multitude have not the right to exercise the functions of sovereignty, and the *present* multitude, therefore, does not exercise it, or those persons do act in the sense described, the result being the same as if they did not. This is the myth known by the revolutionary name of *popular sovereignty*.

If Democracy supplants the personality of the sovereign, if it appropriates from the nation the exercise of sovereignty, and if the substitution of the person and the usurpation of power are definitely exemplified in an impossibility of such action, then Democracy is not a perfect political system, much less the most perfect, and not even an imperfect system of government. Democracy, in the political order, NON EST; or, in other words, it constitutes an absolute error. The words with which Paul Bourget expressed this idea will never be excelled: "It is admirable," he said, "that every hypothesis upon which Revolution has been raised should have been diametrically contrary to the conditions which our philosophy of Nature, resting upon experience, indicates to us to-day as the most probable laws of public welfare."[1]

Consequently, if Democracy is a *nonentity*, how are the people governed in those countries where it is enthroned? Applied to France, Charles Maurras has explained the phenomenon in a manner apposite to all the peoples of the world, the accuracy of which will not be surpassed: "The practical man will ask himself who are the men to whom is due the reign of Democracy in France. The most superficial examination of the question supplies the answer that they are not men. Men capable of putting so extraordinary a

[1] Charles Maurras: *Enquête sur la Monarchie*, p. 116.

thing into practice, of making it endure, are simply non-existent. Let us consider that the greatest, the most ancient, the most venerable spiritual power on the one side, and on the other, material force, those who carry a sword or shoulder a rifle or aim with a cannon, are doomed to failure and are persecuted by a system of institutions and ideas: Democracy! In the administration of this institution, of this system, men would have become divided, discouraged, discordant; they would have devoured one another. So it is needful to assume something else: an organization or organizations, definitely *historic organizations*, physical or psychological families, states of spirit, of sentiment, of will, inherited from father to son through centuries, dynasties. France has been placed by the Revolution in a material state appreciably near to democratic individualism. All *national* organizations were shattered, and the individual disconnected, as a molecule of dust. Since then, *foreign* organizations have not ceased to grow, and have become rooted in French society because their interior discipline was maintained and strengthened by our social dispersion. The Jewish, Protestant, Masonic and Metic organizations form the predominant majority, foreign or semi-foreign, by which contemporary France is governed."[1]

To sum up, in exemplary fashion the "democratic disease" must be removed from every State, and very especially from the New State which we are erecting, because it is evil, because it rots the nation. For the sake of human dignity it must be eliminated. I have said it before. The outstanding imbecility of the Liberal State may be described by saying that its substantival essence was being worn away by its qualifying element. The State was allowing its ethos to be extracted by something that was adjectival to it.

[1] Charles Maurras: *Gazette de France*. July 27, 1904.

CHAPTER VI

ORIGIN OF SOVEREIGNTY

BECAUSE sovereignty—as has been said[1]—is superiority in kind and plenitude in the temporal end of a human society, it connotes the Aristotelian category of *relation* which is an *accident*. In consequence, because of its condition, it should be found adherent to some essential feature of society. It is now opportune to investigate this.

The forms of activity of the associates, both as regards intelligence and as regards will, are not determined either by Nature or by an exterior object or by a sensitive appreciation of the latter. The difficulties which this universal fact causes to arise in the conduct of a single individual, are multiplied *ad infinitum* when they are opposed to a *social* conduct. So the perfection of a society demands their disappearance, that is, the existence therein of a principle conveying harmony to the minds of the associates, agreement to their wills, co-ordination to their means and to their acts. This principle of unity has, at all times, been called *authority*. Without it, the multitude of men would not make up *society*, for the specific characteristics would be missing. Thus authority is an essential feature of every society.

The idea of authority arises, then, from the concept of society, not from that of the individual, although the latter may be presupposed as a material element

[1] Part II, Ch. V.

of the former. It is true that authority would not exist without the natural rights demanded by society, but these do not create it, just as they did not create society itself which has its origin in the community of destiny and of its attainment through the common action of the associates. Natural rights are not authority, nor do they consistute it by means of their sum or partial addition;[1] but they are a condition for the exercise of authority which is not directed to the particular good of anyone claiming such rights, but to the good of the society. Authority has, in consequence, a beneficent character, and thus it comes about that the connection between superior and subject is a bond of love.

Leo XIII has explained this doctrine in the following terms: "No society can exist or be conceived unless there is someone to moderate the wills of the associates in order to reduce plurality to a certain unity, and to give it an impulse, according to law and order, towards the common good."[2] "Hence it follows that every civilized community must have a ruling authority."[3] As a natural consequence of this idea of authority, Pope Leo fixed the extent of its exercise by circumscribing it to the "benefit of the citizens, because the principle of ruling and commanding is precisely the guardianship of the common weal and the utility of the public good." Therefore, "if authority is constituted to watch over and to act on behalf of the totality, it will be clearly seen that never, under any pretext, can it be exclusively devoted to the service or to the comfort of a few or of one alone."[4]

If society, by its nature, exhibits the note of

[1] Taparelli: *Theoretic Essay on Natural Law*, Bk. II, Ch. V.
[2] Leo XIII: Encyclical *Diuturnum Illud*.
[3] Leo XIII: Encyclical *Immortale Dei*.
[4] Leo XIII: Encyclical *Immortale Dei*.

authority as essential to it, concrete societies—the
product of the consolidation of the natural law of
sociability in certain transcending realities—will show
concrete authorities. These are seen respectively in
the family, the township, the region and the nation.
Their action will be limited by the ambit traced by the
specific end. Within this and in everything concerning
it, there will be plenary action. *Autarchy* consists
precisely in this fullness. But only one of these
authorities and one of these autarchies shall be
sovereign: the authority of the government of the
nation whose plenitude, it has been said, lies in the
genus.

Authority is, therefore, like society which manifests
it as an essential note, a work of Nature. This was
proved and is now recollected. Further, as God is
the Creator of Nature and its law-maker, there is
nothing more true, more just and more accurate than
the assertion of the Apostle: "Authority comes from
God."[1] In spite of its clarity, this sentence requires
some explanation on account of the ambiguity which
the revolutionary spirit has raised about it.

In the words of Mella, it has been said before[2] that
"the political monarchy of divine right, be it absolute
or limited, has always been rejected by the Church."
To affirm now that authority proceeds from God,
might appear to some to be contradictory. Nothing
could be more unreal. "The *non est potestas nisi a Deo*,"
says Mella, "at issue with the Byzantine Cæsars many
centuries ago, was proved by St. John Chrysostom to
refer *to authority itself;* but in no way to the subject
or to the form of government. Authority, like all
human rights, is founded on natural law, which is part

[1] St. Paul: *Epistle to the Romans*, Ch. XIII, 1.
[2] Part II, Ch. V.

of eternal law, which objectively is identified with God. Thus the entire juridical order proceeds from Him as legislator, and from Him, as Creator, every being comes into existence."[1] In the text of St. John Chrysostom quoted by Mella, we read that "the Apostle does not say that *there is no prince* unless he comes from God. But he speaks of the thing itself, saying: 'there is no power unless it comes from God.' "[2]

In several passages of the admirable Encyclicals of Leo XIII, the doctrinal concept is reiterated. Deducing authority from the very nature of society, as has just been shown, the great Pontiff concludes: "God has willed, then, that there should be men in society to govern the multitude;[3] an authority which, like society itself, arises and emanates from Nature and, therefore, from God himself who is its author."[4] *"Public authority, per se or considered essentially,* proceeds only from God because He alone is the true and supreme Lord of all things, to whom all are necessarily subject and who must be obeyed and served. Indeed, all who have the right to command, receive their prerogative from no one but God, Supreme Ruler and Sovereign of all. *There is no power but from God."*[5]

This distinction must be made clear and firmly established. It is true that authority comes from God; but God does not concrete its exercise into one subject nor into one form of government. It follows that authority is never illegitimate, because it is an essential condition of society, and that what may be taxed with illegitimacy is the embodiment of that authority in a subject or in a form of government by illegitimate ways and means. "In its noble and proper

---

[1] Vázquez de Mella: *Complete Works*, Vol. II, p. 130. [2] Homily 23.
[3] Leo XIII: Encyclical *Diuturnum Illud.*
[4] Leo XIII: Encyclical *Immortale Dei.*
[5] Leo XIII: Encyclical *Immortale Dei.*

sense"—we read in *The Right to Rebel*—"*power* is the conjunction of authority and force. . . . But sometimes, power is understood as if it were exclusively the possession of that physical force which is its lowest and material element. In that case, power, divorced from the moral right of authority, becomes reduced to the common category of *a mere fact . . .* and then, one may say of power what could never be said of authority. Power, that power, may be illegitimate; authority cannot be."[1]

Because it is a right having as its object "the guardianship of the common weal and the utility of the public good"—as was said before—the subordination claimed by authority does not stifle individuality but completes it. Revolution introduced to the natural relations of the holder of authority and of his subjects an impious word: emancipation. The slave is emancipated from his master; but slavery is the opposite of social subordination. For the slave, the disappearance of the connections which bind him to his master is a boon; for the citizen, the cleavage of those others with which authority guides him is an evil. Authority is, for man, not an enemy which robs him of his proper activities, but a support and a complement even in the annoyances which human unproficiency may bring about in the exercise of its protective action. Often enough the air, too, is an obstacle to the flight of a bird; yet without the help it gives, no bird would be able to fly.

It is certainly not a question of regarding equally the links binding us to authority and those uniting us to the person exercising it. The fact of the possession of authority has not entered into the reflections that have been made, except to distinguish it radically and

[1] Castro Albarrán: *The Right to Rebel*, Bk. I, Ch. I.

categorically from the right which authority implies. Not only is there no difficulty in acknowledging that through possession, the proper relations of authority are transformed into tyrannical relations, but also that reality offers not a few examples of this. Revolution, which sought the ruin of authority, has confused it with the person wielding that authority—even illegitimately—in order to succeed in its purpose. Little attention is needed to detect the clumsiness of the confusion.

From what has just been said ensues the enunciation of an arduous problem. If authority is something distinct from the person in whom it is embodied and who subsequently exercises it, society, as such, and in relation to an essential property which belongs to it by nature, does not exercise authority. Why does society not exercise it? Who exercises it and how? Where are the titles of that exercise? What are the relations which alone exist between society and the person who assumed its authority? Especially because this is the formal object of our investigations, what are the relations scientifically existent between the nation and the person invested with sovereign authority? This is not a suitable place for replying to all these questions; but it will be done opportunely. The reader will remember that in the scheme we proposed, the government of society constituted a part of our study, different from that in which we were to consider its nature, a subject which will be finished with in the present chapter where our attention must still be occupied with the errors through which that nature has been perceived. Once their refutation has been accomplished, the next chapter will be devoted to that great problem known in political science under the heading of "The Localization of Authority."

Society arises from human nature; authority is an essential note of society. This is proclaimed by the reality of things illuminated by reason, that is, by science. Revolution—which is anti-scientific as it is anti-patriotic—denied, as we have seen, that the origin of society lies in the nature of man, and placed it in social convention. It had to be logical in its error and maintain that authority is not an essential note, but a second result of society. This was indeed the case. Rousseau formulates in this matter another proposition as dogmatic and as false as all those heretofore examined. "As no man," he says, "has natural authority over his fellows, and as Nature does not produce any right, there remain the conventions as a basis of all legitimate authority among men. . . . If there were no previous convention, what would be the source of the obligation of the minority of submitting itself to the election of the majority, unless the election were unanimous? By what right do a hundred who want one man, vote for ten who do not want him? The very law of plurality of the suffrages is a fixing of convention, and assumes, at least once, a previous unanimity."[1]

If true philosophy were content with the mere presentation of texts of an opposite meaning in refutation of a fallacy, we should not have to go far to find one that would contradict those transcribed. In the midst of errors which are outrages, Rousseau succeeded in saying this truth: "The family is, then, if you will, the first model of political society; the head is the image of the father, the people is the image of the children."[2] A few lines before he had recognized that the family is a "natural society" (the only one for

---

[1] J. J. Rousseau: *Social Contract,* Bk. I, Ch. IV.
[2] J. J. Rousseau: *Social Contract,* Bk. I, Ch. II.

him). So it might be affirmed, with Rousseau's
assent, that the father exercises authority *naturally* over
his children; and to exercise authority *naturally* is to
exercise it with a right caused by Nature and not by
convention. What other meaning could this word
have in family relations? The authority of the parent
over his children is the greater as the latter are more
incapable of negotiating or coming to terms. It
could not, therefore, arise from a convention—one
blushes at writing the word—between parent and
children. Nor could it proceed from the social
compact—assuming it existent—because, apart from
the fact that Rousseau puts it forward with very
different jurisdictional characters, the children, either
future or present, as such, have no part in it.

But the involuntary acknowledgment of Rousseau
as to the inconsequence and falseness of his thinking
is of minor importance. Ignoring in human nature
the immediate origin of rights—among them that of
authority—and placing it in conventions, it was
incumbent upon Rousseau to justify the relation of
dependence between convention and authority, and
the origin of the power of contracting. As always,
Rousseau shirks this elementary obligation of fairly
honest dialectics, and is content with an affirmation
devoid of proofs, or with an arbitrary negation. So
he passes off as axioms: that no man shall have natural
authority over his fellows—although this is contradicted in the reality of the family—that Nature
produces no right; and that, in consequence, as if the
hypotheses about the possible sources of right had been
exhausted, and without even troubling to show that
amongst them are conventions, he finds in these the
basis of all legitimate authority among men.

As may be inferred from what has just been set

down, the problem is rather more complex than was imagined by the shallow philosophical brain of Rousseau and by revolutionary presumption. Both assert that legitimate authority among men is founded upon conventions. But why do men need authority? And what, in turn, is the support of conventions? By what mysterious process can a convention have the force to bind those who are absent from it, or even those who participated in it? Neither Revolution nor its high priest even suspected that common sense would ask these questions. When a new State is about to be constructed because the work of Liberalism, amid curses, has fallen to pieces, these questions must be taken up and answered.

It has been said that Rousseau, in order duly to establish the avouchment of the general will, demanded that no partial society should exist within the State and that each citizen should opine exclusively for himself.[1] "This postulation," he adds, "is indispensable for the constant manifestation of the general will and so that the people may never err."[2] "In a body politic so organized," he concludes, "what generalizes the will is not so much the number of votes as the common interest uniting them; because in this institution, *each one necessarily submits to the conditions he imposes upon the rest.*"[3] If all this be true, what is authority for? If the general will is always manifested, if the people never errs, if each citizen *necessarily* submits to the conditions imposed by him upon the others, what is the rôle of authority in such a society?

Moreover, just as Revolution remains half-way in so essential a question as that of the necessity of authority, it falls short of a decision in so far as the

[1] Part II, Ch. IV.
[2] J. J. Rousseau: *Social Contract*, Bk. II, Ch. III.
[3] J. J. Rousseau, *Social Contract*, Bk. II, Ch. IV.

conventional order is concerned. It is easy to say that if authority is not born of Nature, it should spring from convention. The difficulty is to indicate the origin of the latter *outside Nature*. If the right—that of authority—*inter alia*—arises from a convention, where is the source of the faculty by which men agree amongst themselves? Either the question has no answer, which would mean definitely that the Rousseauan affirmation is totally irrational, or it would have to be found in the very nature of man. Thus, after advocating convention as the origin of the right of authority and after denying that causality in Nature, it must be admitted that such a right actually does emanate from Nature because the faculty of agreeing is produced therein.

Nothing has yet been said regarding what is the fundamental principle of the doctrine of Rousseau: the necessary effects of a compact between men. That they are clear in our doctrine may be perceived without the use of many words. The duty of *veracity*, betokened as one of the social obligations immediately derived from human nature,[1] binds all men to make their acts and words conformable to their thoughts. The corollary of this is that those who institute a convenant are mutually accountable for its fulfilment. But where, in the thesis of Rousseau, are the antecedents of this latter obligation? If no right is born of human nature, neither can there exist any obligation proceeding therefrom, whether it be considered anterior or posterior to the right. Where, then, does the compulsory force of a compact arise? Not in Nature, because Rousseau rejected this theory previously; not in the compact itself, because this would presume the duty of *veracity* and, therefore, a law

[1] Part II, Ch. I.

contrary to the *independence* of man which it limits; and Rousseau, in his *Social Contract,* enters upon a state of absolute independence. Further, if there is no way of finding the basis of the obligation made binding by the compact upon the contracting parties in the revolutionary doctrine, what derangement would not the supposition of obligation entail before an authority which did not intervene on their behalf in the agreement which constituted it, or denied acquiescence in such a constitution?

Though without drawing the conclusions of his discovery, Rousseau stumbled upon the substance of the questions set down. The compact does not hold compulsory force within itself. "To say that a man delivers himself gratuitously is to say something absurd and inconceivable. Such an act is null and illegitimate on the sole ground that he who performs it is out of his reason. To say this same thing of a people is to assume a people of lunatics, and lunacy does not create rights. Although each one might alienate himself, he cannot alienate his children. . . . Such an offering is CONTRARY TO THE ENDS OF NATURE AND EXCEEDS THE RIGHTS OF PATERNITY. So for an arbitrary government to be legitimate, it would be essential that *in each generation, the people should be empowered to accept or to reject it;* but then, this government would have ceased to be arbitrary."[1]

The whole of the revolutionary doctrine so laboriously prepared is brought down by the onslaught of its own creator. If a compact *which opposes* the ends of Nature does not produce any kind of effects, the convention acquires its compulsory force from Nature itself. What was affirmed as a vital foundation of our doctrine comes to be recognized incidentally by

[1] J. J. Rousseau: *Social Contract,* Bk. I, Ch. IV.

Rousseau, and even reinforced by another statement, thoughtlessly made like the previous one. If *paternal rights* exist, as has already been noted, they cannot arise from any convention between parent and children, and so, right in general and therefore, the right of authority, must have an origin distinct from convention.

The way now appears clear of obstacles. The supposedly primary contract of social life, entirely unproved, was incapable of constituting authority not even by the very words of Rousseau. It was not sufficient to prove the existence of *unanimity*—to which all reference was omitted—but that its concurrence in the compact should be a reality. But granted such credulity, such an authority and the laws under which it might be organized could nowise bind the children of the contracting parties. Moreover, there would be no remedy in what Rousseau proposes "that, in each generation, the people should be empowered to accept or to 'reject' such laws, because generations do not succeed each other periodically and *en bloc* but, at every moment, the mass of citizens is modified with the disappearance of some and the advent of others to public life, as was already remarked when studying national sovereignty.[1] Authority in the democratic system is, then, finally condemned to be illegitimate very soon after its consecration, or else declared to be non-existent, for continuous change is equivalent to this.

All this comes about by deficient perception of reality. It is obvious that no man is, by reason of the essential notes of his specific nature, superior to another. But besides these, there are others integrated therein under the denomination of *proper*, constituting

[1] Previous Chapter.

L—u

a predicable, which, while not pertaining to the essence, are necessarily united to that nature. Sociability, demanded by authority, is placed, in respect of the human essence, in that same relation of necessity whereby authority has its origin in Nature. As men, that is to say, essentially, there is no inequality between father and children who, nevertheless, are unequal through *natural relations*. Even Rousseau acknowledged this. So Leo XIII, opposing with philosophical accuracy the frivolous impression of Rousseau, did not say, like him, that "no man has natural authority over his fellow," but that "no man has, *in himself* or *through himself*, power to bind with ties of obedience the free-will of others," for "to God alone, creator of all things and legislator, belongs this power, and those who exercise it must do so as communicated to them by God."[1]

In reality, authority in democratic systems participates in the two mortal vices above remarked. As it is not possible constantly to substitute it, even starting from the same principles proclaimed by Revolution, it is stigmatized as illegitimate immediately after being set up; and as its false dogmas demand the change, the action of authority is shackled with deficiency. So society suffers, in her Dantesque affliction, from the effects of both constitutional vices. The sensation of illegitimacy exasperates the citizens and encourages indiscipline and animosity. The feeling of deficiency leaves social needs ungratified, and irritates privations by the conviction that they will not be remedied.

Protest and the movement of indignation against unavoidable effects of the causes, are useless and fruitless. If the new State aspires to something more

[1] Leo XIII: *Diuturnum Illud.*

than to deplore the situation in which the world is found, it must base its principle upon the foundations which Nature herself indicates as unique and inviolable, destroying without scruple those which Revolution wrought with sophistry and arbitrariness.

THIRD PART

THE GOVERNMENT OF SOCIETIES

CHAPTER I

THE LOCALIZATION OF AUTHORITY

NOT infrequently, with reference to the forms of expression used by Christians in relation to their God, revolutionaries have said, with contemptuous gesture, that they could not conceive the Divinity except with the conditions and defects of man. This is Revolution; it feels not the least pity for human weakness. But besides, Revolution, in so far as the imputation is uncommendable, is just as it imagines believers to be. It conceives the nation exactly as a man, feeling, desiring, remembering, speaking and acting as a man. This is not only untrue, but it is the opposite to the truth. The nation, which is a reality, is not, however, a leviathan, that is, "a colossal man," according to the simile of Henry George, of which the individuals were corporal atoms. Hence, the nation, *per se*, does not feel, think, desire, remember, speak or act. It has no personal conscience; the impulses that a collective conscience would perceive as proper have no support in any part of its being; only by analogy can a personal conscience be attributed to the nation.

Hence, after what has been set down in previous chapters, unless there is no possible doubt of the existence of the essential note of authority in the national entity, we could never conceive the *direct* exercise of its own sovereignty by the nation. We are certainly not moved to this by the same reason as that which induces us to acknowledge a child's right, only to deny him its exercise. The metaphor of "peoples who have not come of age" must be put aside for ever. It has served, with the goodwill of some and the evil intentions of others, as an explanation of a phenomenon, the cause of which was entirely ignored. There are no "minor" peoples in the sense of authority being charged with remedying their juridical incapacity. The child who has a right, and does not exercise it on account of insufficiency of years, will some day exercise it. The nation which neglects to exercise its right *directly*, through lack of the use of reason, will never be able to exercise it, illustrious as its civilization may become. When emancipated, the child dispenses with guardianship. The nation, emancipated from birth because it is sovereign, would cease to be such if it were wanting in authority.

All this ensues from the very nature of collective persons. Having no principle of activity of their own, they can only develop activity through the physical persons of which they are composed. Otherwise, no act could be imputed to a collective being, because no form of activity would emanate from it. Experience leads us to accept as a mode of activity of the collective being, the *indirect* mode of other individual or moral persons that are elements of collective persons, without reflecting too much on the content of this far-reaching social phenomenon. But a little meditation will show that for the individual person to exercise a social activity and the right corresponding to it, a circumstance is necessary by which that person may act legitimately on behalf of the community, and the operation may be imputed to the latter.

The ordinary legal mechanism by which the acts of one person are imputed to another and are transmitted validly and by obligation, is delegation or mandate; but in the exercise of national rights there can be no mandate or delegation. The same reason as prevents the nation from exercising its activity, of itself, *directly*, would preclude its delegation. We shall see later how basely Revolution has attempted to evade this iron law which overthrows its most fundamental principles. For the present, let us follow our line of thought. A collective personality without a proper principle of activity, which it lacks by definition, is incapable of any *direct* act and, consequently, of delegation or mandate. Nobody, through the ordinary mechanism of delegation, would be capable of holding national representation.

In spite of the foregoing, not a single point of what has been asserted previously about national sovereignty needs rectification. National sovereignty exists and resides primarily in the nation, which is a living reality and informs its authority which carries out the legislative, executive and judicial functions. Yet all this does not authorize falling into *anthropomorphisms*. The nation is sovereign as a collective, not as an individual being may be; and it legislates, executes the laws and sits in judgment, just as a moral, not a physical person may perform these duties. To convert an analogy into an identity is the inconsistent foundation of the revolutionary myth which crumbles in one's hands. To pass from this identification to its opposite by converting the national unity into an inorganic multitude, is the means—as will be seen—which Revolution employs for the working of its leviathan-nation. Truth does not identify what is contrary nor what is analogous; and it must be remembered as a fundamental principle of all this matter that the composition of society is not *mechanical* but *organic*; yet that *organic* composition does not mean *organicist*.

How can the exercise of national sovereignty by one or several physical persons, without any act of delegation of dominion on the part of the nation, be explained?

Before entering upon the examination of the capital question formulated without ambiguity or circumlocution, without restrictions or evasions, the *revolutionary fact* of this exercise must be emphasized. Indeed, Revolution, which based its legitimacy upon *delegation*, if not as an absolutely pure origin, as a means enforced by reality—points that will be opportunely developed—has neglected, in practice, its own doctrine. Invoking the principle set down in the Table of the Rights of Man that in case of oppression, insurrection is the most sacred of all duties, Revolution has urged it against every institution opposed to its ideas. After triumph, it has seized all the organs of sovereignty which it has exercised without any act of delegation having previously legitimized the conquest. The nation has, as a general rule, been faced with the *fait accompli*. If Revolution has afterwards requested ratification, the hypocritical petition was conditional upon the modes the factious government imagined and imposed, and upon the conception which it might form of the nation. The latter, silent under its oppression and disconcerted in its natural organs, the multitude usurping its attributes, was allowed to speak only according to the will of the factious band which audaciously embodied the Revolution. History is full of these spurious localizations of national sovereignty by *revolutionary realities* in which the least attempt of delegation cannot be discovered. It is also full of bombast applied to them by those who boasted of their revolutionary spirit.

Having recorded it as an antecedent of the solution that should be given to the question asked, it is equally interesting to state that Revolution, even in pure Rousseauan doctrine, in one form or another, denies to the multitude, which it placed on a level with the nation, the faculty of exercising sovereignty.

That this should be limited to legislation or that *government* should be considered as a function foreign to sovereign activity, is not justified by any reason whatsoever. But Rousseau, overcome by reality, vindicating his doctrinal failure through the separation of the executive function from the order of sovereignty, writes thus: "It is easy to observe, by the principles before established, that the executive power cannot correspond to the generality as legislator or sovereign. . . . The public forces need, then, a proper agent to assemble them and to place them in action according to the directions of the general will, to serve as a communication between the State and the sovereign. . . . In my view, *government* or supreme administration is the legitimate exercise of the executive power, and prince or magistrate is the man or the body charged with the administration."[1] In pure Rousseauan doctrine, *election* is the normal means

[1] J. J. Rousseau: *Social Contract*, Bk. III, Ch. I.

for the appointment of princes or magistrates. In the revolutionary system created by the stress of social needs, it is extended to the designation of representatives.

Election, although the precentors of Democracy have avowed otherwise, does not presume, in a final analysis, a *delegation* or *mandate*, even from the multitude—by no means from the nation—but a fact which insists upon the localization of sovereign authority in one or several physical persons. That the doctrinaires of Revolution do not care to view it in that way, is one thing; that it actually is so, is something quite distinct. This has been one more revolutionary fraud that has perished under the attacks of political criticism. In fact, election, unless it be an operation of maniacs, postulates characteristics of superiority in what is eligible over what is rejected. That the superiority may be of very varied nature does not weaken the assertion. One man, when it is a matter of election of rational beings, may be superior to others in consideration of certain conduct and of certain purpose, and inferior when the operations and the end vary. But election, if it is to be a human thing, must have as a motive a note, a habit, a quality or an aggregate of notes, habits and qualities that, being superior in the person elected, decide the inclination of the will.

So, when the election is concerned with the designation of the physical person or persons called upon to exercise *directly* the national sovereignty, what it pursues is the localization of authority in them by means of a reality which is none other than *that of the personal conditions of the elected*. Definitely, the election will be simply the *means of designation* of the person *fit to assume the localization of sovereignty*, and in no way does it confer delegation. Thus, the elected would be invested with authority exactly according to hypothesis, not by delegation, but by the *fact of the dignity of the person*.

Although the contrary may be imagined, Rousseau has not declared himself in opposition. In the light of subsequent events his words, when comparing the monarchic government with the republican, take on a burlesque aspect provoking sneers or sarcastic laughter: "an essential and inevitable effect which will always make the monarchic government inferior to the republican, is that in the latter the public voice scarcely ever elevates men to the highest places, unless they are notable and capable and fill those offices with prestige; while those who reach them in the monarchies are nearly always meddlers, rogues, schemers. . . . *The people err much less in this election* than the prince; the man of true merit is almost as rare in the ministry of a monarchy as is a fool at the head of a republican government."[1]

Whether this occurs or not in practice would take us very far and, besides, its investigation is unnecessary after two centuries of experience and the well-known caustic phrase of Clemenceau: "I vote for the biggest fool." But the localization of sovereignty, even in the revolutionary doctrine examined in its deepest foundations, and not merely observed in the saying of its sycophants, is produced by *a fact* and not by an act of *delegation*.

It is useless to protest against what has just been affirmed. What the partisans of popular sovereignty try to pitch through the window comes back to them through the door. Boasting of it before the dunderheads who listen to them, they localize sovereignty, in practice, in exactly the same way as the Catholic

[1] J. J. Rousseau: *Social Contract*, Bk. III, Ch. IV.

doctrine—this will be seen at once—through a *reality* totally foreign to any sense of delegation, and sometimes even to the social order. Here may be seen the enormous inferiority of the revolutionary doctrine even where it ephemerally coincides with Catholic teaching. The means of election—the only one accepted by the former as a way leading to the *localizing fact*, and that as such may be legitimate if certain circumstances concur in it—is only one of many that can show such a character and certainly not the more frequent. A nation, as already remarked, is indeed an historical product and cannot be formed unless the sovereignty has been localized *historically*, for it has been proved that authority is an essential note of every society. The fact by which national sovereignty is localized in a physical person must be, then, coetaneous with the originary national realities, that is, as historical as they.[1] Even reducing its political import to the limits indicated, it does not follow that election will be, philosophically, the means of localizing sovereignty. This can be so when, with the full evolution of the societies, there do not exist other realities having the virtue of localization in one or several physical persons. The glorious history of Spain gives the world an example of this subsidiary character of election in the plege of Caspe.[2]

After all that has been set down let us make a conclusive statement. If the nation is sovereign and cannot exercise its sovereignty of itself, nor by delegation in. a physical person, only through a transcending reality constituting the latter in a social

---

[1] Suárez: *Treatise on Law*, Bk. III, Ch. II.
[2] Pledge of Caspe (*Compromiso de Caspe*): celebrated parliament assembled at Caspe, in the province of Zaragoza (Aragón), in 1412, which settled the dispute of the succession to the throne of Aragón. On the death of King Martin, *el Humano*, who died childless, there were six claimants. (Translator's note.)

organ can sovereignty be exercised, the acts performed by the individual person being transmitted to the nation as from the organ through which it exercises sovereignty. Any conceptions elaborated beyond those specified, presuppose in political society conditions gratuitously dispensed in the likeness of man. They are not, therefore, of a scientific order, but the product of a mere projection of the human being upon social reality, a phenomenon peculiar to primitive civilizations.

Humanity owes to the Catholic Church the zealous preservation of this doctrinal treasure, like that of so many others, through the course of time and in spite of peoples maddened by the revolutionary poison. To-day it seems incredible that the chimera of the delegation of sovereignty should ever have had followers; but examining the circumstances of the epochs in which it was formulated as an evident truth even worming itself into the very sanctuary, it is hard to understand how the Church could weather the storm of barbarism and continue to instruct men in the transcending principle. With stately language, attaining perfection in the precision and application of the words, Leo XIII, in his Encyclical *Diuturnum illud*, once again consecrates it; and Pius X confirms it in his letter condemning that sect that would have done away with the Catholic sense of authority, and was called, by antiphrasis, "Le Sillon," thus rendering to civil society one of the most eminent services to be found in the catalogue which Catholicism could draw up. The great Pontiff says: "It should be here remarked that those who are called to preside over the republic (in the sense of a political society) may in certain cases be elected by the will and opinion of the multitude, a proceeding not inconsistent with or opposed to Catholic doctrine; but through this election *neither princely rights are conferred by the multitude nor is dominion transmitted* (neque mandatur imperium). It is a mere *determination of the person* who is to exercise this power."

An election by the multitude for the purpose of appointing a prince is quite within Catholic doctrine; but it is not the only means to that effect nor is it even the normal procedure. "In certain cases," says the text transcribed—and the kind of exception or infrequency here referred to, need not be emphasized. So although a prince may be designated by different means, so long as these are legitimate, his legitimacy cannot be placed in doubt. Those three words have saved humanity from ignominy. As there are untold indignities inherent in election, were it the sole means of localizing authority, nearly all those exercising such a preponderance would be without the moral prestige indispensable to the assumption of power. Whichever may be the instrument or the vehicle, the fountain-head of authority ever remains pure and clean. No specifically human means transmits dominion. By whichever means power be localized in a physical person, it is no more than a matter of installation. The nation *exercises* its sovereignty through the person, a power with which God, its author, endowed it, as *through an organ*, in virtue of the organic composition proper to it. The prince, in the broadest sense of the word, king or president of a republic, is no more than this, but he is actually this. Either he must be the organ of the sovereignty of the nation or he is nothing. He is not its guardian nor its master in any tutorial sense; but he is its most eminent organ. That should be his honour, and therein lies the reason of his being.

To this conception of the prince, two contrary errors are opposed: that which makes the nation his patrimony in the private acceptance of the word, and that which sees in the prince a mere symbol of external national unity, depriving him of every content of sovereignty. We shall see, in due time, in what sense —purely analogous and relative—can the nation be spoken of as patrimony; for the present, we must confine ourselves to dealing with the direct and ordinary interpretation according to which the nation does not belong, and cannot belong, to anybody but to the Creator of Nature. If, as has been said, the prince is an organ, even the most eminent organ of the nation, the nation is not subordinate to the prince, rather is the prince the servant of the nation. Moreover, the nation is not a thing but a person; and only under the supposition of slavery are persons ascribed to the patrimony of others. So, when the nation did, in effect, belong to the prince, it was enslaved, and consequently the prince set himself up as a tyrant. Nevertheless, it is a matter of justice to recognize that the monarchies known as *patrimonial* in Spain were not tyrannical. The reason is obvious. They were so considered by their enemies because they were tainted by an error which deserved generous extenuation. It is not that medieval kings ever believed that the kingdom was their property and dominion, but that they were the fathers of the people; and taking their royal prerogatives further than the analogy allowed, they incorporated in the political order that which pertained exclusively to the family order. To this, and not to reprehensible sentiments of a tyrannical prince, were due the division of the kingdom among the sons of the king, heedless of his public status.

If it is an elemental truth that the nation is not the patrimony of the prince, between the one and the other there is something more than the relation which may exist between the thing and its symbol. The prince is the organ of sovereignty which, by the eminence of its function, cannot be confused with those of other political functions. Once he is reduced to a symbol, the derangement of national life is the penalty. The prince must be neither tyrant nor despot; the head-piece of a State and, therefore, of the New State, must be an organ, not a symbol. Thus a prince worthy of the name may, and should be, styled the representative of the nation; and in order to distinguish one form of government from any debasement of the same, it should be called "representative." If it is not such, illegitimacy will condemn it.[1]

For the mere effects of controversy, enough has been said to justify our doctrine in regard to the localization of authority. If in one way or another, the conclusion was reached whereby localization was brought about, even in the revolutionary thesis, not by an act of delegation of the nation, but by *a fact* even alien to the latter, by what right will our adversaries demand the production of another series of titles of legitimacy of social authorities? But a consonant reason is never sufficient for a natural truth whose seekers are urged to discover the foundation upon which it so firmly rests. This motive moves us to justify our doctrine in itself, dispensing with the arguments with which prodigally, though involuntarily, revolutionary philosophy has provided us.

Rousseau, in his *Social Contract*, explained the birth

[1] In dealing with a rational being, we believe—in contradiction to other schools of thought—that there can be no distinction between *organ* and *representative*.

as an immediate natural result of a moral and collective body, a public person formed by the union of all the particular persons of the contracting parties, with its unity, its common *ego*, its life and its will. He goes on to affirm that this public person, at one time, took the name of *city* and now takes that of *republic* or *body politic*. Why stop at *city*? Why not move along in the stages of social evolution? Had this been done, one of the realities that historically have localized sovereignty in a physical person, would have been perceived most clearly and unhesitatingly. It has been said, indeed, that a city was nothing more than a tribe settled in a territory after losing its nomadism. In the tribe, social authority, then also political and sovereign, was localized in the patriarch. For the tribe was not, as Rousseau imagined, a composition of individual members freely united without any outstanding fact fixing upon any one of them the superiority characteristic of authority, but a succession of families proceeding from the same trunk. When the city became a republic, by the association of several families the political representation of the city was embodied in the patriarch, or in him who by connected events might succeed to the office. Therefore the localization of authority in the new body politic had as a basis, not the multitude of the various cities which became associated, but its social authorities which were the legitimate representation of the cities.

In the social process, to discover the law regulating localization of authority, one may and ought to go higher. It was said before that the family, in the evolution of its being, has formed every known political society; and the family is based upon matrimony of which the free and mutual election of the spouses is an essential requisite. In no other social institution, by reason of the very simplicity of its conformation, can the part played by election be studied with greater lucidity. Further, it is plain that in the act of electing, neither partner transmits to the other any right affecting, in the first place, the conjugal society and, afterwards, the family, for the obvious reason that they have possessed none previously, nor do they hold any at the moment of the election when the man is not a husband and the woman is not a wife. The rights of both consorts, when of the natural order, have their origin in Nature; those of the supernatural order proceed from the Sacrament. Mutual election did no more than to actuate them, to establish and to fix them in the persons elected.

Respecting the family society, if those who have produced political novels inspired in crazy delusions, had followed history supported by philosophy, they would not have passed over so far-reaching a social reality as *fatherhood* which is there, within sight of all, in the evolution of human societies. So notorious is it that Rousseau did not fail to perceive it, although without drawing from it any consequence of a political order which, nevertheless, was sufficiently indicated. Completing this, let us remember what was previously transcribed from that author concerning family authority. "The oldest of all societies and the only natural one," he says, "is that of the family. *Once the children are free from the obedience they owe to the father, and the father is released from the care he owes to his children, they all equally recover their independence.* . . . The family is, then, if you will, *the first model of political societies; the head is the likeness of the father, the people are the likeness of the children.*" [1]

[1] J. J. Rousseau: *Social Contract,* Bk. I, Ch. II.

M—n

We leave aside what, in the sentences reproduced, is extravagant and manifestly erroneous; and we emphasize that to the mind of Rousseau, the family is a natural society in which the children owe obedience to the father, and the care of the children devolves upon the father. It follows that family authority is localized in the father, and that the localization has been produced by *the fact of paternity*, not by delegation, which would be out of the question. Moreover, it must not be forgotten that in the first family, as to-day in the nation, the temporal human destiny was attained and that, therefore, paternal authority was a sovereign authority. Nor must it be overlooked that the entire social order arose from the evolution of the family.

Rousseau's forgetfulness was the mortification of the world. If, when tempted by the snare of a social compact, he had imagined the contracting parties as the heads of families or tribes, and not as isolated and totally independent individuals, the idea would have prevented his sinking deeper into his abstractions. In order to see the "sovereign" in the "component particulars," he had to dispense with facts so universal as matrimony and paternity, which were the first to establish and to localize authority; and to take for granted that the parties to the contract sprang from the earth like spontaneous vegetation.

CHAPTER II

FORMS OF GOVERNMENT

THE localization of sovereign authority does not demand fundamentally conditions other than those stipulating that it be invested in persons who have within them the principle of activity, and that it should result from a reality of sufficient transcendence to make them an organ of the nation worthy of acting on its behalf. The forms under which this is brought about will, therefore, be legitimate whatever their character. A monarchy or a republic, so long as it is *national* in the full sense of this word as clearly determined in previous statements, may, in consequence, be endowed with the august and immovable note of legitimacy. But this does not warrant indifference in this matter, not even in the abstract order. Neither does it authorize attempts at nationalization of those forms of government not possessing that essential requisite; nor warrant the enforced demand of a citizen's allegiance to a political régime opposed to the principles established, solely on account of the possible abstract legitimacy of its form. The mere statement of the thought—it is so clearly rational—would be sufficient to claim the assent of everybody; but political matters are, unfortunately, so prone to be darkened by passion that it is essential to develop and establish it in the consequences.

All that was said in the Introduction with reference to the substantivity of political matter, may be con-

sidered reproduced here; but it should be added that
the legitimacy of a form of government is not the same
as its perfection. The perfection or imperfection of
the forms of government belong to the technical order;
its legitimacy to the juridical and moral order. From
the confusion of these orders comes one of the several
aspects of the theory—it does not reach the rank of a
doctrine—of indifference to forms of government. The
transference of conclusions, adopted in the moral or
religious order from an individual point of view, to the
technical—political order, is a real deception in regard
to the citizens, and an irreverent abuse in respect of
ecclesiastical authority. For it must be acknowledged
that the Church, when stating her indifference concerning forms of government, clearly reduces this to
what is outside her jurisdictional orbit. Her attitude
is not properly one of indifference; it is one of restraint.
When Leo XIII, in his Encyclicals *Diuturnum Illud*,
Libertas and *Sapientiæ Christianæ*, declares "there are
no reasons why the Church should not approve the
rule of one or of several," he is careful to add the
limitation to this difference, even for the Church
herself, in these other words: "always provided it be
just and tend to the common good." In the Encyclical
Au milieu, he even recognizes in the citizens their
right to prefer a certain political régime to another.
"In fact, however," he says, "public authority is not
always to be found under the same form; each State
possesses its own. This form arises from a combination of historical or national, though always human,
circumstances which in a nation give rise to its
traditional and even fundamental laws, and by these
is determined a particular form of government, the
basis of transmission of power." How could the
subjects of a nation contemplate with indifference a

form of government born of a union of historical or national circumstances which create their traditional and even fundamental laws and *is determined* by them?

It is imperative, then, to investigate the requisites of a technical order integrating the perfection of forms of government in order to compare, afterwards, monarchy with republic as forms of localization of the sovereign authority of a nation. It is clear that if the latter enjoys *unity*, the national authority must also be one, for if by definition the nation is sovereign, its authority must be *independent*. If it develops successively in time, the authority must have the requisite of *continuity*. If this authority, although sovereign, is not absolute, it must, in some form, determine the limitation. If authority is an essential requisite to government, it must be in agreement with its *interest*. Finally, if the mission of authority is the direction of the national subjects, the form of government charged with exercising it must possess *capability* for the office.

Revolution, as its conclusions proclaim, arbitrarily and gratuitously had taken pleasure in adorning with all sorts of perfections the form of government of its predilection which, apart from any doctrinal indifference, it adopted as its own: the republic. In the previous chapter, and for other motives, were transcribed the words of Rousseau tracing the course of Revolution in the matter.

Experience has placed on record the fantastic character of these speculations; the setting up of the republican form in political societies has brought, amid great evils, this decisive good: the regretful lament that the "Republic was fair in the days of the Empire," has become a household word. It is now indisputable and unquestionable that in the political systems emanating from Revolution, authority is *various, dependent, discontinuous, irresponsible, disparaging of the national interest and incompetent.* But even more can be said. A comparison of those republics most highly praised on account of the purity of their democratic origins, with decadent monarchies, leaves the latter favourably placed with no little advantage.

It could not be otherwise. The vices that corrode revolutionary political systems are not accidents amenable to correction, but issues of constitutional infirmities. In them authority is *various*, not only because a conception which elevates functions to powers would be unable to find a means of making them into a unity, but because once access was given to all the organisms coveting the possession of authority, they would oppose one another in unending internal strife. It is *dependent*, because, originating in political parties, it is bound to be subject to them. It is *discontinuous*, because there is no *continuity* in those who grant it. It is *irresponsible*, because, being the organ of the party victorious in the contest, the latter defends and vindicates authority, with all its eagerness of domination, against the most substantial accusations. It cannot represent the *general interest*, because primarily it represents the faction to which it is beholden. It is *incompetent*, because no reason of competence inspired its localization; which deficiency has become a topic, in view of the spectacle of the leaders of Democracy feverishly engaged in the investigation of means with which to endow their authorities with competence in their decisions and with efficacy in their modes of action. Time has given a categorical answer to Lincoln's question, full of uneasiness: "Is there fatally an element of weakness in the nature of every republic?"

It was not only a mystical and religious conception

of the world that suggested to Spanish philosophers and theologians their preference for the monarchic form; it was also the perception of the concrete reality of a nation. If in the latter there was unity consequent upon its end and upon the means requisite for the achievement of that end, the organ of its representation, that which was to embody the unity of sovereignty must be *one* also. A man who, being the organ of sovereignty of a nation, represents it in his physical unity, constitutes precisely the monarchic form of government with a representative character. Evidently this physical unity is not sufficient, but it is necessary. The attacks more frequently suffered by the monarchy have been due to the fact that, apart from unity, it did not possess, on account of degradation, any of the other requisites of authority.

The monarchy in its full effectuation, that is, the traditional, hereditary monarchy, exhibits the note of independence. The king does not owe investiture to any oligarchy or plebiscite; he holds this office by virtue of a fundamental law of the nation establishing the call to the throne by blood and not by election. The king is, therefore, in the origin of his institution, independent of oligarchies, parties or classes. Indeed, he is subject to nothing save to that which was created by those who have passed on the law. The king, as a man, may depend on favourites, minions or courtesans; but to describe that as a defect of the monarchy is to accuse the institution of what is the sin of humanity. The history of the French Republic, in spite of its brevity, offers examples of this last kind of dependency in its presidents. What is man's weakness in any form of government cannot be imputed to the monarchy as a constitutional vice. Examined in this way, it will be seen that the dependence of public authority in the monarchies is *anti-constitutional;* in the republic it is *constitutional.*

The self-same origin of the independence of the monarch—the law of heredity—is the cause of his continuity. This virtue is so notorious in monarchy that nobody denies it. Its enemies limit themselves to bringing forward the question of birth. Heredity, it is said, causes the nation to be ever contingent upon chance. Even taking for granted a dynasty created by a prince of exalted intellectual status, it is added, his successors may be reprobates or imbeciles. They may be indeed; but monarchy should not be judged by mutilating it or by incomplete conduct in the government of the State. Monarchy is not only the king, but the whole formed by the institutions surrounding him, and among them are to be found those which repair the effects of chance and, often enough, remove it altogether. But is there no hazard in election? Renan answered this question in the affirmative, and subsequent experience has given credit to his statement and emphasized the reasons upon which it was based. It has already been remarked[1] that the assertions of Rousseau concerning nominations realized by election, are arrant nonsense. Party zeal and interest in an election urges the electors to vote "for the biggest fool" according to the phrase before quoted from Clemenceau. The few and exceptional cases in which the gravity of the circumstances restrains the vehemence of parties, confirm the rule.

In no political regime that is not bereft of logic, can an authority, sovereign through its functions, be subjected to responsibility. Otherwise, an organ empowered to enforce that subjection would exist in

[1] See previous chapter

the nation and that organ would be the sovereign. Parliamentary inviolability is the clearest manifestation of the irresponsibility of revolutionary regimes. Parliament, in which national sovereignty is held to be delegated, is, by reason of that inviolability, irresponsible although it is not the sovereign, but only his delegate. But the fact that the sovereign authority is not subject to responsibility on the requisition of another organ of the nation, does not mean that it is irresponsible. As absurd is the idea of responsibility by requisition as that of irresponsibility. There is no other solution to the apparent antinomy than to affirm responsibility, leaving the sanction to the inevitable historical and moral reactions. This is not definitely equivalent to irresponsibility, for it carries with it contrary effects. The most powerful incentives of paternity and self-interest forewarn the judgment and the sanction of the acts of the monarch, who cannot doubt that, in spite of his solicitude, they may some day fall inexorably upon his successors.

Virtue is the noblest impulse of man, and therefore should not be wanting in any one: king or president of the republic, authority or subject. But if it is noblest, it is not the most frequent, and social institutions—which require virtue—cannot be founded upon their heroic action nor even upon their normal influence over men who act as their organs. An institution formed on the supposition of the natural goodness of man would give rise to shocking catastrophes, and Montesquieu condemned the republican form to death from the moment when—according to Jean Jacques Rousseau—"he has considered virtue as the basis of the republic."[1] For he did not claim it as a generic condition of every human institution, but as

[1] J. J. Rousseau: *Social Contract*, Bk. III, Ch. IV.

specific and without which that form of government could not subsist. "The monarch," he says, "who by wrong counsel or by negligence omits to cause the laws to be carried out, can easily remedy the evil by changing his advisers or by correcting his own negligence. But when, in a popular government the laws become impotent, as this cannot but accrue from the corruption of the republic, the State is lost."[1]

Setting aside an occasional entirely incongruous word, it is certain that if the principle of the republic is truth and without it the impairment of the laws is irremediable; and on the other hand, in the monarchies, legislative negligence finds easy correction, then republics do not possess the strength of self-preservation with which monarchies are admirably endowed. Moreover, in the latter, the undeniable inducement of private interest is directed to the advantage of the general interest. Jaurés—who could not be unaware of the fact—termed this tendency "the intelligent selfishness of kings." Maurras did not excuse it but considered it as a foundation of the monarchic order. Tauxier expressed the thought in these words: "Monarchy is an institution which makes public interests the personal and private interests of one man." But long before then, almost seven centuries earlier—to the shame of many Catholics who have forgotten it or who have never known it—the truth had been perceived by Saint Thomas, who recorded it thus: "Kings and princes must act, in regard to the common good, through their own good which proceeds therefrom; the contrary is to follow the course of tyrannical government."[2] In this sense alone can monarchy be called *patrimonial*.[3]

[1] Montesquieu: *The Spirit of the Laws*, Bk. III, art. 3.
[2] St. Thomas Aquinas: *De Regimene Principum*, Bk. I, Ch. X.
[3] Part III, Ch. I.

This does not mean to say, nor does it say, that rulers should pursue inevitably through their actions their own good, always seeking, therefore, the common good. What it does mean, and actually says, is that the monarchic institution exclusively offers this admirable note of harmony between public interest and the private interest of the king. A non-hereditary head of the State feels the clash between his interest and that of the nation. A monarch, when he harms public interest, acts directly against his own interest which sooner or later will feel the injurious effect. Definitely, and this is what matters, it facilitates, by its own nature, the action of public authority and removes from its path the obstacles which other forms of government, through their nature, cause to accumulate. This reality is explained by that which has been before presented as the foundation of the notes of independence, continuity and responsibility of public authority in monarchies: the law of heredity. From the moment when the mechanism of the institution connects the private actions of the monarch with his representative conduct as an organ of sovereignty, and as a consequence of the close union between the two orders, responsibility for the detriment of the public interest is reflected in the private interest, the concern of the nation becomes normally concordant with that of the person in whom, by heredity, sovereignty is embodied.

But these are not the only virtues of heredity. It has a more creative phase than that of succession by decease. It is caused during life in the atmosphere of the family and within this, in the professional medium. Gently assimilated by the children, it accustoms them to the comprehension of acts of this

character, enables them easily to use the befitting
vocabulary, prepares them for the acquirement of
ideas of a technical order, awakens in them sentiments
and vocations which would otherwise go unheeded,
and guides their activity in the same direction as that
of their elders. At the outset, this heredity holds a
vast treasure of advantages, extended by the distinctive and intensive features of a traditional education with refinement and ever increasing advance-
ment as time passes. So, from their cradle, princes
learn *their kingly office* under conditions such as no other
man may learn his trade or profession.

When stating this, we must repeat what was
previously said concerning other circumstances of the
monarchic form. It is not meant to affirm that princes
are fated, as if by enchantment, to derive the benefits
of the excellences offered by the system, but that these
exist in the institution *specifically*, and are not present
in other political régimes. With them, monarchy
contains within itself the means to correct the hazards
of birth, reinforced by the advisory institutions
surrounding the king and which, as will be seen in
due couse, are the corner-stones of the monarchic
State. The *competence* attributed to it is not idolatrous
adulation of persons, just as the *incompetence* of democracies—to-day recognized even by their leaders—is
not a calumny of their adversaries. To prejudge the
competence of kings as *personal* simply because they
are persons is an abominable fetichism. The authority
in monarchies which in practice observe their laws,
is *competent* by the hereditary preparation of the princes
and by the complementary institutions which, like
the brain of man, elaborate social thought. It is not
so in democracies, because they lack preparation and
councils; and these cannot be held to exist in democ-

racies, because it would mean the latter denying themselves. Every democratic institution must owe its origin to election; that is, to the masses and to the party vote, which are *incompetent*, by definition, in the juridical, professional or technical order, and very particularly in the *truly* political order. Evidence in this matter is so overwhelming that the reality only brings lament from the lips of pre-eminent democrats. Gastón de Jèze, not to be suspected of fervour, has summarized the result of the hapless experience in these words: "One would have to be blind not to see that the most intelligent, the most honourable and the most zealous men in public life are not elected at the polls. *No electoral reform would bring about any great change here. Let us harbour no illusions on this score.*"

The forms of government concretely applied to nations, and considered in their organic whole are known by the denomination of State. As sovereignty and authority are national notes, their localization makes the State the seat of the sovereignty of the nation and not a sovereign entity with its own sovereignty. The nation is not for the State; the State is for the nation; or, in other words, the State, in principle, must be national. All the confusion raised about the State on account of sovereignty is dissipated with these words. It may be termed sovereign forasmuch as the organ of sovereignty originates in it, but not as the subject of it. The doctrine of nationalities, upon which dividing and revolutionary nationalisms have been based, is not false in its enunciation but in its applications. For the exercise of a right, the natural faculty is not sufficient; the concurrence of legitimate facts determining the merely abstract right granted by Nature, is essential. These facts, within the natural order, in the matter of nationalities are two: equality of spirit, and legitimate superiority in the organism that is to constitute the national State over those pertaining to the partial States. It behoves us to say a few words concerning this most interesting subject.

The societies constituted by the breaking up of the universal human society, in the course of time, at the moment in which the associative events stimulating efficaciously the instinct of natural sociability occurred, could be informed by social spirits that would classify them under their respective signs. Those identically assigned would coincide in what is fundamental in a nation, and would thus become fragments of one destined to gather them naturally to itself. The doctrine of nationalities, of the name given to each of those societies of identical national spirit, clearly does not err when prescribing their union in the national society under one State alone. It offends, however, when it sets up violently and unlawfully as a national State, that of one of the nationalities to the detriment of the others, or an organism which no outstanding fact has endowed with superiority.

Enough has been said to refute the other aspect of the doctrine of nationalities, but it has been made clear that the idea of nationality cannot be confused with the idea of the nation.[1] Because a society is possessed definitely of a national spirit, *it has no right to constitute itself a nation exclusively per se*, severing the social connections binding it to others of the same spirit, a union which, precisely, would constitute a national body.

If the form of government or State is to be national, its Constitution can scarcely be otherwise. Revolu-

[1] Prat de la Riba, in his work *Catalonian Nationality* (p. 52), is obliged to acknowledge this although, immediately after, he makes assertions as if he had denied and refuted it.

tion, which invoked the antecedent when it suited its purpose, has entirely forgotten the consequence. Worse still, it has denied it in public life. The revolutionary Constitutions have been wrought out of sight of the nations, and imposed violently upon those who were to be ruled by them. The world tragedy lies there. The written law does not accord with the traditional law which, as we have seen, provided the internal Constitution of political societies. Cánovas del Castillo,[1] not partial in the matter, saw the evil although he aggravated it by sponsoring an anti-national Constitution. Here are his most notable words in which he expresses traditional thought in respect to the existence of internal national Constitutions prior to the written codes: "Whoever has said, or now says, that nations always have an internal Constitution *anterior or superior to the written texts*, the easy eclipse of which is shown by experience . . . has uttered, or now utters, a truth so plain and so convincing that it can hardly bear rational contradiction. . . . It may, then, be resolutely affirmed *that such a régime is, amongst us, anterior and superior to every written text*."[2]

Spain has a double good fortune in the midst of her present grievous afflictions. She possesses the plan of the New State. Her internal Constitution propounds, without any doubt, the representative monarchy as a national form of government. Science points to it as the most perfect of all political forms. Its very adversaries have felt bound to recognize it. This testimony is from the pen of Poincaré: "In monarchic

---

[1] Don Antonio Cánovas del Castillo (1828-1897), leader of the Conservative Party, mainly instrumental in the restoration of the monarchy in the person of Alphonso XII. (Translator's note.)

[2] Introduction to the Royal Decree of December 3, 1875, summoning the first Parliament of the Restoration.

countries, the king may yet, without doubt, appear to his people as the pure likeness of his country. In a republic, an elected president is but a politician who yesterday came from the crowd and to-morrow will return to it."[1] There is no room for hesitation There is nothing to be done save to develop the plan so that the good State shall be the New State. Nobody, on any account, may claim the allegiance of national subjects to an anti-national State nor fix a time-limit for its nationalization.

[1] Poincaré: *Au Service de la France*. L'Union Sacrée, Vol. IV, p. 121.

CHAPTER III

FUNCTIONS OF SOVEREIGNTY

THE note of sovereignty of the nation, already set forth,[1] does not create national functions; it only gives them sovereign character. If a function is sovereign because it belongs to a sovereign society, it does not follow, it cannot mean that it is a sovereign power. Power, which is nothing but authority in action, must of necessity be *one* like the being to whom it belongs; and *one* like the authority of which it is the operation. If three functions exist in a nation, there are not three sovereign powers; the note of sovereignty of the function does not proceed from the latter but from the nation to which it corresponds.   The bombastic ineptitude of the eighteenth century not only did not perceive these most simple truths, but elevated their antitheses to the standing of doctrines. It did not stop to consider that the existence of three sovereign powers implied that of three sovereign authorities, and, therefore, that of three different societies in that aggregation which, by definition, ranked as *one*.

What Montesquieu proposed was so obviously contradictory as to be reformed by the very defenders of the régime called, by antiphrasis, constitutional. If in a society there existed three independent powers, social unity, already broken by the mere fact of their existence, would be utterly ruined in the event of conflict among them, this being indeed more frequent

[1] Part II, Ch. III.

than a state of agreement. Benjamin Constant added a fourth to these three powers: the moderating power, charged with settling the differences that might arise among the other three. But it is clear that if that power judged the acts of the others, came to resolutions concerning them and forced its decisions upon them, it would eventually be the sovereign power. If it meant the vindication of common sense, it also meant a deep rift in constitutionalism, and an arbitrary attempt was made to close it. The moderating power would exercise its specific functions through the executive power. Thus, the judgment and the action of the latter could not fail to be warped. "The question remained as before," says Mella;[1] "parliamentary progress came to a stop. All subsequent efforts have only served to modify the technicality. The substance continues identical."

Rousseau stated his thought about the matter in the following terms: "Every free action has two causes which concur to effect its production: one, a moral cause, the will determining the act; and the other, a physical cause, the power executing it. . . . The body politic has the same principles of motion which are distinguished also in the same way by power and will: the latter under the name of *legislative power;* the former under that of *executive power*. Nothing is or ought to be done without the concurrence of both. We have seen how the legislative power belongs to the people and cannot but belong to it. On the contrary, it is easy to observe, from the principles already established, that the executive power cannot belong to the people generally as legislative or sovereign, because that power is exerted only in particular acts which are not within the province of the law, nor

[1] Juan Vázquez de Mella: *Complete Works,* Vol. II, p. 9.

consequently within that of the sovereign, all whose acts must be laws."[1]

In this paragraph, apparently plain and sensible, there is nothing but confusion and arbitrariness. Every free action has not two but three immediate causes: reason, will and the power of motion. But the mediate cause, excluded by Rousseau and of which reason, will and the power of motion are only faculties, is no other than human nature which—as already stated[2]—is the origin of judgment, of will and of the external and physical act. To distinguish these human operations of so diverse a condition cannot be anything but legitimate; but there is nothing so absurd as to regard them as *totally* separated in life. The only power that manifests itself thinking, willing and acting, resides in the human being. So, in order to continue the similitude, Rousseau is obliged to speak of the *body politic* as the substantiality of what he calls *executive power* and *legislative power;* but instead of concluding that both belong to the sovereign power, for he uses the appellation in describing the body politic in its relation to the subjects, he attributes to it only the former, and clearly and categorically denies any such affiliation in the case of the latter.

The likeness established by Rousseau between the body politic and man—which to a considerable extent and within certain limits, as before stated, may be considered legitimate—is an argument against his doctrine. If the body politic, like man, needs diverse impulses in order to act, and in man all these are proper to him, why should not those of the body politic bear the same relation? Why should he who legislates as a sovereign not carry out what he

---

[1] J. J. Rousseau: *Social Contract*, Bk. III, Ch. I.
[2] Part I, Ch. I.

legislates? If the body politic and man are of a nature that does not admit similitude, why analogically deduce the conditions of life of a society from those which pertain to a being of a different nature?

The analogy established by Rousseau, and at once denaturalized, between man and the body politic does not even allow the identification of the will with the sovereign. In man the will is *his own*, but it is not man himself. The will is a power of his mind as the limbs through which he executes his volitions are organs of body substantially united to the soul to form human nature. It cannot be said that man is his own will. If such licence were permitted, it might be said, likewise, that man is his own motive power.

In consequence, Democracy has mutilated the nation which, as observed, is the orthodox name for the *body politic* or *sovereign* of Rousseau. After pompously declaring its sovereignty he falls into this monstrous contradiction. He ascribes to it the power of legislating and denies it the power of executing. To whom does he impute this?

In order to escape from the quandary in which his frenzied imagination has placed him, Rousseau brought forth even more preposterous notions. "What, then, is government?" he asks. "An intermediary body established between subjects and sovereign for their mutual correspondence, charged with the execution of the laws and the maintenance of civil and political liberty. The members of this body are called magistrates or *kings*, that is to say, *governors*, and the whole body bears the name of *prince*. Thus, those who hold that the act by which a people profess submission to their chiefs is not a contract, are quite right. It is, in fact, nothing else than a commission, an employment in which *as simple officers of the sovereign*, they exercise in its name the power it has vested in them and *may limit, modify, and take up again when it pleases.*"[1]

Let him who can, understand the paragraph transcribed. If the sovereign power "is only formed by the *individuals composing it,*"[2] where is the need of an intermediary body for their mutual correspondence? Even if this need were proved, the government being only constituted "by simple officers of the sovereign who exercise power in its name," how has it been stated "that the executive power cannot correspond to the people generally as legislative or sovereign, because that power is exerted only in particular acts which are not within the province of the law, nor consequently within that of the sovereign?" How could the sovereign "limit, modify and take up again when it pleases" a power to which it is not entitled? Finally, where is the origin of this "intermediary body" which is the government? It does not proceed from the compact, because were that so, it would be as supreme as the sovereign itself; and if the compact alone is the source of the legitimacy of political societies,[3] whence come the governments in democratic régimes?

The hopeless weakness is exposed. In democratic régimes, governments have no legitimate foundation. They are simply intrusive bodies without which systems could not live, but which from the first moment every effort is made to eliminate. Let no one waste time trying to strengthen their authority.

One sole power in society with three different functions does not consequently mean three powers; but neither does it mean one sole organ which in turn

[1] J. J. Rousseau: *Social Contract*, Bk. III, Ch. I.
[2] J. J. Rousseau: *Social Contract*, Bk. I, Ch. VII.
[3] J. J. Rousseau: *Social Contract*, Bk. I, Ch. I.

performs the three different functions. One power with three substantially distinct functions implies normally as many organs as functions. As when examining the problem of the localization of sovereignty we inferred that an organ of sovereign authority exists in every nation, it follows from what has now been said that a legislative organ, an executive organ and a judicial organ must likewise exist. The three take the note of sovereignty from the only one who can grant it, who is supreme and personifies the whole nation. This is why laws are made and carried out, and judgment delivered in the name of the king. This does not mean to say, and it never has been said, that the king personally and exclusively legislates, executes and judges, but that the power of legislating, of executing and of judging is held by the respective organs derived from the sovereignty vested in the king as representative of the nation.

What in the democratic system is meaningless is here significant. The organs of the legislative, executive and judicial functions of a nation must be independent *one from another;* and because democracies were inspired in principles contrary to those stated, it will now be understood that their independence—absolute in the predications—did not exist and never can exist in the functions. Montesquieu, in his asseveration that "when the legislative power is joined to the executive power in one same person or body, then there is no liberty,"[1] condemned every democratic régime the world has seen, although they were meant for a contrary purpose. Experience, indeed, has made clear the practical impossibility of obtaining, in democracies, independent action between the organs of public functions.

[1] Montesquieu: *The Spirit of the Laws,* Bk. XI, Ch. VI.

In Italy the commission set up by the government for the study of constitutional reform, records the following in its notable report: "Substantially, the faculty of resolving crises was accorded to Parliament alone. The government was merely its instrument. The doctrine granting pre-eminence to the Chamber of Deputies over the government had gradually prevailed. . . . Hence, parliamentarism is the most serious and dangerous degeneration of political customs; it constitutes a complex deviation and usurpation of power." In France an opinion of the highest standing, by reason of the double status of the author and the conditions in which he emitted it, joined what is fast becoming a chorus of voices crying out for the separate action of the legislative and executive functions in the Liberal State, which made it dogmatic. Poincaré has given as a formula for the remedy of its evils "the extirpation of the hypertrophy of Parliament, the reduction of Parliament to its due function, the clear separation of the legislative from the executive power." In Spain, Count Romanones, after defining the parliamentary régime as that "in which assemblies perform the executive besides the legislative functions, for the former are exercised by a representation of Parliament and cannot exist without the confidence of the same," concludes emphatically, without distinctions or attenuations: "in parliamentary governments all is lost, because within them *that division of powers cannot exist*."[1]

Yet perhaps the greatest evil does not lie in this invasion of the functions of one organ of the State by another. The worst is that the organ performing a function not proper to it, ends by fulfilling its own defectively. Two obvious reasons may be adduced in

[1] Alvaro de Figueroa: *The Parliamentary Régime*, Ch. VIII.

support of this statement. First, the loss of the habit that perfects and facilitates the operation. Next, the adaptation of a function extraneous to it. Thus it is observed in revolutionary régimes that the legislative organ, when it invades the executive sphere, executes badly but legislates worse; and that the executive organ, when it overrides the legislative function, legislates deplorably and executes recklessly and negligently. In the light of these last reflections, the testimonies previously cited amply explain the discordance and infecundity of parliamentary regimes, even considering spearately each one of the organisms therein styled *powers;* but I cannot resist quoting another from the Italian presidential commission which is like a synthesis of all that has been set out: "In the parliamentary régime," says the report, "the Chambers exercise attributions belonging to the executive power; and replace the Crown by refusing it the exercise of that supreme directing and integrating function, indispensable for the harmonious co-ordination of the powers of the State . . . and naturally, under pressure of the necessity created by parliamentary demands, the interferences of the executive power with the exercise of the judicial power are frequent."

Moreover, experience concordant, general and unequivocal is not the result of infraction of the laws pertaining to revolutionary régimes, but is an unerring manifestation of the very principles upon which these systems are founded as already indicated by the texts brought forward. If there is no organ of independent sovereignty and all *power* emanates from the people— as the parliamentary jargon has it—the latter, through the political parties that are the means of its action, will be considered as exercising sovereignty, and therefore, the parties assembled in Parliament after the elections will claim that sovereignty for themselves, and, as a consequence, the subordination of the executive organ. This, in its turn, having at its disposal the resources of public administration and through these, a hold on the electors themselves, will aim at constituting Parliament by its own regulation and authority, for according to parliamentary doctrine, the independent power has no reason to recognize any superiority in Parliament. The assertion of the independence of functions in democracies must now appear totally contradictory to the doctrinal foundations from which it was held to be derived.

It ought not to be sufficient for us to recognize by a first intuition from the diversity of public functions, the necessity of mutual independence in the action of their organs; the indeclinable necessity of their separate action should be drawn from Nature itself. We are assisted in this direction by the contents of the aforesaid report of the Italian presidential commission of constitutional reform. "The State," it declares, "needs continuity and rapidity of action in international relations no less than in those of an interior order. This need is felt even more in modern life. The complexity of international relations that have many reactions in every field of our activity, requires a strong, free, lasting, self-determined government, qualities which parliamentarism certainly cannot guarantee. The co-ordination of the infinite demands of the country, the formation of the degrees of authority in relation to the possibility of satisfying those demands, the prevision of the utility of those relating to remote ends of a superior order, presuppose government acting above parties and not continuously undermined by their possible fraudulence. . . . When extra-

ordinary events like a war or a public calamity have
ravaged a country, the activity of Parliament has been
considered embarrassing or superfluous. In the modern
life of States . . . extraordinary events are the reality
of every day."

Already in man himself, reflection and action are
different things. The former claims rest and time; the
latter spiritual and physiological tension, and rapidity.
They are likewise separated and distinguished by the
fact of their acquired habits being totally different.
It is known that without habits which elevate incal-
culably natural dispositions, the world would move
with the slowness of a tortoise. For the purpose of
reflecting as well as of acting, man needs to attach
habits to his nature. No great effort is needed to show
that the habit of reasoning is entirely distinct from that
of action.

But what produces the greatest difference between
the operations pertaining to these is the quality of the
impulse. Both being human, it is unnecessary to recall
that the elements of the double nature of man should
participate conjointly in them; and that, in consequence, reasoning and acting equally require the
concurrence of body, mind and muscle. But it is very
evident also that in the former function, the greater
part is of the spiritual element, in the latter it is of the
organism. We might say that reasoning is essentially
internal and has nothing external save what is indispensable to any human operation; and that action is
predominantly external, possessing nothing internal
beyond what is requisite for its rationality.

It is not surprising that the differences observed in
man in the operation we are analysing should also
appear in the analogous operations of a political
society. Circumstances, habits, régimes and the

impulses that bring them about, make legislation something substantially different from execution. But besides, the discrimination between the two functions is still greater in political societies than in man by reason of the new factor taking part. The individual, when reflecting, deliberates with himself, and may nearly always dispense with outside suggestions. The deliberation proper to political societies, on the contrary, enforces discussion among a plurality of individuals, and demands the intervention of different public elements to furnish what might be called the general principles of the matter to be debated. On the other hand, satisfaction cannot be afforded the requisites of the executive function if this is entrusted to a deliberating Chamber. The dictates of Nature must be obeyed. The executive function, carried out or mediatized by many, will always be accomplished badly; and exactly the same must be said of the legislative function given over to an organ appropriate to the executive order. As the functions are distinct, so distinct organs must be established; otherwise, there is nothing but a stupid resignation to be badly governed.

But this does not in any way exclude an organ of State from exercising surveillance over the others. The glorious Cortes of Castile, of Aragón, of Catalonia and of Navarre scrutinized the acts of the royal power. It was simply the expression of their supervisory faculties acknowledged by the most powerful kings, the statement of grievances presented at the opening of the period of sessions. There is a real gulf between the revision of acts of pure government and of those connected with the execution of laws. If it is accepted that one organism of the State may not interpose in another *in the element proper to the latter*, it is just as obvious that it may interpose in all the others *in what concerns its own element*. If the element of the legislative organ is the law, the legislative organ may scrutinize the executive organ in the application of laws in its acts of government. But its scrutinizing faculties cease there; they cannot be extended to the discretional powers that human prevision, whatever the political régime may be, is incapable of enclosing within regulated forms.

It is well known that the circumstances, habits and impulses which characterize the judicial function are totally distinct from the habits, circumstances and impulses proper to the legislative and executive functions. The reasons given for the maintaining of the independence of the two last are also valid respecting them and the judicial function. But there is also another, exclusively touching the latter which, of itself alone, cannot be ignored. The judicial order affects *concrete* rights which naturally cannot be acknowledged at once—like abstract or natural rights—in every individual forming a social category. When deciding upon them the judge does not merely concede them; he deprives somebody of their enjoyment according to a pre-established standard to which he must rigorously submit. Furthermore, concrete rights are not interpreted in the same circumstances or under identical forms. Accuracy in this requires a constant application of activity to the function and a state of spiritual balance, as much in the moral as in the intellectual sphere, that should not be perturbed.

Nothing of this can be asked of human weakness unless efficacious support is given to it. Heroism may be binding upon the conscience of an individual, but it cannot be taken as a foundation, as was said before, of a society that is for everybody and counts a small number of heroes. Thus, it depends upon the institution which, *as a natural consequence of its organization*, must offer its members encouragement for study, serenity of mind for decision, sufficient protection so that conscience may be able to resist every urge. Only then will the discreditable ones be eliminated. Nothing can be cured unless there is a healthy foundation. In weak natures with sources of infection, with morbiferous inheritance, little or nothing can be done by the physician who, paradoxical though it may seem, cures healthy but not corrupt natures. The judicial organ must, in consequence, have characteristics distinct from the legislative and executive organs; and its structure must be an obstacle to the pressure of both.

These functions of sovereignty, by definition, have the limits of sovereign action itself. Like this, they are bound[1] above, by religious society and below, by the social autarchic personalities in regard to the orbits of jurisdiction drawn by their respective ends, thus terminating in the matter delimited by these. But it is also plain that they may not be exceeded by societies which contain organically the national functions. From this it is inferred that the natural law in social matter is infringed equally when the nation takes upon itself functions belonging to the Church or to sub-sovereign societies, as when it shares with one or another in functions that are exclusive to such societies. There must be neither regalism nor "subjection to anybody in temporal things;" neither centralism nor delegations of power.

But once this is affirmed, it must also be remembered in order to avoid appreciations as erroneous as they are harmful, that the proper matter of the jurisdiction

[1] Part II, Ch. V.

of societies which are elements of the national society, is not outside the nation but inside it, and it affects subjects which are national. Hence, these come under several jurisdictions so that although the nation must not invade the prerogative of the others, this does not mean that it may not legislate, execute and judge, having as subjects the same as those for whom, in their own matter, the Church, the region and the municipaltiy legislate, execute and judge. The jurisdictional orbits of the respective component societies of the nation or co-existent with it, do not affect territories but matters. It was anticipated and is now made clear that if the municipality has the right to legislate, to execute and to judge, in relation with its exclusive end through the respective municipal organisms, the region and the nation legislate, execute and judge in the municipality and beyond the municipality, in what concerns the regional and the human destiny; and the nation, in the region and beyond the region, in what refers to the temporal end of man.

CHAPTER IV

THE KING

IT has been said that the king is the organ of sovereignty. To recall it is to assert implicitly that the function fulfilled by the king in the State belongs to him and to nobody else. The function of sovereignty, therefore, should be fulfilled by the king and by the king alone. Ministerial sanction, in the sense of rendering valid the royal decision, not in the sense of attestation, constitutes real fatuity. "In order to be effective and not nominal"—Mella has said—"sovereignty demands that its functions be not dependent upon the authorization of another; because, with independence as its attribute, if its exercise were to depend upon the authorization of another entity, this would be supreme."[1]

The argument is unassailable and it is unmoved even by the possibility of absolutism. With ministerial sanction, it would not be avoided but transferred or shared. If the king may fall into it, there is no reason whatever why the minister who countersigns should escape it; and if it is argued that the danger is nearer the king than the minister, it may be objected, without proving the hypothesis, that in a non-representative monarchy it might be possible, but not in that which is the object of study in the present work. Thus, for example, in the parliamentary monarchies of which ministerial approval is an essential institution,

[1] Juan Vázquez de Mella: *Complete Works*, Vol. II, p. 101.

ministerial absolutism is not only possible, but its existence has been admitted and recognized. This text is from Count Romanones: "When the representative régime was established" (the Count, with a certain demureness, thus describes the *parliamentary* system) "and the irresponsibility of the king and the responsibility of ministers proclaimed, the whole power of the absolute monarchs passed to the ministers, that is, to the executive power, which became, as Azcárate says, '*the heir and successor of the old royal power.*' "[1]

Indeed, it could not be otherwise, much as Revolution might embroil the affair. In the revolutionary view, national sovereignty is unlimited; in the Catholic mind, it is limited.[2] Its organ, according to the revolutionary notion, would consequently have, in spite of concealment, absolute faculties. They are not so in a Christian monarchy. The representative monarch moves in the same area in which national sovereignty may be exercised, determined by the end of the nation, according to the natural law, by the superior power of the Church and the autarchies belonging to the sub-sovereign societies. As these are organic and not mechanical, that is, resulting from the constitution of the State itself, the king encounters them in continual action against possible tendencies to the abuse of his sovereign faculties.

But the king, in a representative monarchy, has the complement of personality already pointed out:[3] the institution of the councils. Our national mind did not fail to see that kings could not be omniscient or impeccable in their sovereign functions; and it found, in the organic nature of society, the means of supplying

---

[1] Alvaro de Figueroa: *The Parliamentary Régime*, Ch. IV.
[2] Part II, Ch. V.   [3] Part III, Ch. II.

personal deficiencies and of repressing wrong inclinations. It set up, to this effect, consultative bodies that
advised the king in procedure and in decisions,
transmitting to him the political lore they treasured
and the experience and uprightness which distinguished them. These councils, by the prestige
with which tradition endowed them, were cordially
received by the Constitution of 1812 in the following
words expressing their purpose: "A Council of State
has been organized to afford the government the
character of stability, prudence and system required,
to ensure affairs being directed according to fixed and
known principles, and to provide that the State be
henceforth guided, as it were, by maxims and not by
the isolated ideas of each one of the Secretaries of
State which, besides the possibility of error, are
necessarily variable on account of the transitoriness to
which ministers are subject. It is the sole council of
the king who will hear its opinion in grave matters of
government, and particularly for the purpose of
granting or refusing sanction to laws, of declaring
wars and of making treaties."

The national mentality was not content with the
creation of such efficacious guarantees against the
abuses of the absolutism of kings, the legitimate
personal exercise of whose sovereign faculties was,
notwithstanding, never the object of expropriation.
Another wonderful institution, living and acting,
corrected *a posteriori* the royal encroachments in the
exercise of sovereignty. I refer to the *Justice*[1] of
Aragón, a juridical organization covering the *sobre-*

---

[1] A supreme magistrate in the kingdom of Aragón who was charged with the
protection of the people's privileges and who might oppose the king if he
invaded them. It has been said that he merged in his own person the powers
of the Lord Chancellor of England with those of the Supreme Court of the
United States. (Translator's note.)

o—

carta[1] of Navarre, the *pase foral*[2] of the Basque Provinces and, in general, the *"obey but do not comply"*
traditional throughout Spain.

There were four *processes* with which the *Justice*
could prevent royal encroachments without the
necessity of denying, through sanction, any of the
functions proper to sovereignty. They were called
judgments of *apprehension,* of *inventory,* of *manifestation*
and of *juris-firma* which, as a foundation of the jurisdiction of the *Justice,* took into account force or
violence done to property or to persons. They are
allusively termed *forales.* Under the first process, real
estate was sequestered pending settlement of the
litigation caused by the oppression. Under the
second, movables and papers that might be the object
of the inquiry were placed in safe custody. The third
was the means principally of compelling the judge
concerned to produce the person who had been the
victim of legal despotism, and if the criminal action
calling for this *manifestation* were to be sustained, the
alleged culprit was kept in the prison of the *Justice*
under his protection. The fourth process was the
instrument for the defence according to the *Fuero*
(constitutional law) of the proper jurisdictional orbits

[1] *Sobre-carta:* a second or ulterior award or adjudication pronounced by the
Court upon the same matter when, for some reason, the first has not been
observed. (Translator's note.)

[2] *Pase foral:* an institution of supreme political importance which prevailed
in the Basque provinces and in Navarre though under different names. It
reveals the significance of the *Juntas Generales,* a real legislative power retaining
the fullness of its sovereignty even after those provinces had been incorporated
to Castile. By virtue of the *pase foral,* the *Juntas Generales* examined the regulations decreed or directions imposed by the central government upon judges in
commission and others for the exercise of jurisdiction within their borders,
for the purpose of ascertaining whether there was any order or resolution
against their *fueros,* laws and prerogatives. In such an event, the *Junta* applied
the paralogical formula: *"se obedece pero no se cumple"* ("obey but do not comply")
which held good until the king or the Court which issued the offending
regulations or directions had received and considered the complaint of the
province, and acquiesced in a modification resulting in conformity with the
fueros. (Translator's note.)

against any authority whatsoever—including the king —who might override them.

Zurita says of the *Justice* that "he was ever the protection and defence against all violence and force . . . and it was not only subjects who had recourse to him, for oftentimes kings would appeal to him for protection from rich men. In the aggrandizement of the kingdom, he was the protector and chief defender so that kings and their ministers should not act against that which . . . was allowed them by their privileges and customs." Rodolfo Reyes expresses with spirited precision the nature of the office of the *Justice* in the following eloquent sentences: "His ascendency . . . was, above all, for the purpose of compelling the royal power to respect rights and privileges and limitations imposed upon it, and to receive the oath determining those limitations. Both functions fall within the clear anticipation of the unconstitutional. By his authority, personal or corporative freedom was shielded against aggression, *even did it proceed from the king himself*, by means of complaints among which the *greuges*[1] were a classical form. He was empowered to adjudge grave responsibilities, also a repressive form of guaranteeing institutional bases; to settle contentions of authorities among themselves or in relation to the king. Finally, even that most modern institution which, expressed in English, interests us so deeply, the *advisory opinions*, has also a precedent there, for the *Chief Justice* and his *Consello* fulfilled the offices of interpretation and consultation respecting the *Fueros* (rights and privileges). The representative of the monarch, the other judges in consultation, and by adjournment of their proceedings, the Deputations and Regencies of

[1] Old Catalan word meaning the complaint ordinarily made in the Cortes of Aragón when laws or rights were assailed. (Translator's note.)

the kingdom, and every person suffering wrong, could all appeal to this tribunal."[1]

So, without any invasion of the proper functions of sovereignty, the king, in order not to exceed his due prerogative, is subject to these organic restrictions which, besides, are his *support* in the exercise of his exalted office: the Church, a spiritual society supreme in its kind, which, as a religious authority, imposes, in conscience, public and private duties, and respect for the fulfilment of pledges; the traditional Constitution reflected in the fundamental law of the nation, which the king may not modify, by himself, or transgress in any way; the Cortes, an organ of the common good —as will be seen—whose concurrence is indispensable to him for the promulgation of laws; the autarchies of the sub-sovereign societies; the decisions of his Council, and, finally, with a corrective character in its case, the Court of Justice conveying an efficacy of action unanimously acknowledged.

Against this picture of insuperable perfection, in which order prevails as each institution figures in its appointed place, Mella has outlined the perspective of revolutionary governments: "If the sovereignty of the Cortes," he has said, "depends on that of the king

---

[1] Rodolfo Reyes: *Constitutional Defence*, Part I, Ch. II. The English historian, H. E. Watts, thus describes the powers and functions of *the Justice* of Aragon: "He was the highest interpreter of the law, the keeper of the king's conscience, and the final referee in all disputes, not only between subjects, but between the subjects and the sovereign. He could interfere, of his own authority, in any cause, and remove it to his own jurisdiction. He could review the royal decrees, and declare whether they were agreeable to law or not. He could exclude any of the king's ministers from the conduct of affairs, and call him to account for maladministration. He was *ex officio* a permanent counsellor of the king, and had to accompany him wherever he went. He was regarded as a power between the king and the people—the controller of the one and protector of the other. . . . There is no doubt that the *Justicia*, whose very existence under that name is a proof of the liberty claimed by the Aragonese, did exert a powerful influence in the government, superior to that of the Judges in Castile, and of a kind which is without parallel in any contemporary European State." Summary of Spanish History from the Moorish Conquest to the Fall of Granada, p. 156. (Translator's note)

under sanction of the Cabinet, and the sovereignty of the people with personality and citizenship, through suspension of guarantees, depends upon the authority of the Cabinet, then there is nothing more to be done but to give this Cæsar, who is more powerful than all the Cæsars, the name of prince or principate in the imperial Roman sense and even in that which it received—with no reference to the monarch—from our political writers of the sixteenth and seventeenth centuries, from Guevara y Ceriol to Saavedra Fajardo, when describing its doctrinal filiation (that of the Constitutions born of Revolution). Its paternity goes back to the first century of the Christian era, and the genealogical tree even extends to the Assyrian empires; but its juridical formula lies in the so-called *lex regia*. . . . What freedom do the citizens enjoy according to these codes? The freedom that is not prohibited or placed in abeyance by the law. What is the law? The will of the Cabinet which assumes and unites in itself, with the suspension of guarantees and with ministerial sanction of the acts of the king, every attribution. . . . The will of the prince is strong because the people transmitted to him all its powers by the *regal law* which gave him supremacy. Let us now alter the names. Where it says "prince" (in the precept transcribed from the Institutions of Justinian), let us put "Cabinet" or "ministry"; where it says *lex regia*, "sanction" and "suspension of guarantees" should be substituted . . . and . . . the new *lex regia* as a juridical synthesis of the Constitution and as a compendium of parliamentary freedom is established![1]

Why should this be so? Why, in a democratic régime, cannot the organic restrictions before enumerated, co-exist with the specific action of the head

[1] Juan Vázquez de Mella: *Complete Works*, Vol. II, p. 110.

of the State in his exclusive functions, while the only mechanical constraint is the ministerial sanction which annuls his authority?

One needs little reflection as to the origin of society according to the democratic doctrine previously expressed,[1] before reaching the conclusion that neither the Church nor the sub-sovereign societies have any place there. The compact did not even touch the religious order nor could the Church, not being a society originating from a contract, be considered legitimate. Logically, democracies, revealing their anti-religious nature, consider religion as a private affair when they are in a benevolent state of mind, and persecute the Church when they are out of humour. It is also plain that sub-sovereign societies with their own autarchies are unacceptable because it has already been said that for the right enunciation of the general will, according to revolutionary principles, every partial society within the State must disappear, each citizen exclusively expressing his own opinion.[2] The *sovereign power* in the revolutionary doctrine thus has no external restriction, but it is also without the internal restraint consisting in the natural law concreted in a traditional and reflected in a written Constitution. More than one will be surprised at this assertion which exposes the emptiness of the subjection, under the revolutionary system, of everybody, citizens and authorities, to the fundamental law of the State. Yet nothing is more true.

"One half plus one," it was said during the analysis of the spurious forms of nation,[3] "would be, henceforth, the fount of justice and liberty" and "oracle of the general interest." Democracies, then, lack an objective juridical principle for their acts, seeing that

[1] Part II, Ch. I.   [2] Part II, Ch. IV.   [3] Part II, Ch. III.

the individual will, merely by repeating itself in
sufficient number, makes its line of conduct vary with
its volitions. Definitely, the democratic power does
not know how far it may advance the next day or to
what extent it should draw back. Who is to hinder it,
or who is to urge it on, is an unknown number at all
times. The reiterated phenomenon of the violation
of the revolutionary Constitutions is now explained.

What has just been stated should be reproduced in
regard to the Cortes. If the fundamental law is not
restrictive of power in a democratic régime, the organ
which ought to be legislative will be much less so.
But further, there is in respect of this, a specific
reason. Parliaments, in democracies, consider themselves the real sovereign and with a sovereignty that
oversteps normal bounds. For them, it does not
emanate from the nature of society but from convention;[1] and, in consequence, the revolutionary
power not only is not constrained, as before stated, by
the fundamental law of the State, but the latter is
itself similarly unchecked. Moreover, this unlimited
latitude of power, and not its unity, constitutes
absolutism.[2] Those who imagine it with one head
alone have a totally false vision of reality. In a
greater or a lesser degree, it has always come from
communities. Socialism has already told us: "The
State is an absolute power."[3]

It was anticipated[4] that the nature of democracies
was in contradiction to the institution of the councils
in regard to the *competence* of authority. But contradiction also lies in the idea of *selection* which that
institution entails. An advisory organ pre-supposes,

[1] Part II, Ch. VI.　[2] Part II, Ch. V.
[3] Speech delivered by Largo Caballero at Geneva (June 1933) to the amazement of the whole world and probably of himself.
[4] Part III, Ch. II.

in the members composing it, discrimination respecting their knowledge of political science and their moral virtues, or at least, clear cognisance of ethical standards. The hypothetical law of equality is thus set at nought not by purely social inequality, but by one inscribed in the political codes. The alternative becomes clear: either the institution of the councils, constituting an organic restraint of power with negation of Democracy, or the acceptance of the nature of the latter by repudiating the councils. It should be added that, in regard to the former option, the democratic virus would very soon pollute and crush the institution.

This has been clearly shown by the very brief experience of the Court of Constitutional Guarantees. A tribunal intervening in the legislative order under the legal supposition that the decision of the majority is *true* law, is a senseless idea. If the vote makes the law, what is the meaning of its examination by somebody who does not claim the right to the vote? It is not a question of the possibility of an ordinary enactment infringing the constitutional law of higher standing, for both derive their *revolutionary* legitimacy from the majority representing the general will. That solicitude for the establishment of a Court for the judgment of laws, observed in every country in the world, is an unconscious tribute to this resplendent truth of Christian philosophy: that a law must contain requisites above the collective will even legitimately expressed. Through its rejection, every doctrine concerning self-limitation of the authority of the State has ended in failure.

The legal supposition mentioned shows the question in its true light, and with it, the jurisdiction of a Court upholding constitutional legality becomes perfectly obvious. It decides, on its own authority, matters of legislative and generally political competence among the different public societies of the State. It deals with the unconstitutional nature of all measures dictated by sub-sovereign organisms and of those which, proceeding from the sovereign power, are likewise in default through the absence of legal requirements. It intervenes, with other organs of the State, in the examination of laws not conforming to the Constitution. The conduct of this inquiry appears no less clear. The law, having been dictated with constitutional requirements so that it may not be a mere act of the will, is impugned as unconstitutional before the Court which will examine the foundation of the appeal, and if this is esteemed justifiable, the Court will remit its judgment to the king, proposing the repeal or modification of the law in dispute. The proposal will be dealt with by new Cortes as a motion confirming, abrogating or reforming the law impugned which, meanwhile, will remain in abeyance. The new law to be prescribed will be definite in character.

So a law within the competence of the sovereign power may not be abrogated by its own organ not possessing legislative faculties; but the abrogation, confirmation or modification of the original text, should this be expedient, will be invested with the most ample guarantees that can be conceived and established. No invasion will have denaturalized the original faculties of the legislative organ; but what is mutable in it has undergone variation for the fulfilment of the purpose desired. Moreover, a new national element has been incorporated in its work in the juridical and technical aspect befitting it, and new motives adduced for the most complete study of the question. In this case the entire State has been converted into a palladium of one who was considered a victim of unconstitutional procedure.

Of a State whose life was long regulated by those admirable institutions which, in their old age, are new to the intellectual classes of to-day, forgetful of and ungrateful to their ancestors, Murillo could say: "Here there are no annoyances to trouble the poor, because everything must be done according to law, and there are efficacious remedies to ensure the law being observed. Here the monarchs *have never made use of absolute power*, rather have they always prided themselves on respecting the *fueros* and keeping faith with what they have sworn. Here, indeed, the road is closed to every kind of oppression, for in order to save themselves from this, the Aragonese have two forms of security: the *manifestation* and the *juris firma*.[1]" So our new State will not, like so many others, be contrived in the land of chimera and brought down by contact with reality. It will emerge from the latter which has set upon it the double seal of justice and of life.

If the national interest, as its name indicates, is the interest of the nation as a collective personality, obviously it is not the sum of the interests of the private persons who compose society. This notion scarcely calls for refutation. But neither can it be the sum of the specific interests of social classes; because, apart from the fact that the acceptance of this supposition entails the same difficulties as oppose the previous one, the classes—by definition—act not only for themselves, but also as natural organs of society, and their specific interests, being heterogeneous, do not permit addition. The national interest, then, can be no other but the

[1] Carlos López de Haro: *The Constitution and Liberties of Aragón and the Chief Justice*, Ch. XVI.

synthesis or integration of the specific interests of the classes.

This conception demands the concurrence of two organs: one, to reflect, in each problem, the expression of class interests; the other, for the accomplishment of their harmonious synthesis. The first will be considered later, and will now be merely mentioned. It is the Cortes. The second is the king and precisely so because, as the national interest springs from the integration of class interests, he who is charged with its accomplishment must, from the very beginning, be above them all, and, by reason of his position, must identify his own with the national interest. Louis XIV, in his *Memoirs*, set forth, without possible emendation, this harmonious procedure of the king. "Far from favouring any class," he writes, "at the expense of the others, we must strive to raise them all, if this be possible, to perfection; and be convinced that the very class which we might unjustly desire to distinguish, would not on that account bear us more affection or greater esteem, while the others would rightly indulge in complaint and censure."

So clear has this beneficently integrating and harmonious mission of kings appeared to the adversaries of monarchy, that they have been forced to acknowledge it. Kautsky, the Austrian Socialist, flung in the face of his associates the undoubted fact that in no other country in Europe—nearly all were then ruled by monarchies—had more proletarian blood been shed than in France during the twelve preceding years (1903). Bebel addressing in the next year the Socialist Congress at Amsterdam, said: "To a certain degree, I ought to be the advocate of monarchy. . . . It cannot engage deeply in class strife. It must count upon the people." Only too

recently, more than one of the leaders of Spanish
Socialism has expressed his disappointment in the
republican form of government, openly declaring that
the atmosphere of an impaired monarchy, such as that
of England or Belgium to-day, is much more beneficial
to the worker.

The extent and nature of the intervention of the
monarchic State in the economic order is thus
established. If there is a national interest, if this
springs from the synthesis of the different class
interests, and if, finally, an organ of national interest
exists, it is evident that the specific interests of social
classes cannot be alien to that State, although the
latter may not supersede those classes in their natural
function of promoting their own interests. The
mission of the monarchy is narrowed to *harmonizing
them* synthetically in order to produce the flower and
fruit of national interest. But within that orbit, it is
substantive and, like everything concerning this State,
it comes under the juridical order. It follows, therefore, that as the partial corporations[1] are integrations
of classes in relation to a certain object, the intervention of the State in the manner shown is essential
to them, that is, not for the purpose of their creation,
but to preside over their juridical life once they have
been constituted. This mission of the king, shaping
the national interest through the synthesis of the
specific interests of the social classes, is possible
because the very origin of these classes, as already
explained,[2] reveals the existence of a *natural* harmony
between one another. Democracy, and therefore, the
republic, denied this with the supposed law of *the
struggle for life*, a corollary of the social composition
patronized by it. Later, this principle, applied by

[1] Part II, Ch. IV.   [2] Part II, Ch. IV.

Socialism to social categories, was taught in the form of *class war*. Only a monarchy based upon Christian foundations can logically provide authority with those faculties of supreme arbiter, not in contention—already denied—but in discrepancies, reconcilable by nature, of class interests, conveying to the nation the boon of juridical peace without which human fellowship is totally impossible.

CHAPTER V

REPRESENTATION

Rousseau, in his work, *The Social Contract*, speaks of representation, an institution looked upon by many with superstitious respect. Yet he is in error who might think the father of Democracy would erect an altar to it whereon the worship of human generations should be offered. To Rousseau, representation implies a reproachful declension in democratic fervour. "So soon," he declares, "as public service ceases to be the main concern of the citizens, and they would rather discharge it with their purses than with their persons, the State approaches ruin. When they should go to war, they pay troops to fight for them, and stay at home; when they should go to council, they send deputies and again stay at home. By dint of indolence and of money, they contrive to employ soldiers to enthral their country and representatives to betray it."

"Sovereignty cannot be represented for the same reason as it cannot be alienated. It consists essentially in the general will, and this cannot be represented; it is either itself or it is something else; there is no middle term. The deputies of the people are, therefore, not its representatives, nor can they be such. They are only its commissioners; they may not decide upon anything definitely. Any law not ratified in person by the people is null and void; it is no law. The English people believe themselves free. They are gravely mistaken; it is only so during the election of the members of Parliament. As soon as they are elected, the people become enslaved; they are nothing. In the brief moments of liberty, the use they make of it is such as to deserve its loss. The idea of representatives is modern. In the old republics and in the monarchies, the people never had representatives; the word was unknown. Looking into it all, I do not see how henceforth, it is possible for the sovereign to retain, among us, the exercise of its rights, unless the city be very small."[1]

He who has ears must have heard. The nomination of deputies is a sign that public service no longer interests the citizens, and is the best means of betraying the country. This is what Rousseau tells us, and when he assures it so categorically, he must have a reason, always within the idea of representation elaborated in his contradictory brain. At all events, those who invoke Revolution, which is to invoke Rousseau, are not authorized to hold the contrary in this matter without incurring the condemnation of the Genevan philosopher, a condemnation that, down to the present, at least, does not appear to have been fulminated. The adversaries of Revolution would need no more powerful reason to bear out their conviction. In Democracy there is no room for representation; and if through it, any physical or moral person were to claim the exercise of sovereignty, it could be assured that such a demand would be nothing but fiction and imposture. Rousseau has proclaimed that "sovereignty cannot be represented."

There was already something absurd going the round of political and intellectual circles inspired by Revolution. Within the ambit of human logic, no

[1] J. J. Rousseau: *Social Contract,* Bk. III, Ch. XV.

way has been found whereby popular sovereignty might be proclaimed and parliaments might be defended against or in face of the people to which it is attributed. Even starting from the existence and legitimacy of a popular delegation of sovereignty in assemblies or individual persons, it was inexplicable that the mandatory should exert the attribution delegated against the people who delegated it, and that he should be considered as being indefinitely invested with such authority without intervention in its exercise on the part of the body originally possessing it. But the fallacy reaches proportions so fabulous as to be inconceivable when the whole thing is preached as true doctrine, denying its suppositious fundamental support: the possibility of delegation.

The modality of modern revolutionary doctrine is precisely the result of admitting, in spite of the Rousseauan thesis, the full and absolute transmission of popular sovereignty to assemblies elected by the multitude, namely, parliaments. But the worst of the case, the idea being deeply rooted, is that people, learned and unlearned—those styled learned actually urge it more heatedly—proclaim the error with utter good faith and with a perfectly clear conscience, deceiving themselves with the greatest candour and the most picturesque ignorance of revolutionary dogmas in their former purity.

Let us draw the practical consequence of all that has been said. Parliaments elected by universal suffrage are not legitimate national representation, *not even within pure revolutionary doctrine.* When they claim to possess the attribute of sovereignty, they simply commit usurpation. The deputies, so proud of the popular vote, are not the elect of the people. They are, according to Rousseau, the authentic testimony of its degradation and the agents by whom the country may be betrayed.

Rousseau agrees to vouchsafe one function alone to parliament and deputies: that of the *commissioner*, understood in the sense that whatever is done through that medium must be ratified necessarily by the sovereign, that is, by the people, with the expression of the general will. Democracy, according to this, has only one legitimate form, the plebiscite. But the worst is that this also stands condemned by the doctrine of Rousseau. "Looking into it all," he says, "I do not see how, henceforth, it is possible for the sovereign to retain, among us, the exercise of its rights, *unless the city be very small.*"

To this strait has come the fraud that turned the brain of peoples. Its ideal is a chimera. Only a social Constitution which lies in the opposite pole to that proved by universal experience to be the human aspiration, would allow the institution of Democracy. The confession cannot be questioned, not only because of its origin, but because reality confirms it. To submit all laws to plebiscites in nations of somewhat numerous population is materially and morally impossible, unless to the fiction which a plebiscite implies in itself, it is desired to add that of a multitude voting for what it has not discussed, does not know and does not understand. Following up the argument, this corollary is reached: if the practice of Democracy is impossible *unless the city be very small*, the imagined possibility does not even arise from the event of Democracy being operative under those conditions, but from the fact that the short radius of civic action permits appreciation of common concerns as if they were private affairs; and the simplicity of most people finds sufficient guidance in the principles of natural law written in the heart of every man. But that does not constitute a political order suggesting a form of government, but a state of social anachronism which, fortunately, must be temporal in every human society.

Democracy, as the régime of a people, would consequently be confused with pre-civilization. Democracy and a primeval state would be the same thing, which, on the other hand, cannot be surprising from the moment when a narrow social ambit was recognized as a condition of its existence, universal society—as before said[1]—being the proper object of man's vocation. Democracy then, boasts of what it lacks: the spirit of progress; it hinders this aspiration with its doctrine, and through its canons, establishes impassable gulfs between peoples and rulers, for such is the sentence of death which, in the phrase of Rousseau, would automatically be applied if the social ambits were extended. The capital question is not resolved by the attribution to political parties of the power of representation of national sectors, by which the nominees of the parties in Parliament would integrate the representation of the nation; because apart from what has been said against the arbitrary supposition,[2] the anathema of Rousseau against complex and extensive societies as seats of Democracy would equally include them. But besides, they are particularly and exclusively condemned by the Genevan pseudo-philosopher. They constitute, indeed, the foundation of the system of the English Constitution and this, as the transcribed text has already shown, Rousseau held to be an origin of slavery.

Let it be recorded simply: in Democracy there is no place for representation. Whoever claims to exercise sovereignty therein with such an authority is a usurper.

[1] Part II, Ch. I.   [2] Part II, Ch. IV.

This problem does not arise in counter-revolutionary political régimes. The localization of sovereignty[1] constitutes the prince, as the organ of the nation, its genuine representative. But a nation is not only the sovereign authority which appears as its essential note under the form of the State. A nation is a social body, an organism which must be—like its authority— represented. It is now time to study the representation of society under this last aspect.

That the multitude has no capacity to represent the social organism is inferred from what has been previously stated.[2] The multitude is nothing more than the inorganic matter of society, common to very different and quite distinct bodies. This statement is sufficient for its exclusion as a medium of representation which should affect what is proper and peculiar to the thing represented. Nor can political parties represent the social body, as may be deduced from what has just been explained concerning their radical incapacity for acting as a basis of representation in sovereignty, and because the political party—as before stated[3]—is something ephemeral and circumstantial, the disappearance of which has no relation to the life of society nor to the features of its immutable and unequivocal personality. Thus excluding the multitude and the parties, and recalling that in the analysis made of social composition, classes and bodies appeared as social elements, it must be concluded that society, as an organism, can only be represented by these. Moreover, as their condition of social aggregations or collective entities demands their representation being conferred upon physical personalities, the final conclusion emerging from all this is that society, as a body, as a political organism, is embodied

[2] Part III, Ch. I.   [1] Part II, Ch. V.   [3] Part II, Ch. IV.

in the representatives of the social bodies and classes. We are now in the middle of the great problem of election. But before entering upon its study, a few observations will be very helpful in the matter. Election is not the only means of conferring representation.

It has already been seen that the representation of sovereignty, which in certain cases may be concreted by election, issues ordinarily from absolutely different means. There is no need to recall—the fact is so general—that *natural* representations exist (that of minors, that of a wife, etc.) in which election has not the least part. This is due to a principle of representation considerably more general than that of the will. It is enunciated by asserting that in every collectivity *hierarchically* organized, such a form being demanded by its nature, representation corresponds by right to its own authorities, *antecedent to other personalities*. But besides those *immediately natural* representations from which election is banished, there exist others *by the very nature of the function*, qualified, regulated and even subordinated to facts which, being entirely unrelated to the social body, are caused by its representatives appointed in one form or another. Here we shall mention one example alone which in the revolutionary régime has no justification whatever and which, in the counter-revolutionary system, we shall justify at the right moment: the specific representation of the members of the executive organ who, in republics, are elected by those who, in turn, owe their representation to election.

Definitely, the latter is not a means of representation except when that which is represented is endowed with proper activity to confer it, while election must not, of itself, constitute any determination in the representative. Hence the nation, in respect of the concept of sovereignty implying hierarchy, is represented by its authority. Likewise, graded bodies of the State such as the army, navy, magistracy and diplomacy should be represented by their own authorities. Finally, it follows that election, for the purpose of representation of the social organism, is inevitable in so far as law is concerned, and because by the equality of the elements constituting categories, there are no natural or functional facts to determine a hierarchy.

If it is by classes and not by the indistinct multitude that the social body, in its organic aspect, is represented, it is evident that for the election to provide representatives of classes, it must refer to each one of them. The representation of the social organism therefore requires, conclusively, separate elections in each social class. In consequence, the one census usual in the revolutionary régime must be replaced by a special census for every social class existing in the nation, in which, respectively, all the citizens existing therein shall be inscribed in categories. This brings to the ground the empty claim of the revolutionary systems concerning the universality of the suffrage. If the latter is indeed the attribute of everybody forming part of a class, its universality in the traditional régime cannot be surpassed, for in a well organized society there is no citizen who does not belong to a class. But further, as the title to the suffrage is class and not personal circumstances of age and sex, its extension encounters no limit in sex or age. Every man or woman, adult or minor, exercising functions proper to a social class, has the right to nominate a representative of the same. The fact that there may be incapacity for the exercise of this right, thus requiring completion of personality in the political order, is nothing new, for the institution is only too well known in the civil order.

The mere statement of the manner in which the suffrage by classes is exercised, emphasizes the legitimacy of the function. Whoever votes—if he claims to effect a *human* operation—must know the subject concerning which he is going to vote, and afterwards freely desire the object of his vote. Should either of these conditions be missing, the suffrage is little more than an act of *gregarious animality*. The elector, as an element of a class, knows what he is voting for because he does so with a view to the social interest, an aspect of the general interest which the class represents and which is his own private interest. He desires what he votes for because it affects his interest, and he desires it freely because no pressure from any other class is possible, and equality exists within each of them. Representation of a class conferred through a suffrage of the same name possesses, then, the conditions of capacity necessary in what is represented, and the specific condition of public interest indispensable if it is to be an element of the representation of the social organism.

By contrast, it may be already anticipated that the inorganic universal suffrage neither confers legitimate representations, nor is it endowed with the necessary political character so that the representative nominated through its agency may be enabled to represent the national organism. By saying that universal suffrage contains the "vote on everything" and recalling that the political party is not an "element of the national organism," the conclusion surmised would be sufficiently justified. But it is worth while going into the matter more fully. "To vote on everything," is very different from "everybody votes." It

has been seen that the latter is a natural consequence
of the inevitable location of every citizen within a
certain class which makes his vote, whatever be the
question at issue, an appreciation of the object
perceived through the known interest of class. "To
vote on everything" is to value what is known and
unknown as equally important, and places the learned
and the ignorant on the same level. "To opine on
problems that are ignored," says Anatole France—a
witness beyond suspicion in such a matter—"constitutes, definitely, the substance of that monstrosity
known as universal suffrage."

The fanaticism with which Revolution enslaves its
followers is great, but the absurdity of the system was
bound to cause misgivings among them. This is
Castelar's judgment: "Each election is a calamity,
each assembly a market, each elector a slave, each
minister a sultan, each candidate an abettor of public
immorality and each deed of election a record
of scandal and ignominy."[1]   Count Romanones
expresses himself as follows: "So far as the elector is
concerned, the function of the suffrage is completely
unknown, this being due *not only to human nature* but
also, in great part, to the *special conditions of the
parliamentary system* which, with the existence of parties
and the need of majorities, has developed the *selfish
instinct of man.*"[2]   Don Santiago Alba has written:
"Universal suffrage which, with the institution of the
jury, formed the ideals of our early youth . . . has
rendered active an element of extraordinary parliamentary and social corruption, namely, money. It
is parliamentary corruption because of the kind of

[1] Quoted by D. Gumersindo Azcárate in his work *The Parliamentary Régime
in Practice*, Ch. IV.   Don Emilio Castelar (1832-1899), President of the
First Spanish Republic. (Translator's note.)
[2] Alvaro de Figueroa y Torres: *The Parliamentary Régime*, Ch. III.

persons who, with the greatest ease, may enter
Congress.   Any wealthy block-head, any coxcomb
prodigal with his income, the upstart who likes to cut
a figure, and the adventurer who finds it convenient
to 'cover his retreat' by the acquirement of administrative rank, may succeed in obtaining a seat in
Parliament quite simply, by the mere operation of the
opening of a safe.   It is social corruption because there
is nothing so pernicious, so devastating, so repulsive,
as those auctions of votes in which an entire people,
intoxicated with an incredible cynicism, has been
already sold like a flock of sheep, and in which success
does not go to the most intelligent, to the most cultured
or to the most distinguished person, but to the one who
pays best."[1]   Cambó makes this confession: "The
right to vote, by express or tacit delegation, by
purchase, by theft or by forgery was exercised by the
directors, the rulers, those who after the election,
controlling their desire to laugh like the augurs of the
lower Empire, presented themselves before the
assembly of those anointed by the popular will,
seeking its light and its strength, the light and strength
of the national will."   Finally, Azcárate, high priest
of Democracy, thus portrayed universal suffrage:
"When elections are more political, parties appear on
the scene which frequently obtain by trickery and
falsehood what they ought to obtain only by the
courage of their convictions and the reputation of their
men, sacrificing everything to success.   Preventing
living people from voting and making the dead leave
their tombs to vote, the evaporation of suffrages that
are polled and the apparition of others that have not

[1] Santiago Alba: *Problems of Spain.*   Don Santiago Alba (1872),
Leader of a Left group in Parliament, and Minister of the Crown.   He
welcomed the Republic and was Speaker of the Cortes under that régime.
(Translator's note).

been polled, the fabrication of election returns showing events that have not occurred, and not recording others that did take place, are esteemed accomplishments worthy of reward and of which their authors are proud and boastful. . . . And so electoral corruption afterwards brings in its wake parliamentary and administrative corruption, and as a consequence o these, social corruption."[1]

If the vote, in order to be a human operation, demands free will in its emission and knowledge of the subject at issue; if in universal suffrage, the elector, by nature, is ignorant of the problem submitted to his judgment and so lacks freedom to resolve; if, for greater accentuation, a continued experience accepted by its most fervent promoters clearly shows that the elector is ignorant of the function of the suffrage (Count Romanones), that he puts up his vote for auction (Alba and Cambó), is a victim of forgery or causes it (Cambó and Azcárate), is supplanted by rulers (Cambó), and moves in an atmosphere of immorality that explains every corruption (Alba and Azcárate), it must be concluded that the vote in universal suffrage lacks its essential requisite: it is not a human operation. Its motto of "one man, one vote," should be replaced by that of "one animal, one vote."

It is plain that anything so exalted as the representation of the nation as a political body could never come from such a cesspool. But, furthermore, the advocates have acknowledged it explicitly. Alba has said it: universal suffrage gives victory not to the worthiest but to him who pays most. Cambó describes the makers of the supposed national representation as great hypocrites who keep back their laughter

[1] Gumersindo Azcárate: *The Parliamentary Régime in Practice*, Ch. IV.

at the sight of the work of cynicism and fallacy. Azcárate shows us the waters that should cleanse the representation, befouled in their sources. What more could we ourselves add?

In the erection of the New State, no doubt whatever can be entertained as to the system of representation of the political organism. The investigation now made carries us to the conclusion that there is but one legitimate system, and this must be adopted; just as there is only one legitimate manner of suffrage, the organic manner proper to that system, because all the circumstances demanded by the purity and efficacy of the election concur therein.

CHAPTER VI

THE LAW

IN few subjects can the contradictory spirit of Jean Jacques Rousseau be better sounded than in that dealt with in the present chapter. From the most orthodox assertion to the most unwarranted consequence, the Genevan pseudo-philosopher traversed the whole gamut of thought.

"Whatever is right and conformable to order," he says, "is so from the nature of things, and independently of human conventions. All justice comes from God. He alone is the fountain of it; but could we receive it immediately from so sublime a source, we should stand in no need of government or laws. There is indeed a universal justice emanating from reason alone; but this justice, in order to be admitted among mankind, should be reciprocal. Considering things from a human standpoint, we find the laws of justice vain and fruitless for want of natural sanction; they tend only to the advantage of the wicked, and the disadvantage of the just. While the latter observes them in his behaviour to others, nobody regards them in return. Conventions and laws, therefore, are necessary to couple duties with privileges, and to confine justice to its object. In the state of Nature, where everything is in common, I owe nothing to those to whom I have promised nothing; I acknowledge nothing to be the property of another but what is useless to me. This is not the case in a state of society in which all rights are fixed by law."

"We come at length, then, to consider what is law. . . . But when the whole people decree concerning the whole people, they consider only their whole body; and if a relation is thus formed, it is between the entire object under one point of view and the entire object under another point of view, without any division of the whole. In this case, the matter of the decree is general like the will that decrees. Such is the act that I call a law. . . . Laws are properly only the conditions of civil association. The people, being subjected to the laws, should be the authors of them; it concerns only the associates to determine the conditions of association. But how will they be determined? . . . How would a blind will, which often knows not what it wishes because it rarely knows what is good for it, execute of itself an enterprise so great, so difficult, as a system of legislation? Of themselves, the people always desire what is good, but do not always discern it. . . . They must be made to see objects as they are, sometimes as they ought to appear. . . . Hence arises the need of a legislator. . . ."

"The legislator is, in all respects, an extraordinary man in the State. If he ought to be so by his genius, he should be not less so by his office, which is neither magistracy nor sovereignty. This office is established by the republic but does not enter into into its constitution; it is a special and superior office having nothing in common with human government; for, if he who rules men ought not to enact laws, he who enacts laws ought not to rule men. . . . He who frames laws, then, has or ought to have no legislative right, and the people themselves cannot, when they so desire, divest themselves of this incommunicable right, because according to the fundamental compact, it is only the general will that binds individuals."[1]

The French Revolution, in article VI of the *Declaration of the Rights of Man and of the Citizen*, of 1789, defined the law saying it was "the expression of the general will."

Let us emphasize it simply for the confusion of the political systems based on secularism. "All justice," confesses Rousseau, "comes from God." If it comes from God, it comes from nowhere else, unless the second cause be a providential instrument, which would imply indirectly repeating that the origin of its acts is in God. The confession cannot be weakened by the arbitrary supposition that "could we receive it immediately from so sublime a source, we should stand in no need of government or laws." Because in the state of innocence or that in which man received justice from its origin, mankind was subject to laws and governments, that dependence being a condition of its sociable nature.[2] Moreover, God speaks to man not only through Revelation, but through Nature and through reason, at first so extolled by Revolution only to be afterwards discarded.

But even coming down to earth, Rousseau is wrong in esteeming human laws and conventions as necessary to unite rights and duties, and to confine justice to its object. They are not called for by the supposition that the standards laid down by justice are unavailing on account of the lack of natural sanction, the wicked receiving good and the just evil when the latter observe the rules of justice towards others while others fail to do so by them. This is the alternative:

[1] J. J. Rousseau: *Social Contract*, Bk. iii, Ch. VI and VII.

[2] St. Thomas Aquinas: *Summa Theologica:* 1a. Qu. xcvi, art 4.

either those conventions and laws have sanctions that can be also established for the fulfilment of the precepts derived directly from the principle of divine justice, or they have not, in which event they will continue to dispense good to the wicked and evil to the just. There is no escape; if all justice comes from God, the prescriptions that govern human societies must proceed from that justice and from no other; because the law must be just and it is acknowledged that *all justice* comes from God. Revolution, in times when it seeks to accommodate itself to men, utters words which later it repudiates violently, but which it is unable to recall. This is one of them. There will be no peace for humanity while legislation is not inspired in the divine legislation, where there is no injustice, because ALL JUSTICE COMES FROM GOD.

By the arbitrary hypothesis affirmed to this effect, Rousseau seeks a different origin for the laws, and places it in the *general will*. This is manifest to him when the whole people legislates upon itself, establishing a relation between the object in its entirety, regarded from one point of view, and the whole object, considered from another aspect, but without any complete division. Although more than one ambiguity obscures the meaning of the phrase, its explanation is not indispensable, for it would be a useless labour. What follows is more than sufficient to throw into relief the inanity of ideas in all this play upon words. The people that must legislate upon itself is incapable of doing so. Its will is blind. Frequently it knows not what it requires because it rarely knows what is most befitting. Though it may always desire good, it does not always perceive that good. That general will creating the law, even granted it is always conscientious, is guided by a judgment not always clear. They are not our words; they are just transcribed in letters of fire. So deeply have they sunk into the minds of the revolutionaries that after long periods in which they were silenced, they rise again with remarkable vigour. One seemed to be listening to Rousseau when Lerroux despaired of the salvation of Spain because he saw her between "two great incapacities: one (that of the king), through decadence, and the other (that of the people), *through incompetence.*[1]" What is most eminent in the government of peoples—the creation of the law—Revolution puts into the hands of a manifest *incapacity* through incompetence, fleeing from God from whom all justice issues!

With the people bound to set up the law without knowing how, revolutionary indelicacy imagined a solution would be found in the introduction of an element, the exact condition of which is not defined, denying the magisterial and sovereign character of its function. An extraordinary person comes between the two aspects of the people which, in their mutual mystical penetration, produce a third of the same substance: the law. He dictates it and delivers it to the people. The people, so inspired by the skill and wisdom of the extraordinary person, votes for the law proposed which thus emanates from the sovereign authority.

What a power is truth! All this nebulous exposition of things; all this eagerness to unite will and reason after proclaiming the law as the work of the general will; all these falsely mystical processes coming from

---

[1] Alejandro Lerroux: *In the Service of the Republic.* Alejandro Lerroux (1864-0000) was, during the monarchy, a tireless agitator against religion, social order and property. He was the author of most violent publications against the principle of organized society. Under the Republic, he became the leader of the Radical Party. (Translator's note.)

timorous attempts to appreciate different personal
entities in the people, are solely due to a secret necessity: that the law should appear as a work of reason.
But the revolutionary desire was too strong for this
intentness; and so, when Revolution assumed power,
it limited itself to placing reason—suitably profaned—
upon an ephemeral altar, and to defining the law,
with utter disregard of the extraordinary person, as
"the expression of the general will." Fatally, upon a
law so defined, the imperfections of this vague revolutionary concept would be impressed.

It must be remembered that in view of the impossibility of rendering accordant the *general will* and
individual sovereignty and independence, Revolution
compels the minority *to be free*, proclaiming as the
general will, not that of the totality of the members
of the so-called body politic, but the majority of the
electors.[1] The will of *one-half plus one* would become
definitely, as was anticipated, the source of justice in
the revolutionary law. But in reality it is not even
that. The juridical sense of the law is bestowed upon
a handful of electors who, leaning to one side or to
another, give the majority to or take it away from
the aggregations which in the midst of a people have
been formed for the purpose of attaining or impeding
the promulgation of a legal precept. Even if indifferent to the problem under discussion, an inconsiderable minority may be the decisive factor of its legislative solution. In the end, the *one-half less one* with
one mind and one will, may be vanquished by the
one-half plus one without unity of will or mind, and
with no other link save the negative one of coinciding
in the rejection of the mind and will of the *one-half
less one*. Thus, definitely, the relative majority becomes

[1] Part II, Ch. III.

subjugated by a heterogeneous sum of absolute minorities. In revolutionary régimes, not even oppression is oppression by the greater number.

Revolution made the multitude supreme, and at once declared it incapable of dictating a law. It proclaimed that the essence of a law lies in the expression of an indifferent majority. Revolution raised the standard of justice and ignored it as the fount of laws. The revolutionary embolism appears so manifest that it is amazing how noble intellects became its victims and how all the peoples of the world suffered submissively its effects. It has been no little good fortune that the work of destruction has not been brought to a finish. The alarm has shaken humanity which, in need of law, returns instinctively to the paths that lead to its true conception. Let us illumine them with the torch of Catholic philosophy.

The sound of the word "law" immediately awakens within our minds ideas of "government" and of "submission." That the whole universe is subject to an order is clear from the teleological law mentioned when dealing with finality in man.[1] Plato has spoken of that government of the universe and, in consequence, of its law. That which he described as *divine* was denominated *eternal* by Catholic theologians in order to avoid the double meaning of the term. By this law—it is no other than the reason of the government of the universe[2]—all things are ordered to their ends by convenient means.[3] There is, therefore, no being—all are subject to the eternal law—which does not participate in this, in one way or another, for its effect is the inclination of each towards his own acts and ends. But this participation is very different in

[1] Part I, Ch. I.
[2] St. Thomas Aquinas: *Summa Theologica*, I^a-II^{ae}, Ch. XCI, art. 1.
[3] St. Thomas Aquinas: *Summa Theologica*, I^a-II^{ae}, Ch. XCI, art. 3.

beings endowed with reason and in those not possessing
it. In the former, the inclination to proper acts and
ends is free under the direction of the intelligence;
and opposition means infringement of the law.   In
the latter, it is governed by the force of necessity. So,
in regard to the former, the said participation is
called "natural law," and in regard to the latter, it
is termed the "necessary relation resulting from its
nature."

On the other hand, only by placing the origin of
the law in God, can "submission," which is the consequence, be satisfactorily explained.   Indeed, the
mere simple submission of one man to another would
have no meaning, unless it be something ignominious.
The submission demanded by the law presupposes
superiority in the person ordering it, and all men are
equal in their essence.[1] The difficulty is not avoided
by applying it to a multitude instead of to a man,
because the submission required by law is not of a
material but of a moral order, and therefore, the
superiority must be qualitative and not quantitative.
So it has been necessary that the eternal law respecting those participating in it, should contain the
motives by which certain men should be subject to
others, and then, the submission acquires the reason
of its dignity.   That the creature should obey its
Creator and, through His mandate, should obey
another creature is just and honourable; but there is
no distinct foundation whereby a rational being is
subject to another of the same nature. While it is true
that this nature produces rights,[2] it should be borne
in mind that it participates in the eternal law with
which God governs the world.

But man is not only a "nature." He lives in time

[1] Part II, Ch. VI.   [2] Part II, Ch. VI.

and space, he has a temporal destiny, and he attains it in a society composed of rational beings.[1] This last consideration would of itself justify the existence of human laws derived from the principle of natural law by means of its application to social reality. To this, it should be added that the other circumstances affecting man cannot help producing determinations in the order of pure nature. Logically, in this way, there arises the positive human law regulating civic acts as they are carried out in the life of society. Suárez sets forth their purpose as follows: "It is based on the fact that man is a sociable animal; his nature requires the civil life and communication with other men and, therefore, he must live uprightly not only as a private person, but also as part of the community which greatly depends upon the laws of each one."[2]

From the foregoing, let us draw the conclusions that may serve as guidance in our speculations about human law, which is what interests us directly. If all things are subject to laws of their own nature; if, among these, there are some requiring for their execution the concurrence of our freedom; if positive human law may not oppose natural law and is, as the name implies, the work of man, it must be affirmed that though laws exist which may be infringed by the wrong use of liberty, it is not for us to create them, to abrogate them or even to modify them, in so far as they are absolute. Neither the eternal law, nor the natural law, nor those laws governing irrational beings, nor even positive human law itself, inasmuch as it is a likeness of natural law, is at the mercy of the will, the behest or the opinion of men, even be they considered as an entire community. The sphere of action reserved

[1] Part I, Ch. I and Part II, Ch. I.
[2] P. Suárez: *Essay upon Laws*, Bk. I, Ch. III.

for them in the law may be still further indicated. The law, in the positive order, must regulate human acts, as before said, bearing in mind the immutable nature and changing circumstances. Respecting the former, neither man nor society imparts anything specific to the law. Natural law provides for this. Concerning circumstances, man and society add to the fitting natural principle the determinations demanded, within reason, by circumstances. Only through this addition and in consideration of it, may the law subsist or perish, be reformed or substituted. Only thus may it vary with time or place, be useful to-day and harmful to-morrow.

So we have come to establish the concept of positive human law. In so far as it contains injunctions of natural law, it is *an ordinance of reason to an end*; in respect of its circumstantial determinations, that end *is the common good* of the members of a concrete society; and finally, as a human work, *it must be promulgated by him who cares for the community*.[1] Its enunciation alone brings into striking prominence its three essential requisites. Every legal precept adopted for the government of a society must be *rational*; it must have the *common good* as an end; and it must be endowed with a moral force possessed by the *will of authority*. A rational precept without relation to the common social good will have but the appearance of a law. An irrational precept, even if, by accident, it should produce the common good, will be an injustice. A precept lacking the coercive force of authority, though it be in agreement with the common good, will be a counsel worthy of fulfilment, but not a law.

In order duly to be dictated, the legislative organ should, in consequence, be formed by three distinct

[1] St. Thomas Aquinas: *Summa Theologica*, I^a-II^{ae}, Ch. XC, art. 4.

elements: that which is the source of the rational principle, that which affords the matter of the common good, and that which seals it with the power of sovereignty. With the spontaneity of everything natural, in these words are already reflected the three institutions which, in their proper spheres, co-operate in the formation of the law in a State organized according to right: the King, his Councils and the Cortes. Furthermore, it is made quite clear that the law is not a mere act of the will. It is neither an act of the will of a man (the prince in the despotic régimes), nor of the will of an assembly (the parliament of the Liberal régime), nor of the will of the multitude (the people in plebiscitic absolutism). The mere act of the will may be irrational and unjust; but it is impossible for the law, as an ordinance of reason, to be so. So, in the order of justice, there is no difference between a command issuing from the will of a despot, from the majority of an assembly, or from the hazard of a plebiscite. All three lack the essential condition of ordinances of reason; each is a work of unipersonal or collective arbitrariness.

The idea of the *common good* is not so clear. It is evident, after what has been said about the national interest, that it is not made up of the sum of particular goods of associated persons or of the social classes of a nation.[1] Rousseau hints in vague terms, either purposely to allow equivocation or through lack of clearness in the conception, that such a name can be given to the specific good of those associated, or to a part of it supposed by the father of Revolution to have been alienated by individuals in the social compact.[2] But this is obviously unacceptable. In both suppositions, society would be a needless artifice,

[1] Part III, Ch. IV.   [2] J. J. Rousseau: *Social Contract*, Bk. I, Ch. IV.

for, the specific good of man which is its final end
being beyond the reach of human society, the latter
could hardly claim it as its own. To determine this,
what has been stated about the temporal human end
and the nature of society must be called to mind. If
the latter is characterized by the conspiracy of wills
towards an extra-terrestrial end, and if the temporal
human end consists in maintaining the tendency
imposed by that unearthly end, in so far as concerns
the present life,[1] the common good—in the social
order—will originate in the possibility first, and in
the harmonic realization afterwards, of the fact of
the spiritual conspiracy, and as a consequence of
efforts into which wills resolve within the vital order.

As the powers with which men fulfil the duties
impressing moral necessity upon their acts—and
therefore, upon those of the conspiracy—are their
rights, and the realization of the conspiracy demands
regulation of the varied co-operation afforded it,
the *common good*, essential requisite of the human law,
will consist in the consecration of the rights claimed
by social needs and in the ordering of elemental
activities towards that which, as a product of the
conspiracy, is considered social. That consecration and
this ordination bring with them, for the peoples in
which they have flourished, the consequence of the
possession of all good: temporal happiness.

If the New State aspires to be a State organized
according to right, it must not be without any of the
organic elements required by the elaboration of the
law. Neither the King, nor the royal Councils, nor
the Cortes must be absent from it. It will be said
of both that they are co-legislators with the king.
Nevertheless, on no account may it be said they are

[1] Part I, Ch. I and Part II, Ch. I.

co-sovereign with him. It was one of the grossest
ambitions of Revolution to make parliaments par-
ticipators in sovereignty in order to depose the king
immediately after, because sovereignty could not be
shared. But the King, the Councils and the Cortes
of the New State will not be so in name or in mere
appearance. A king who is not sovereign cannot
endow the law with coactive force. Incompetent
councils, with no juridical sense, with private interests
and without independence, cannot impart to the law
the element of reason. Cortes that do not represent
the country cannot feel its needs or realize the oppression in which perchance right may be found, or sense
the clashes of some social elements with others through
the absence of harmony in mutual co-operation. The
statement alone carries with it the expulsion from the
New State of the monarchy subject to sanction; of
the councils run by political parties; and of the Cortes
whose representative foundation does not dwell in the
very roots of the nation because they are not composed
of its legitimate representatives.

The mechanism of the elaboration of the law in the
New State is perceived in all clearness. Whatever be
the initiative, the law, after its presentation to the
Cortes has been authorized by the King, will be the
object of their deliberation in the form to be set forth.
Once voted, it will pass to the Council which will
consider it, not from the point of view of necessity and
convenience—circumstances that belong to the competence of the Cortes—but from the juridical and
constitutional aspect. The King will approve it or
not. In the latter case it may be reproduced before
new Cortes; in the former, it may be the object of an
appeal on the ground of unconstitutional action.[1]

[1] Part III, Ch. IV.

The State will thus be the true organ of right, for reason and not will is the source of the law. It will be the juridical regulator of social co-operation, ordering that of individuals in classes, and that of classes in society. It will be the promoter of the satisfaction demanded by social needs which will be authentically expressed; and, as a consequence, the integrator of the diverse social interests in the general interest. For all that, the State will not replace, absorb or supplant the various elements of society.

CHAPTER VII

THE CORTES

THE parliamentary régime, namely, that which constitutes the legislative organ with the more or less impure representation of political parties, set up by inorganic universal suffrage, is to-day in a condition of culpable bankrupcy. The study made in previous chapters of the principle of representation, of universal suffrage, of political parties and of the law, forejudged the conclusion which historic events, with cruel rigour, have imposed upon the several nations of the world.

To conceive, for the purpose of legislating, an organ which by its own nature, by its intimate contexture, should, in a fatal and irremediable manner, incorporate in the law, not the common good, but the interest of party, is not to draw apart from the imperfection attached to everything human, but to accumulate, from the first moment, all the imaginable contradictions of the end to be attained. To propose for the nomination of legislators a procedure eliminating in their electors indispensable elements without which the election cannot be rational, yet allowing the play of the lowest passions, the impulse of personal interest clearly antagonistic to public interest, the predominance of concupiscence, the outburst of covetousness, is not to frustrate, to oppose, much less to repress the movements of the animal part of man, but to favour them, to encourage them and even to justify them. That is why the application of the system could produce nothing but pernicious results, so much so, that nobody now defends it. Moreover, the acknowledgment of the constitutional defects of the parliamentary régime does not date from the present.

Count Romanones considers it thus: "Experience painfully teaches that such perversions, degenerations and abuses are not abnormal and remediable, but constitute *the essence of the parliamentary régime* wherewith parliamentarism constitutes a whole, because it is the necessary, inevitable and logical result of the fundamental principles of the system which, *considering the conditions of human nature, cannot be put into practice by men without becoming degenerate.* . . . Now I ask the defenders of the parliamentary régime: Do you believe there are means of preventing this eventuality? I know one that is infallible, but I believe, without any desire to offend, that it lies beyond your reach, although the means is simple. It consists solely in *completely changing the nature of man and creating a new human species.* Unless this is done, I repeat once more, these defects will subsist because they are *inherent to the very essence of the system.*"[1]

On his part, Don Santiago Alba devoted to the matter the following racy lines: "Unanimous thoughts and wills move towards the ideal—*as a perfect ideal*—of a composite representation in harmonious relation with every national force. Hence the increasing goodwill with which, as a *scientific aspiration and as the sole possible and immediate formula* for the suppression of present-day immorality, *representation by classes and guilds,* so ably advocated in Spain by Señor Perez Pujol, has been in many parts received. On the contrary, it may be assured without incurring in any exaggeration, that the number of representatives in

[1] Alvaro de Figueroa: *The Parliamentary Régime,* Ch. III.

the Cortes" (he referred to the Spanish Parliament), "more or less interested in the budgets, amounts to 150 individuals in a Chamber where the figure of 300 is very rarely reached in the number of members taking part in a division! Is the *increasing discredit of the parliamentary régime* now explained? Numbers are more telling than reasons. The success of the system of observation is legitimate. Behold the soul of a régime in a positive cipher. Behold the secret of so much fruitlessness above and so much hopelessness below: THE GREAT COALITION OF APPETITES!"[1]

In his turn Cambó contributes to the process this terrible diagnosis: "The crisis in the prestige of parliaments *is a general phenomenon* if one excepts England and the Scandinavian countries. This discredit began before the war; the war but accentuated and emphasized it. There is one fact to which I would especially draw the attention of my readers, because, to my mind, it throws definite light upon the evident crisis of the parliamentary régime in the majority of European States. The moment when the myth of popular sovereignty became a living reality was when, in many countries of Europe, Parliament lost all efficacy and fell into the greatest disrepute. Why? Precisely because the myth became a reality! CAN ANYTHING WORSE HAPPEN TO A POLITICAL SYSTEM THAN TO BE UNABLE TO RESIST THE PROOF OF REALITY?[2]

The appreciation anticipated by Azcárate may be taken as a conclusion of all these partial judgments. "On the whole," he said, "the result is that after so many efforts directed to the establishment of the government of the country by the country and *to the removal of all personal government*, THE PARLIAMENTARY

[1] Santiago Alba: *Problems of Spain.*
[2] Francisco de A. Cambó: *Italian Fascism.*

RÉGIME IS, IN PRACTICE, A NEW FORM OF THIS in which the leaders of parties are, *as it were, Cæsars and temporal dictators* taking turns in command. Maybe someone will say this is a necessary step in the transition from the old régime to the new, rendered necessary by the lack of political education affecting certain peoples, to which we would point out two things. In the first place, if this is so believed, it should be proclaimed to the whole country, for there may be reluctance to admit the possibility of a *Liberal dictatorship*" (underlined in the original). . . . "Secondly, such a manner of education is, in truth, very strange, and if we are to judge by the fruits, it also produces contrary effects, for each day the pupil becomes less apt for the life of liberty, and the tutor or teacher is daily more corrupt and more inspired by his own selfishness when exercising the eminent ministry attributed to him."[1]

There is no appeal against the sentence passed upon the parliamentary régime and upon the legislative institutions monstrously engendered by it, pronounced in moments of sincere consternation by its own votaries. Let us again turn our attention to the doctrinal foundations that have been laid down in the course of this work so as to draw from them the secret of the constitution of the legislative organ pertaining to the New State.

It has been said the the *common good* is constituted by the consecration of the rights demanded by social needs and the ordering of partial activities in relation with that which, as a product of human concurrence, is described as social. In this statement, two entirely distinct aspects may be clearly perceived. Both the consecration of a right, as a mere act, and the ordering of activitites, as a fitting disposition of the same, are

[1] Gumersindo de Azcárate: *The Parliamentary Régime in Practice*, Ch. V.

operations of the reason. Accordingly, their determination should correspond to the organic element having the duty of conveying the rational principle to the law, even when it affects the very matter of the *common good*. But rights, needs and activities that must be consecrated, satisfied and ordered respectively, refer, in an exclusive way, to social man; that is, inasmuch as he forms the diverse components of the national organism through which he suffers this oppression caused to his rights, he feels the needs that are to be satisfied, and he endures the dissensions produced by disparity in the total co-operation. Inasmuch as the *common good* is the basis of the rational operations that are to give it juridical form, it requires an organic element of specific expression distinct from that which furnishes the law with its rational principle. For this reason, such an organ is inconceivable unless formed by representatives of bodies and classes which, when studying human social evolution, were discovered as its components in the heart of society. The Cortes—under which denomination, in Spain, the organic element of the *common good* has always been known—will therefore be constituted by the representatives of the bodies and classes of the nation. Once more, at this advanced stage, it becomes manifest that the individual—in the meaning given to the term—is not an organic part of society, but is the substance of those parts integrating society. It is likewise evident that as the rights consecrated by society with exclusive faculties, are those based on positive human law, the guarantee of the *natural* rights, namely, those pertaining to man by reason of his nature and regulated by natural law, is imposed upon him just as the duty of respecting natural law, when elaborating any law of a positive character, is also imposed.

The Cortes are now constituted by the representations of social bodies and classes, and the proportion corresponding to each of their elements in the whole must be fixed. A simple consideration would appear to determine this. In a well organized State, no social interest can be quantitatively stronger than another. Assuredly, on account of differences of quality, a gradation may exist among them, but not superiority of a physical order. As the State has need of all the bodies and classes which analysis showed to be indispensable to its economy, it must prevent any one from obtaining material advantages at the expense of others, and also prevent its suffering from numerical inferiority. Besides the absence of any motive justifying quantitative inequality in the representation, one of the principal functions incumbent upon the State is precisely—as we have seen —to re-establish, should the case arise, the balance between the several interests. Hence, an equitable composition of the Cortes will not tolerate in any body or class—indispensable to the State in so far as it represents different social interests — a greater numerical strength than others. In other words, the Cortes must be formed by as many sections of representatives as there are interests represented, and in the case of aggregations not instituted by individual or social freedom, the number of representatives is to be exactly equal.

At this point, revolutionary hypocrisy again opposes the composition of the legislative organ of the *common good* with the same gesture of feigned repugnance it adopted towards that of society: the supposed encouragement of class warfare. The emptiness of the observation was made plain in the study devoted to it, and there would seem no need but to reproduce now the arguments then put forward. But there is something more to be said. If strife were the principle of the social classes, it would exist with or without a political organization based upon them. As the organic Cortes are not the fountain head of this discord, its hateful sign would likewise be impressed upon the assemblies of the parliamentary régime itself. The indication goes still further. False as the principle of class strife is, there is the extraordinary phenomenon of parliaments being gradually organized in the world as if it were true. Is anybody unaware that there are minorities, and even majorities in them that are described as a *class* in the aggressive sense of this word? Thus, as far as lies in its power, the parliamentary régime has aggravated in reality the efficacy of the false principle.

This fact enables us to point exactly to the very root of the fallacy. In the parliamentary system, *class* parties are inspired in a doctrine, the foundation of which is precisely the impossibility of conciliation of social and economic antagonisms. In the representative system there are no parties, but classes which, being social elements, pre-suppose the harmony of all in the social end. Conflict is thus taken, consciously and doctrinally, to the bosom of Liberal parliaments; and, on the other hand, the sense of possible integration of the partial interests of class in the national interest, is incorporated in the Cortes, consciously and doctrinally. There is something that widens still more the irreducible distance of separation. Class parties are not professional but practical. Pretending to defend class interest, they do not tend to the promotion of this; fundamentally, they strive to gain possession of public authority and to transform the social system. The Communist Manifesto expressed it with its cynical nonchalance: "Every class struggle," it read, "is a political struggle." So, to the mind of Marx, "the organization of the proletariat in a class," was equivalent to its organization "in a political party." In consequence, those who reject the organization of the Cortes according to the principles laid down, on the ground of the false motive of the encouragement of class warfare, reach this refinement of duplicity. They make their parliaments a battle ground in which the disjunctive principle appears indicated by a connoting sign, and they impute that circumstance desired, sought and created by them, to an institution which repudiates everything standing for irreducible dissension, both in the order of doctrine and in the order of reality.

It is time to observe, for the delucidation of concepts, that the negation of the strife of classes does not assume the inexistence of conflicts between them. Class war means to Marx, according to the explanation given by Engels—and in this sense is the phrase understood in the political and social order—the fatal fact that "since the dissolution of the ancient common property of the soil, the whole of history has been a history of conflict between classes, of conflict between exploited and exploiting classes, directed and directing classes, whatever the degree of development they may respectively have reached."[1] To put it in words more clear and concise: Marx holds that class strife is an inevitable social law because the antagonisms dividing the classes are *irreducible and incapable of being brought to any form of understanding or settlement.*

The constitution of the organic Cortes contains the fundamental condition upon which, in the practical

[1] F. Engels: Preface to the German Edition of the Communist Manifesto, 1883.

order, depends the efficacy of the doctrinal conclusion we have set up against the Socialist theory, deduced from the very nature of the classes, that is, the natural harmony of their interests, and consequently, the possibility of replacing antagonism by agreement. For this condition is none other than that the classes themselves should intervene in the making of laws that are to contain the conciliatory formula, and that in order to obtain it, they should discuss, deliberate and reflect upon the various points of view. With what authority can the efficacy of the procedure be denied by those who, from its condition of a means, have raised deliberation to the category of an end? How will the absence from their parliaments of the classes assumed to be in a hostile attitude, be justified if they seek to procure peace amongst them? Finally, bearing in mind the fact that every kind of interest is reflected in parliaments, how are laws to be made affecting certain interests of which the legislators are totally unaware? Let us affirm it emphatically. The organic Cortes is the only means of rendering accordant interests, divergent yet susceptible of conciliation, that agitate the world; of imparting to the law the element of the common good in opposition to the party interest which revolutionary parliaments take up; and of avoiding, with sufficiency, the conflicts that might arise between interests. But for greater testimony, it has been seen that the Cortes are crowned by royalty in its character of the integrator of partial social interests and the arbiter who brings about harmony amongst them.[1] Now the irrefutable affirmation has been made, let us establish its composition and procedure in the New State which we shall suppose to be instituted in our country.

[1] Part III, Ch. IV.

R—п

The Cortes, it has been said, must be formed by as many sections of bodies and classes indispensable to the economy of the State, to be composed of an equal number of representatives as there are interests to be represented. The latter will be disposed, therefore, according to the signs of classification of the former. As it is clear, by definition, that the classes promote diverse interests and that, among the bodies, the regions represent a different interest from the rest, it may be concluded that the six social classes and the regions should form corresponding sections in the organic Cortes. All the other bodies of the State (clergy, aristocracy, magistracy, diplomacy, army and navy), rather than promote the exclusive interests of their members, even if they are social interests, endeavour to defend, to safeguard and to further the public interest "directly." This common denominator requires their aggregation in one section. Finally, national bodies and corporations that do not affect any class in particular nor the State exclusively or directly, should be grouped in the last section, in which the number of representatives will vary, because national bodies and corporations depend upon individual or social initiative. In the organic Cortes of the new Spanish State, there will be, therefore, nine sections in which the representatives of bodies, classes and corporations will be assembled.

In an attempt to outline the organic Spanish Cortes it would be irrelevant to justify the figure adopted for the number of representatives, identical, as was remarked, in the first eight sections. It will be sufficient to state that it is fifty; that in its adoption, mere considerations of population have not been kept in mind although they have not been absent in the computation; that the setting for the election of the

representatives of the classes could be no other than
the region, seeing that the very fact of its existence
colours all public interests with a local sense; and that
starting from a *natural system of representation*, the most
equitable *system of election* could and should be applied:
that of proportional representation when the region
has to elect more than one representative of each class
or of the region itself. The structure of the organic
Spanish Cortes of the New State now appears in
outline. They would be made up of four hundred
deputies distributed in eight sections of fifty each, to be
called: agriculture, commerce, industry, property,
manual labour, professional labour, regions, and
State bodies. As the components of the last section
are of diverse nature, equity demands the distribution
of the number of deputies assigned to it among the
several component bodies. So, the fifty deputies of
the section will be apportioned to the five bodies
forming it at the rate of ten for each. The structure of
the Cortes will be completed by the ninth section of
national bodies and corporations in which will be
represented entities of a public character with ends
of a moral order duly allocated. These may be already
existent, or may arise from private or social initiative,
or by the public dedication of the State, eventually
reaching the figure of the deputies fixed for the other
sections.

The features offered by the Cortes thus formed stand
out so prominently and, above all, they indicate so
marked a difference from the assemblies of the
parliamentary régime, that there is little need of
excessive comment or enlargement for the appreciation
of the importance of their legislative work. Still,
attention should be drawn to one of the consequences
that the substitution of Liberal parliaments by organic

Cortes would involve. It is that the latter, by reason of their composition, would be endowed with real efficacy and would not lend themselves to the sterile consumption of energy or to the paralyzation of activities. For it is evident that if the sections represent different social interests, they must perforce deliberate separately until each establishes a collective view concerning each point submitted to the Cortes. What in Liberal parliaments was a name—the section—because it contained nothing, will be, in the organic Cortes, a reality expressing in the present social state the "arms" of the traditional Cortes. Instead of one deliberation by more than four hundred deputies, with the confusions, surprises, inconsistencies, and the impositions of empty eloquence upon tardy reflexion, there would be as many simultaneous deliberations in groups of deputies not exceeding fifty as there are sections composing the Cortes. Moreover, the unity of the problem under debate is not broken, because each section must examine it from a different point of view in harmony with the social interest represented. This leads to another far-reaching consequence, namely, that as in the organic Cortes, organic and not individual judgments will be sought, the results of the partial deliberations will establish the decisions of the sections, the integration of which will be effected, as a general rule, by the delegation of one of its members for the purpose of expounding and defending the conclusion arrived at. Thus, the very serious inconveniences of a general deliberation undertaken at the outset will have been avoided. Again, in plenary assemblies, a maximum of nine speeches with replies of the government or its delegates, and consequent amendments, would be normally the limit required for the voting of a law. Lastly, by

fixing a period of two, three or four months in which
each section should emit its opinion, in the absence
of which its conformity with the projected law should
be assumed (nothing could be more reasonable),
there would be an end to the disgraceful obstructions,
to the reprehensible procrastination and to the delay
in providing a remedy for delicate situations of national
economy.

The sections, in this type of Cortes, will be, by their
composition, real laboratories, and the assemblies,
which will relinquish everything trivial to them, will
recover their ancient splendour. Questions, interpel-
lations within matter affecting the Cortes, incidental
propositions, etc., etc., should be ventilated in the
sections, and except in the form of a resolution, they
should not be brought to the knowledge of the Cortes.
The same proceedings will apply for the purpose of
procuring the response of ministers to the call of a
deputy.

But not only by their composition do the organic
Cortes offer these advantages. Through it they also
bring about, in practice, the separation of the legislative and executive functions. The government,
indeed, has no part in their origin, for none has a
political colour, and the government does not owe its
existence to them. Nor do the Cortes, on their part,
interfere in the action of the government, for by
definition, they limit themselves to providing the law
with the element of common good. Nor, lastly, is
there pre-eminence of the government over the Cortes
nor of the Cortes over the government, because they
move on totally different planes. The extirpation of
the need of a majority from the Cortes means the
disappearance of the double consequence that either
the government shall make the majority or be made

by it, an alternative that in either of its members leads to the confusion of the specific functions of the respective organs. The solution, obvious in our thesis, was impossible in the revolutionary teaching. The organic Cortes, as they have been outlined, are inspired in certain and incontrovertible principles. But by affirmation, no people can be promised that their institution will produce an earthly paradise. The footsteps of Revolution cannot and must not be followed in promises. Truth does not fear, rather does it seek the light. No social or political régime can be perfect and free from blemish, because, as has been observed,[1] man bears within himself the tendency to evil and communicates it to everything related to his nature. Hence, the purpose of social and political institutions that will never obliterate the effects of the fall of man, is to "oppose and reduce them." The organic Cortes reduce them and do not favour them, while revolutionary parliaments aggravate them by encouraging them.

[1] Part I, Ch. II.

CHAPTER VIII

THE GOVERNMENT

Azcárate raises a difficulty concerning the proper jurisdiction of what he calls "executive power," described in the present work as "organ" of the executive function. "At first sight," he says, "it seems that every law, once made by the legislative power, in order to subsist, needs the help of the executive power whence, no doubt, the faculty of drawing up regulations has come to be considered one of the most characteristic and important of those exercised by the latter power. Yet such a conjecture is far from being true, for in most cases, beginning with the codes, almost in their entirety, the action of laws takes place without any intervention of the executive power. What happens is that besides the function implied in its denomination, it fulfils two of the most vital offices to which it owes its importance and predominance. They are *administrative* and *gubernative*. In order to appreciate the character and extent of the former, it will be sufficient to notice the contents of what is called *administrative law*, of this congestion of the modern State. . . . In order to esteem, in its just value, the *gubernative* function, it will suffice to advert to the fact that what is modestly called *executive power* has the initiative with respect to proposing laws to the legislative power, and inspires and directs the general policy prevailing in the country through the action of the party in charge of the administration. Hence it follows that given the nature of each of these functions, the *executive* is of least import, and the *gubernative* and *administrative* are the most interesting. Indeed, ministerial *omnipotence* is due to them."[1]

Azcárate would be right if the executive function of the State were limited to the publication of regulations, and if the idea of the law were restricted to the letter of the injunctions so described. But neither one supposition nor the other is correct. The execution of a law is not always carried out through requisitions of a regulated character, nor is the law itself limited to the mere expression of its letter. Any external condition without which the fulfilment of the law would be impossible, when accorded by the executive organ of the State, tends to the execution of the law, and therefore, to be disposed within the executive function. Also a regulation of social or individual activity not explicitly foreseen by the law, not infrequently of a discretional character but in agreement with it and demanded by the facts, is not, definitely, any more than an act of execution of the law. Recapitulating then, the executive function as previously defined[2] is no different from those described by Azcárate as administrative and gubernative, but it comprehends them with the regulating faculty.

This is not contrary to the truth of *part* of the conclusion stated by that politician: the existence in *certain cases* of *ministerial omnipotence*. But he is again in error when indicating their origin. It does not lie either in the administrative or in the gubernative faculties contained within the executive function, but in the very nature of the parliamentary system. A stray word from the pen of Azcárate gives us the key

---

[1] Gumersindo de Azcárate: *The Parliamentary Régime in Practice*, Ch. VI.
[2] Part III, Ch. II.

and explanation of it all. He had seen what he called "executive power" in an organ that "directs the general policy prevailing in the country through the action of the party in charge of the administration." It is clear that if one begins by including in the executive function the direction of national policy and this, significantly, is impelled by the action of a party placed at the head of the State, the party first, and afterwards the government constituted by it, both take on the quality of omnipotence. But it should be noted that the party is an element of the parliamentary régime and this will explain perfectly that when Azcárate spoke of *ministerial omnipotence*, he was giving a general character to a phenomenon that can only be produced in conditions to be found in the aforesaid political system. Removing the direction of the general policy of the country from the executive organ, thus reduced to its condition of one of the organs of the State exercising a certain function, from being *omnipotent*, it becomes a mere co-operator in the conduct of the State.

But if Azcárate went too far when raising a case that could only occur in the parliamentary régime, to the level of a general reality, he was also mistaken in presenting that régime under one form. Not infrequently, *omnipotence* is not to be found in the executive organ but in parliaments. The reason of this subversion was given when studying the functions of sovereignty.[1] In any case, the conclusion of the republican politician must be duly noted as something useful, for he makes it quite clear that the imagined balance of *powers*, the foundation of the parliamentary régime, only exists on paper. In reality, the *omnipotence*, that is, the absolutism, of one of them is the immediate result of the system.

[1] Part III, Ch. II.

The fact leads us directly to the assertion of the need in which the world stands to-day of a radical change of ideas in regard to the executive organ of the State.

From the moment when a régime makes parties into instruments of government, the conflict between the nation and its executive organ is inevitable. The nation demands that the government shall execute and that, therefore, execution shall be its characteristic function. The political party, on the other hand, requires the government's opinions to be in accordance with its own, and that the execution be subordinate to the judgment it may have formed concerning the function. This, indeed, shows the degree of exclusion of political parties from public life. It is not maintained however, that their *total* disappearance is indispensable to the good of the nation. There have always been parties and there always will be. What is meant is that they cannot act as *instruments of government*, just as it was said before that they could not be elements of national representation. At most, their existence— that of the worthy ones, of course—would be comparable to that of the philosophical schools, and their influence would be similar to the social influence of these. In this way they might exert it within the government of the nation, but not govern the nation.

It cannot be urged that the task of government being human, to govern against one's own doctrinal convictions would be unworthy of a ruler. Because, apart from the fact that the same could be said, applied to the order of justice, by those who form the judicial organ, and that the Revolution, which never experienced any scruple towards the oppression caused to conscience, imposed infamous laws upon the citizens, there is not the least analogy. The executive organ of a State which, as such, should have no opinion concerning the function it fulfils, limiting itself to execution, does not forcibly absorb the person governing. He who is not in agreement with its organic procedure may, in the majority of cases, reserve his own judgment, and should it be a matter touching conscience,he may cease to be an element of the organ.

So, only by wresting the government from the political parties, can the vices with which parliamentarism has innoculated it, be corrected. The brief synthesis which Azcárate makes of the parties proves it. "In the first place," he concludes, "those vices result in *a party administration* which, as Mingheti says, is the negation of the essence and of the end of the State. . . . Further, as the State has charge of so many services, the administrative disorder passes to all the spheres of life, and thus, instead of directing, protecting, and illustrating social and individual activity, the State is responsible for its misdirection and corruption. And as all this is done for the satisfaction of individual selfishness, or on behalf of *the interest of a political communion* . . . it happens that many seeming supporters of liberty are, as Tocqueville said, hidden servitors of tyranny."[1]

Let us record it as an incontestable truth: political parties cannot be instruments of government nor would these be created by the Cortes in the New State. When studying the functions of sovereignty,[2] it was made clear that, by nature, they were independent of one another; and this necessarily demands the inexistence of relations of dependence in the formation of their respective organs. It is also clear that if, in spite of the execution of the law being the function of the executive organ, it cannot, according to true doctrine,

[1] Gumersindo de Azcárate: *The Parliamentary Régime in Practice*, Ch. VI.
[2] Part III, Ch. II.

be set up by the legislative organ, a process of exclusion leads to the view that the executive organ must be nominated directly by the organ of sovereignty, seeing that for the same reasons as those adduced when endeavouring to localize the latter, the nation is incapable of exercising any operative act.

Thus the absurdity inherent in the revolutionary doctrine is avoided in the traditional doctrine of representation. As, according to this, the sovereignty of the nation is represented by the king and its organism by the Cortes, not the least objection can be raised to representation proceeding to the other organs with which sovereignty exercises its functions, from the organ of sovereignty itself. A government appointed by the king, when it is acknowledged that sovereignty is localized in him, cannot but represent the nation itself within the proper sphere of its function. It should be noted that representation is alsolutely necessary in every organ of the State, otherwise the actions it performs would be devoid of national character.

What in the traditional doctrine appears quite transparent, in the democratic chimera is presented enveloped in dense cloud, emerging from which is the contradictory sense of its being. With the exception of very few occasions on which the evil of the system has been displayed without the least attenuation, the members of Liberal governments—to a greater or a lesser extent, with larger or smaller restrictions—are appointed by the head of the State, be it constituted in a monarchy or in a republic. This leads inevitably to one of two conclusions: either sovereignty resides in the head of the State, thus denying national sovereignty as shared by the citizens or deposited in the parliaments, or it continues to dwell in the nation or has been delegated to the legislators, from which suppositions it follows that such governments are bereft of national representation. Both terms of the alternative equally undermine Democracy. If the head of the State is sovereign therein, the law is not the "expression of the general will" because the law must be dictated by the sovereign, and the general will, save in brief electoral periods, would not be sovereign. Moreover, if the sovereignty remains untransferred in the people, or at most, is delegated to parliaments, the authority of the governments would be without communication with the source of all power and must needs be set down as illegitimate. It is true that Revolution being a contradiction in itself, could scarcely succeed in avoiding contradictions when applying its fallacies to the governments of people.

It would not befit this work to record in detail the purport of these words in so far as they relate to the executive function of sovereignty. On the other hand, those of Azcárate previously transcribed show that to attempt the examination of what he calls "congestion of the modern State" in order to set apart what should remain from what should be extirpated, would lead to a maze of disputes. But just as it is difficult to indicate details—in works that are not monographs—it is easy to determine the *orbit* within which the executive organ of the State must act. Three texts, only two well known and of very different origin, come near to limiting its field of action. At least, they constitute landmarks that do not undergo alteration.

Campanella said: "The instruments of empire are: firstly, language; secondly, the sword; thirdly, the treasury." Maurras wrote: "Whatever nation he belongs to, man calls upon the ruler to guarantee the integrity of the territory wherein he was born, where he made his home, reared his family, where he grows old and dies. After this security, he may desire the normal multiplication of the members of his community, the progress of material welfare that will ensure or facilitate his subsistence and, indeed, the respect of the higher conditions of a common and prosperous life, those affecting custom and even those of the order of conscience, preference of good to evil and of virtue to vice, the impartiality of justice and law, the dignity of law, the honour of the country and the nation."[1] Leo XIII, in his Encyclicals *Diuturnum illud* and *Immortale Dei*, taught: "The very force of necessity requires every association or community of men to have a ruling authority *so that society be not dissolved.* . . . Each individual knows he can rely upon safe guides and leaders . . . and is conscious that others have charge *to protect his person alike and his possessions and to procure and preserve for him everything essential for his present life.*"

Social conservation, the security afforded to the associates in their persons and in their possessions, are elemental objectives that the executive action of authority may not overlook; and this requires the use of sword and treasury according to the graphic expression of Campanella. In this connection we shall treat concisely of both, after remarking that as the executive functions are of public order, the institutions representing the sword and the treasury must also be public; and that as the State has no source of activity other than those of individuals and no means distinct from theirs, the institutions representing the sword must be organized by individual effort and that of the treasury must be served by individual possessions. In modern diction, these institutions are called, respectively, the army and the public treasury.

[1] Charles Maurras: *Enquête sur la Monarchie*, p. 8.

In civil society, few institutions outweigh the army in importance. It is the arm of the law, the shield of its life, the defence of the territory, the protection of the citizen, the guarantee of national independence. To have allowed these characteristics of the armed forces to fall into oblivion is but one more reason for the restoration of doctrinal order in the matter. It proclaims—in opposition to the revolutionary error already exposed in due detail—that inequality being a law of society through its condition as an organism, it will also prevail in the army which has sprung from that society. The mere statement at once reveals the contradiction by nature existing between the army and Democracy. It matters little that life still imposes, in this political conception, the law of inequality upon the army; the fundamental idea, seeing itself duped by facts, will introduce its virus as far as circumstances permit.

If the army is a political institution, it must be national by definition; and this opposes its being constituted in a caste. It is also clear that, in case of need, nobody may neglect to contribute his military service, since every intelligent being is bound by the duty of self-preservation. But neither reason supposes equality in the social contributions of the individual, nor therefore, a universal obligation in that of the service of arms. Nature, indeed, tells us that although the military profession is not a privileged calling, vocation should inspire its exercise. But the State does not create it, much less can it be made general. Like every inclination of the spirit, it is found in the individual; like all, it affects one social group. The office of a good State is, on the presentation of this phenomenon, to observe revealing facts in order to favour and to utilize it. Only after directing the vocations presented, will it be able efficaciously to assemble around them the efforts which in extraordinary cases must be added to those resulting from vocational influence. In this regard, there is no distinction between officers and soldiers. When differences were fallaciously introduced by Democracy, it prepared in an insidious manner the destruction of the army, first giving it a false foundation so as to attack it later as an oppressive, sanguinary, degrading and parasitical institution.

Yet the professional army is not an army of mercenaries, because it would then cease to be national. It constitutes a profession; but besides the vocation necessary in every profession, its due exercise demands an attachment to the object guarded and protected, superior to that of life itself, since such sacrifice is an essential pledge of its office of defence. Only exceptionally may this circumstance concur in those who are not nationals. The fact demands nationality within professionality, and it is also the foundation upon which compulsory military service, in case of necessity, has previously been justified.

All that has been set down may be contained in this dictum: "voluntary military service in time of peace, and compulsory military education." That is, in essence, the antithesis of the revolutionary system in which military service is compulsory—it has been seen with what sort of final consequences—and military education is voluntary. It could not be otherwise, since the constitutional principles of political society governing the revolutionary system are diametrically contradictory to those regulating the traditional and Christian scheme. This does not mean that strictly, even in time of peace, the army is to be sustained solely by volunteers, because these may not come forward in sufficient number, or because the State may be unable to support in that condition the number of soldiers it requires, or because the law of compulsory education is unfulfilled. The first two circumstances are cases of necessity, and the last demands that military education not acquired outside the army shall be acquired within it. In other words: the terms of the axiom should be considered not as an inexorable realization but as a pointer that leads to the ideal.

When indicating one of the circumstances influencing the extent to which the principle of military professionality may be applied, another matter pertaining to the executive function was adequately stressed: the treasury. It has also been said that the State, which has no patrimony of its own, has no choice but to require the citizens to provide its needful resources. This necessity produces the following consequences: that the State should properly disburse the dues it is legally authorized to exact, and that within its sphere of action, it should promote the development of national wealth. The former entails the setting up of a State system of examination of accounts, and the latter a juridical regime of protection.

The natural assimilation of man—outside all organicism already repudiated—which imposes upon our intelligence the concept of society, suggests the necessary use by the State of two classes of possessions for the support of its economic existence. As in all the other orders, the human being, in the economic sphere, projects his personality towards the future. His disbursements come under two quite distinct headings. Some provide possessions of relative continuity that render service by their use, and others supply objects that are consumed, ·their service being given by their own substance. So there is nothing more logical— setting out from the aforesaid assimilation—than to affirm likewise the existence in political society of needs requiring for their satisfaction goods for immediate consumption, and of others requiring possessions not destined to that purpose.

The very nature of things prescribes, in consequence, that public finance be reflected in two different *budgets*, the term being used in the technical sense, namely, the prevision of requisite expenditure for the satisfaction of certain needs, and of the revenue that can be reckoned to meet that expenditure. One budget is qualified by resources giving service through their use, remaining in substance practically intact; in the other, they are consumed in the course of service. Although the terms are not appropriate, the first is called *extraordinary* and the second *ordinary*. It is evident that if the latter affects daily operations of the State, it must work in periods suitable to its purpose, having a year as a unit, and covering all income and expenditure bearing upon the life of the State during the operative period chosen. This consideration suggests another connected with the source of income of both budgets. The income of the ordinary budget, because it is consumed during the period it is in force, must necessarily be limited to the proportional part detracted from the annual proceeds derived from the public revenue. The income of the extraordinary budget, because it constitutes a *national asset* permitting a national economy, must be fairly distributed amongst the legitimate requirements of the individual, of society and of the State.

Three objections have been brought against the simultaneous maintenance of extraordinary and ordinary budgets. They refer to the supposed condition of their unity and that of the treasury, to the facility for meeting the deficits of the ordinary budget,

and to the danger of *inflation*. But the budget of the
State, considered as ordinary, is not its whole accountability; it is but a partial account known in commer-
cial terminology as *general expenditure*, and is included
in the complete accounts with others, among which is
the extraordinary budget. The standard type of
accountability does not imply and never did imply one
sole account. It will suffice to remark that as the
exchequer figures among the assets, unity of the treasury
must exist whatever the fortunes awaiting the budget.
Likewise, little need be said regarding the facilities
afforded by the extraordinary budget for the purpose
of meeting deficits of the ordinary budget. The
different nature of each prevents any confusion in a
duly regulated system of government. If such is not
the case, there is nothing shameful in denouncing the
damage caused by faulty direction in the working of
the ordinary budget. Lastly, *inflation* does not arise
from the ordinary nor from the extraordinary budget
in itself, but is brought about by overstepping the
limits which the nature of things assigns to the income
of either of the two budgets in relation to the annual
revenue accruing from natural wealth and economy.

If, as has been said, the public treasury is sustained
by the proceeds of private estate, the State, not only
for reasons of the common good, but also for its own
preservation, must concern itself with the development
of wealth. The normal means of promoting this, is a
policy of tariff protection. But as, by definition, it
should be solely and exclusively applied for that
purpose, such protection will only aid production on a
national basis, that is, to mobilize, to utilize, and to
transform natural resources that would otherwise be
lost. This is the only case in which the tax to be paid,
in return for such protection, by privileged producers

and in general, by the other social elements, would, did protection not exist, perforce be paid partly to analogous foreign producers, and part compensation would come from the indirect benefits rendered to priveleged production chiefly through the demand for labour.

Furthermore, the common good—in this case the nationalization of protected productions—requires the tariff margin not to have as a final object— reflectively sought and involuntarily found—the *inflation* of capital applied to protected production, but the strengthening of the same, once the legitimate benefit of the investments effected have been obtained, so that, in time, it may sustain itself in the country without tariff privilege. If the possibility of a future increase of strength may not be presumed—and permanent protection is an indication of this— protection would constitute pure loss.

CHAPTER IX

JUSTICE

ROBESPIERRE said in the Convention: "Let us acquaint the universe with our political secrets. What is our object? The reign of eternal justice whose laws have been written not in marble or stone, but in the heart of every man, even in that of the slave who forgets them and in that of the tyrant who denies them. We want, in France, to substitute morality for selfishness, probity for honour, duty for propriety, reason for prejudice; that is, all the virtues and wonders of the republic for all the vices and falsehoods of the monarchy. The democratic and republican government alone can accomplish these prodigies . . . not only is virtue the motto of democracy, but it cannot exist outside this kind of government."[1] As if it were his codicil, in his last speech he reproduced his main thought in these words: "The revolutions that, until now, have transformed the face of the empires, had as their sole object a change of dynasty or the transmission of power from one to many hands. The French Revolution is the first to be founded upon the theory of the rights of humanity and the principles of justice."[2] So came Revolution: boasting of setting up for the first time in the world the standards of virtue and of justice, and denying others even the possibility of making them their own.

[1] Lamartine: *History of the Girondins*, Bk. LIV-XX.
[2] Lamartine: *History of the Girondins*, Bk. LX-VII.

These ambitious illusions did not last long. The Revolution not only did not bring justice, but being incompatible with it, opened the door to despotism. Of a thousand testimonies verifying this—leaving aside the lamentations we hear daily—I bring forward three, by reason of their national origin. Azcárate wrote of the matter as follows: "In certain countries there is a truly singular contrast between the *impotence* of the judicial power and the *omnipotence* of the executive power. Actually, the manner of understanding and practising the *parliamentary régime*" (namely, that issuing from the Revolution, as we have seen) "has caused the judicial function to be denaturalized, and brought about the incomprehension of the nature and character of the power charged with its fulfilment; because . . . in practice it becomes subject to other powers, especially to the executive power. . . . Afterwards, abuse stresses its disadvantages, and certain encroachments, manifestly illegal, make it appear as if *right* is the least claim to the justice of the Courts *while the greatest consideration is to count upon a recommendation* from the local "boss" to the Justice of the Peace, from the big "boss" to the examining magistrate, from a member of Parliament or a Senator to a Judge of the Provincial Court, or from an ex-Minister of Justice, who is likely again to occupy that office, to a Judge of the Supreme Court."[1]

Count Romanones is the author of these very stern ideas: ". . . it is harder to find an upright judge than a perfect man; and we are so accustomed to this that we consider it an incurable disease. . . . For the evil lies so deep, and, above all, *it is so necessary a consequence of parliamentary governments* that its remedy cannot be sought in partial solutions. . . . This

---

[1] Gumersindo de Azcárate: *The Parliamentary Régime in Practice*, Ch. VII.

considerable intervention of the executive power in the judicial function, which will always exist in Cabinet governments, responds to *their need of obtaining and sustaining those fictitious and factitious majorities* that are an essential condition of their existence. In order to procure this result, to obtain supporters and votes, the Cabinet has at its disposal two unique and powerful resources: *the favours of administration and the favours of justice*; so much so that, as Guicciardini says, IN MODERN GOVERNMENTS, JUSTICE HAS TWO BALANCES: ONE FOR FRIENDS AND ONE FOR ENEMIES."[1] Nearly forty years after writing these formidable words, and embracing almost half a century of Spanish political life, the Count said: "All the circumstances of our political and social life *have caused this evil* (the exercise of government influence upon the judiciary on behalf of litigants) *to increase greatly, as may be seen in the period we are now examining* (1879-1923)."[2]

At the solemn opening of the Law Courts in the year 1922, the Minister of Justice, dwelling upon the situation of the judicial organism, said: "There was a time when, on account of the action of powerful influences for the purpose of the admission and appointment of those responsible for the administration of justice, it was frequently observed that while a case was proceeding, the parties would endeavour to acquire their goodwill, and would use every effort to ascertain who were the respective backers of those judicial officers." The acknowledgment of the evil could scarcely be more explicit and more painful. Maybe, because of this, the Minister who uttered those words attempted to mitigate them by suggestions as to the state of the public spirit at the moment when

[1] Alvaro de Figueroa: *The Parliamentary Régime*, Ch. VII.
[2] Alvaro de Figueroa: *The Responsibilities of the Old Régime*.

they were spoken; but even admitting the evil had undergone some attenuation—a supposition denied by the words of Count Romanones previously quoted —there can be no suppression of the testimony that the parliamentary régime had produced such disastrous effects in the judiciary administration that litigants looked for justice, not to the tribunals in strict accordance with law, but to the chance of the occasional coincidence of the judges and the political personage upon whom they might depend.

The high-sounding promises, the boastful over-estimation, the implacable condemnations of Robespierre, in the end, in face of incorruptible reality, became reduced to the ridiculously depraved fact that litigants in the "reign of eternal justice" would ask themselves when pleading at the Courts: "Who is So-and-So's patron?" If Revolution did not rouse our abhorrence on account of its crimes, it deserves to be derided because of its brazen ignorance. Thousands of years before it defiled the world, these grand words had resounded therein: ". . . Hear them, and judge that which is just, whether he be one of your country, or a stranger. There shall be no difference of persons. You shall hear the little as well as the great. Neither shall you respect any man's person, because it is the judgment of God."[1] "And not go aside to either part. Thou shalt not accept person nor gifts; for gifts blind the eyes of the wise, and change the words of the just."[2]

Indeed, the work of exhumation of the past has again given to us, in the face of the vacuous declamations of the revolutionary platform, the serene and solid conduct of the monarchy in the matter. Here, among many others, are four admirable precepts emphasizing

[1] Deuteronomy: Ch. I, vv. 16 and 17.
[2]   Ibid.   Ch. XVI, v. 19.

the sentiments of justice of the Kings of France—the country over which Robespierre had the audacity to presume to sit in judgment—clearly marking their persistence and continuity in the principles professed. "Be loyal and upright with your subjects," said St. Louis, "without inclining to right or left, rather to the contrary, sustain the pleading of the poor until truth shines forth." "Kings have been established," declared Henry IV, "to do justice and not to take part in the excesses of individuals." "My cousin the Duke of Luxembourg having announced to me," counselled Louis XIII, "that he purposes to prosecute the suit in which he wishes to obtain a judgment from my Parliament of Provence, I have desired to write to you to beg you to be firm so that justice be observed on this occasion as exactly as you are wont to render it to all our other subjects." "Favour," proclaimed Louis XIV, "is directly opposed to justice which is the chief virtue of the prince."[1]

What is to be said of the Spanish monarchy? . . . The civilized world, willingly or not, has had to bow to its admirable principles of judicial order. Since the Middle Ages it proclaimed to all men that "while the king does right, he should be called king; when he does wrong, he should forfeit the name of king,"[2]

---

[1] Gabriel Boissy: The art of governing according to the Kings of France.

[2] *Fuero Juzgo*, title 1, law 2. *Fuero Juzgo*, Body of Laws to which the whole of Spain was subject by the Visigothic Kings. It was anciently called *Forum Judicum* which became corrupted into the vernacular *Fuero Juzgo*. It is believed to have been drawn up by King Chindasvinto (642-652) and published by his son Recesvinto who assisted his father in kingly duties before succeeding to the throne in 652. This code was never formally abrogated, but continued to be quoted in the acts and decrees of the Cortes down to the end of the eighteenth century, being the basis of all Spanish jurisprudence. The version translated and promulgated by order of St. Ferdinand contained nearly six hundred laws tabulated in twelve books, wherein every relation of individual to individual, every obligation of subject to State, is precisely and providently defined. It may be said that so comprehensive is this Magna Charta of medieval Spain that scarcely any degree of offence a man may commit or any transaction in which he may engage, is omitted. (Translator's note.)

a magnificent statement of resistance to oppression; that "wise men also said that the emperor is the Vicar of God in the empire to do justice in temporal things";[1] that "Vicars of God are the kings each in his own realm, placed over the peoples to maintain them in justice and in truth";[2] and that "although Scripture may say that the just man falls into error seven times a day" (which revolutionary fatuity certainly did not bear in mind when judging institutions) "because he cannot yet act as he ought by the weakness of the nature that is in him, nevertheless his will must ever be directed towards good and the fulfilment of the precepts of justice."[3] How different is all this from the proclamation of "republican" justice solemnly carried out by the Second Spanish Republic!

It is possible these maxims were more than once forgotten, the very princes who so magnificently formulated them actually doing violence to them. Yet their infringement was not a *necessary consequence of the political régime* they embodied, but the fruit of the weakness of human nature. The presumptuous Revolution, not correcting but aggravating this tendency to evil, added *the cause that fatally* was to drive justice from its seat and enthrone iniquity thereon. Azcárate and Count Romanones have acknowledged it explicitly, and the text quoted by the latter from Guicciardini—that horrible text of the two balances of justice in revolutionary régimes —reveals that the evil is universal, the product of a principle and not merely of a local or national circumstance. To efface it, no partial solution—as the

---

[1] Partida 2—title 1—law 1. *Partidas:* The *Siete Partidas*, or *Seven Sections*, compiled by order of Alphonso X and published in 1258, are still the basis of Spanish common law. They were a supplement or an adaptation of the *Fuero Juzgo*, and, like the latter, covered the whole structure of society, in the abstract and in detail. (Translator's note.)

[2] Partida 2—title 1—law 5.   [3] Partida 3—title 1—law 1.

Count admits—would be sufflcient. The New State, which could not exist without justice, has one more motive to make it abominate every organization closely or remotely parallel to the political system guilty of forgetting that, deprived of justice, according to the *Second Book of Proverbs*, "peoples are wretched."

The gravity of the evil has suggested, in the agitation consequent upon the alarm raised, a false remedy that would render it still more acute. Under the pretext of safeguarding the independence of the judicial function, its definite withdrawal from the State has been proposed, thus making its organ a super-power. Having proved that there is only one political power, and that is the national power, it follows that a judicial power could not be accepted; and the idea of assenting to the predominance of a super-power of such a nature is still less acceptable. Let us insist upon what was said at the opportune moment. The judicial function is national, autarchic, and can only receive the note of sovereignty due to it within the State from the organ in which sovereignty is localized. Definitely, the judicial function is independent of the legislative and executive functions; but not of the State itself. In other words, the independence of the judicial function and of its proper organ, is independence *within its orbit* drawn by the law in accord with the nature of both.

So the way has been cleared of the obstacles which Revolution had accumulated, making continuation of the mental process in this matter impossible. How is the organ of the judicial function to be constituted? Azcárate saw clearly that "the idea of dependence which naturally arises towards the person from whom the appointment is received, will not disappear, nor can the law succeed in closing all the doors which favour will always strive to keep open." Wherefore, in his judgment, "the only remedy for the evil consists in conferring upon the Supreme Court or upon its President all the faculties to which, in this matter, the Ministry of Justice is entitled." He condenses his thought in this phrase: "Until there be in Parliament beside the *blue*[1] bench, a *red* bench where the President and Prosecutor of the Supreme Court may sit, the judicial power will not be independent."[2]

If the disease was accurately diagnosed, the remedy is inoperative. Who will confer upon the Supreme Court or upon its President the faculties which, in the judicial order, are ordinarily attributed to the Ministry of Justice? The executive organ? The Cortes? But in order to attribute anything, it is essential to possess authority for that purpose, and that would mean the consecration of the superiority of the executive or legislative functions, and therefore, the dependence of the judicial function—the disappearance of which was sought—upon one of the other two. Perhaps the basis would be the supposition that the judicial organ is constituted by direct localization by means of a transcending reality of the judicial functions, as occurs with sovereignty. But even accepting this provisionally, the judicial organ would lack, if not the function of that name, the note of sovereignty only to be derived from the person in whom it is localized. There is no other solution save that already indicated when treating of the constitution of the executive organ. It was then said, in a general way, that the sovereignty of the nation being represented in the king, there was not the least objection to be raised to the representation, absolutely

[1] In the Spanish Cortes in Madrid, the members of the Cabinet used to sit together on a long bench upholstered in blue velvet. (Translator's note.)
[2] Gumersindo de Azcárate: *The Parliamentary Régime in Practice*, Ch. VII.

necessary in every organ of the State, passing to those with whom sovereignty exercises its function—and therefore, to the judicial organ—from the organ of sovereignty itself.

The old Spanish political philosophy had discovered, with wonderful intuition, all these internal connections of the diverse organs of public authority. The Old *Fuero* of Castile considered justice as a thing natural to the lordship of the king "who must give it to no man nor let it depart from him, because it belongs to him by reason of natural lordship."[1] These words did not mean that the king was personally to administer justice, but as the Ordenamiento de Alcalá[2] lays down, he "has supremacy and royal lordship which is for the accomplishment of justice should the lesser lords fail to uphold it."[3] Thus the institution of the judges was regulated, in regard to whom "the people of old did not approve their being placed, in the temporal sense, by the hand of any other than those we shall here name: emperors and kings who have power to appoint those who are called ordinary judges."[4] So that this nomination might never imply "dependence within the orbit of the function," it was proclaimed that "the suits to be heard by them" (the judges) "let them be settled rightly and loyally as quickly and as well as they know how; *and by the laws of this book and by no others*; and that neither for like or dislike, for fear or favour given or promised to be given, must they leave the path of truth and of right."[5] Lastly, lest it be

[1] Fuero Viejo; law 1, title i, Book. I. A compilation of laws published by King Peter the First in 1356. (Translator's note.)
[2] Ordenamiento de Alcalá: Celebrated code of León and Castile promulgated by Alphonso XI (1312-1350). Translator's note.)
[3] Fuero Viejo; law 2, title xxvii.
[4] Partida 3, title iv, law 2.
[5] Partida 3, title iv, law 6.

ever understood that the appointments of judges
should be founded upon the arbitrary choice of the
king, they were required "to have the will to desire
and to love justice wholeheartedly, minding well the
good and the benefits that in it lie; that they should
know how to act as the facts demand, now with
compassion, now with severity; and that they strive
to make every effort to further the end of justice against
those who want to hinder or to oppose it."[1]

Definitely, the judicial organ derives its notes of
representation and sovereignty—like the executive—
from him who is the organ of sovereignty.   But,
besides these, it must possess other specific qualities
without which the collation of those two notes would
be totally inefficacious. Its members must know the
laws; afterwards, they must justify the possession of
that knowledge.   They must love justice wholeheartedly "minding well the good and the benefits
that in it lie"; therefore their spirit must be educated
in the cult of justice. They must have fortitude to
accomplish it; therefore the institution must endow
them with this virtue lest they be wrecked by weakness.
In other words, if the judges derive their notes of
representation and sovereignty from the king—
thereby invoking his name when their decisions are
pronounced—they should be proved honest men of
law entirely beyond any suggestion other than the
impersonality of the law. A whole world of *organic
restrictions* is discerned through the words; but none
severs the connection of the judicial organ with the
organ of sovereignty so that, at every moment, it may
be national by means of a representation derived
from the same. In the present work, it is only possible
to mention these protective restrictions. Nevertheless,

[1] Partida 3—Preamble.

it must be stated that all those safeguarding the members of the judicial body must be instituted in the New State which, finding itself freed from the invincible evil of parliamentarism, possesses the necessary conditions for their efficacious operation. Sufficiency, probity, integrity and honour in the magistracy may be furthered under the following headings: *knowledge* (competitive examinations and experience properly combined), *dignity* (judicial councils, inspections and Courts of honour), and *independence* (ample private means, and freedom from any personal influence in nomination and promotion). If the judicial function consists in the emission of the judgment merited by human acts in relation to the law, the difficulty of forming a clear and exact judgment may arise from the law itself. Intelligible laws are therefore needed. Generally, in parliamentary States, neither substantive nor supplementary laws are easy to understand. There are two self-evident reasons for this. Nothing perfect comes from the hand of man, and his work requires continued creation. Experience alone, by opposing bad faith or subtle ingenuity, indicates the indispensable reforms of what has been legislated. It demands that the legislative organ should legislate; and we have seen how, in the parliamentary régime, so natural a thing is impossible.

Taking Spain as an example, the last of the additional regulations of the civil code prescribes its own reform every ten years. In spite of the fact that four times that period has elapsed since its publication, there has never been even an attempt to carry out a legal injunction of such profound significance. There is nothing to be said respecting supplementary laws not imperatively subject to periodical reform, nor regarding jurisprudence which, with explicit laws and well-adjusted legal bodies, should be a source of light, whereas, actually, with obscure and badly-arranged precepts, it contributes to increased confusion and greater darkness.

Having repeatedly said that the function of judging is the exercise of an autarchic faculty, it cannot be surprising that in the New State—guide of a nation organically constituted—there should be different jurisdictions in the judicial sphere according as the matter is pertinent to the nation or to national elements. Nor can it be considered strange that beside these jurisdictions, yet apart from them, those of another society—the Catholic Church—should exist. The so-called *unity of jurisdiction*[1] is, in itself, an absurdity, for it does not affect the members of a *substantive* social category, but all citizens by reason of their *specific equality*. So notorious has the contradiction been, that only the very slightest effort is required to memorize the numerous special jurisdictions created by the Revolution for the purpose of protection, by privilege, of almost everybody from members of Parliament down to workmen. The difference between *privilege* and *prerogative* has already passed to the condition of a false topic. If prerogative concerns the function, and is granted to the person in consideration of the same, privilege (private law) certainly knew no other origin. Workmen, as such, do not exercise public functions yet, through concurrent circumstances, exceptional jurisdictions have been created for them.

[1] The municipal laws and the general *corpus juris* of the realm were called *Fueros*, e.g. *Fuero Juzgo, Fuero Real*, etc. In current law, the word *Fuero* is equivalent to jurisdiction, more precisely, special jurisdiction, namely, the right and obligation of certain classes of persons to be tried by special Courts of their own class. It also means that certain offences are to be submitted to such Courts instead of to the ordinary Courts. Hence *fuero militar* (military jurisdiction) *fuero eclesiastico* (canonical jurisdiction), etc. (Translator's note.)

The Revolution, which introduced into Spain the exotic conception of the unity of jurisdiction by article 248 of the Constitution of 1812, incurred contradiction, partially at least, when putting it into practice by its decree-law of December 6, 1868. In effect, it recognized, when dictating it, that the *ecclesiastical and military jurisdictions* had proper reasons for subsistence whatever the orbits that might later be marked out for them. Referring to ecclesiastical jurisdiction, the decree says that "it could not be disparaged or restricted," and that "the Church, faithful depository of the privilege, will continue to exercise it just as she received it from the hands of her Founder and as regulated by the canons." Of military jurisdiction it is said: "It will be only competent to deal with merely military offences and common faults stated, when committed by individuals of the army and navy on active service."

Persistent though the endeavour may be to seek justification for the contradiction, its existence is clear. More or less mutilated, the special jurisdictions are recognized through the necessity of Nature itself. For if there are rights and there are duties affecting generally all men, there are some only to be observed in certain aggregations or categories of men. Indeed, even common rights and obligations may appear qualified by far-reaching circumstances that require for their due estimation, adequate disposition in the judicial institution. The fact that the Revolution has been unable to evade this truth, first recognizing the jurisdictions mentioned and subsequently multiplying them prodigiously by successive impositions of the elective régime, makes further elucidations unnecessary and justifies the conclusion formulated in the matter. The distinctiveness of judicial jurisdictions is based upon the nature of civil society, upon vital circumstances under which the common right is presented, or the existence of a perfect society distinct from civil society yet made up of members of the latter. Diversity is thus authorized, but any jurisdiction not comprehended in such authorization stands condemned.

The jury, in criminal matters, is in reality a jurisdiction and is included among those considered reprehensible. Actually, there is no fundamental reason why some offences should come before a jury and others before the Law Tribunals, for the latter, in their normal function, also concern themselves with the investigation of the cases attributed to them; while, in the accused, there is no personal or substantial distinction in the matter of guilt. The jury, in its own order, is nothing more than a usurping institution as Liberal parliaments were proved to be. The proof of this is seen in the identification of the *multitude* with the nation, those appointed by the former claiming to be legitimate representatives of the latter. The monstrous fiction by which a dozen unschooled and not infrequently unscrupulous jurymen represent the nation, is to be found virtually in the revolutionary declamations on behalf of its procedure. Every reason adduced for the purpose of demonstrating the fraudulence committed when striking a balance between the multitude and the national being, is applicable—more intensely, if possible, to this case—for juries are not even empanelled by election. Similarly, the reasons previously stated respecting the representative character of the judicial body, which it derives from the organ of sovereignty, lead to the conclusion that only tribunals invoking the name of the king may lawfully claim to deliver judgment in the name of the nation. So against the justice of two balances proper to the Revolution, the New State will set up the one wherein . . . ". . . a just weight is His will."[1]

[1] Proverbs: Ch. XI, v. 1.

CHAPTER X

EDUCATION

Let us again bring to mind the phrase of Campanella: "The instruments of empire are: 1, the language; 2, the sword; 3, the treasury." The sword and the treasury have been objects of our attention.[1] It behoves us now to speak of the means of expression of thought, not in its technicality, but as a vehicle, that is, under the concept of "education." The first question to come before us concerns the organ to which the function is referred.

Revolution, which proclaimed such contradictory principles as those of equality and liberty, from the first moments paid tribute to the former by sacrificing the latter. Condorcet, indeed, presented to the Committee of Public Instruction of the Legislative Assembly a report dated April 20th, 1792, in which, while it is true that liberty is not denied, principles are affirmed whereby, shortly afterwards, it was to be totally suppressed. Very little later, in Lepelletier de Saint Fargeau, the true revolutionary thought, free from the dross of the past, makes its appearance. Robespierre accepted it and the Convention approved it in the form of a scheme for the organization of public instruction. Its spirit is contained in the following principles issuing from the words of the tyrant. A State, conscious of its authority, cannot forego any of its rights. As the State is everything, and the

[1] Part III, Ch. VIII.

individual and the family nothing, the child belongs to the State in preference to its parents. The schools, according to the plan of Condorcet, have the essential defect of not retaining possession of the children except for a few hours and of releasing them during the remainder of the time. In public instruction, on the contrary, the totality of the children belongs to the State. Everything that should make up the republic will be adapted to the republican model. Boys and girls will be educated in common, at the expense of the republic. The former, from five to twelve years of age; the latter, from five to eleven, there being no distinction or exception whatever between them. For greater equality, boys and girls will wear austere and simple uniforms, and all will be served with the same food without bread or meat. All will be submitted to identical physical education and rudimentary teaching. Boys and girls will be equally devoted to manual work; the outcome of the workshops will serve to augment, to the advantage of the republic, the mass of manufactured products.[1]

The French Republic has followed, step by step, these principles of pedagogy established by the Revolution. In this respect, the words of one of the representative men of the Third Republic, Léon Bourgeois, are important. He says: "A society cannot live in security and peace if the beings who compose it are not united, and as if voluntarily impelled by an identical prevision of life, of its destiny and of its duties. The ultimate object of national education is to give unity of spirit and of conscience to society." All the revolutionary hypocrisy comes to the surface here in this uliginous phrase. The unity of a nation through religious sentiment was combated with

H. Parigot: Revue des Deux Mondes—November 1, 1932.

affected indignation by those who were preparing
its artificial uniformity by means of the spirit of
heterodoxy. In spite of it all, the Revolution has not
hesitated, when it so suited its purpose, to adopt in
regard to education an entirely contrary form to that
definitely proclaimed on the occasion of its triumph
in the year 1789.

This apparent inconsequence will not be surprising
if one recalls its protean character, generally determined by its position with respect to public authority.
When, in Spain, the republic was not advantageous,
Revolution left us an unimpeachable testimony of
this self-interested modification of thought.   Giner de
los Rios, concealing from his unfortunate readers the
fact that it was a specifically revolutionary work,
wrote: "Since the excesses of modern centralism,
when the first French Empire reached its height,
provoked a reaction in the opposite sense, mainly
initiated in Germany, decentralization, among other
interpretations, has come to be understood in two
ways: one, according to which "to decentralize"
means to transfer functions previously performed by
the State (national) to the town or province; and
another, which understands that word to mean the
emancipation of those functions and their respective
ends from official action in any sphere, and furtherance of their constitution as social and free organisms
of life . . . These two conceptions of decentralization
. . . have their expression in the doctrines referring
to the organization of education. The old idea of
decentralization aided by the spirit of governmental
and bureaucratic symmetry, has made elementary
education municipal education. It has taken secondary
education to the province and has allotted to higher
education the splendour of the State which, never-

theless, directs and governs all three. The emanci-
patory conception, on the other hand, considering
that instruction and education are not functions of
the central State, nor of the town, nor of the province,
but of society, aspires to re-establish them with this
character. So this idea has successively created two
solutions that correspond to the two moments of its
evolution: the individualistic and the organic. In
the first of these moments, the problem of liberty of
education is expressed by the right of the individual
to undertake his studies how or where he chooses, so
long as, in due time, he satisfies such conditions as
the State may establish in order to give those studies
official status; the right to found independently,
alone or in association with others, educational
establishments of all kinds; and lastly, the right—
in another sense—of the public teacher in official
centres to exercise his profession according to his
conscience in regard to doctrine, to form and to
method."[1]

This must be made clear. Whatever truth may be
contained in the foregoing transcription of the views
of Giner de los Rios does not proceed from him or
from the Revolution; and Giner knew it, as is shown
by the very affectation with which he speaks of centralism, locating its culmination in the Empire as if
it did not originate in the Revolution. But when
Giner wrote the page quoted, with apparent equanimity and inherent refined duplicity, the weapon
forged by the Revolution for the purpose of introducing its poisonous doctrine—State education—was
not in sufficiently energetic hands for the attainment
of the efficacy at which the Revolution aimed. So it
claimed freedom of education, and as if it were a

[1] Francisco Giner de los Rios: *Education and Teaching*, p. 195.

legitimate consequence thereof, "the right of the public teacher in official centres to exercise his profession according to his conscience in regard to doctrine, to form and to method": a State education binding upon all citizens, in which the only one to enjoy freedom could be he who is paid by those who are deprived of it and who are forced to receive that teaching!

The doctrine of Giner de los Rios, wherin was formed the generation which co-operated in the establishment of the Second Republic in Spain, failed—as it was bound to do—in the very hour of its institution. Freedom of education was violently proscribed from national life. The republic sought inspiration in Robespierre and in the men of the Third French Republic, and laid down in its Constitution, in Article 48, that "the service of culture is the *essential attribution* of the State which will impart it by means of educational institutions connected by the system of *unified schools*, the teaching being secular." In Article 26, besides dissolving religious Orders whose statutes enforce, besides the three canonical vows, "another obedience to an authority distinct from the legitimate authority of the State," the Constitution prohibited all others "from engaging in trade, industry or education." Once more, under this form, the essentially anti-social and anti-religious character of the republic is clearly shown in the concrete realization of its State.

"To teach" is to communicate socially one's own thoughts. If society—as was observed[1]—is the natural condition of man, if it supposes a conspiracy for the common attainment of a good known and desired by human beings, and if social unity demands

[1] Part II, Ch. I.

the knowledge of a truth the good of which men are morally bound to attain, "teaching" is but the medium through which all this may be concretely realized. "Teaching" is, then, a natural function of human society.

By simply stating it, the problem of "State education" acquires unsuspected extent. Through mere historical circumstances, it was placed before the Christian conscience linked to the secular character impressed upon it. For the sake of clarity, these two concepts must be separated. Education may be secular even if the State does not dispense it, and it may be religious although provided by the State. The matter in dispute is only whether it is incumbent upon the State "to teach"; or if, in other words, that "teaching" is its specific function. After this statement, the only logical decision is that—saving the suppletory character referred to later—the State should not be called upon to teach, even were it a matter of religious teaching; no teaching of any kind should proceed from the State. So the question takes on transcending notes. It does not affect this or that State, Catholics or Protestants, believers or non-believers, monarchies or republics. It relates to all countries, under every political form and whatever be the religion they profess.

It is useless for States, now and again, to make a show of equanimity. It is useless to give assurances that the conscience of the child will be respected when education is in the hands of the State. Although this aspect has already been separated from the purely pedagogical consideration, the conscience of the child must be approached necessarily either in a positive or in a negative manner, by transmitting knowledge of a moral order or by depriving it of what it needs in that sphere. Education that does not reach the conscience of the child is a fraud or an immense hypocrisy. An irrefutable proof of what has just been said lies in the idea of public instruction adopted by the Convention above referred to. Another, in the persistence of revolutionary thought, has been afforded by the Second Spanish Republic when drawing up regulations to which "State education," adopted in the precepts of the Constitution, should be subject. The Director of Education who strictly forbade "all political, social, philosophical and religious propaganda" in the school, by the very same enactment in which the prohibition was hypocritically formulated, recommended teachers to "take advantage of this circumstance" (the promulgation of the republican Constitution) "for the purpose of providing their pupils with a series of lessons in which the Constitution might be the *central theme* of scholastic activity." Not content with this barefaced infringement of his own orders, the republican functionary proclaimed "that the teacher must be fundamentally an educator. He must reach the *very heart* of infantile personality."[1]

The attribution of the function of education to society implies, in so far as it is exclusive, that society must be independent of the State. For an identical reason, education must also be independent in what concerns it exclusively, of the region and of the town as political and administrative bodies. Not a few have perpetrated the gross contradiction of claiming on behalf of social rights that the State should surrender its educational powers to the regions and towns. That independence gives its real meaning to what has been called "liberty of education." This ambiguous phrase, so far as it is orthodox, does not

[1] *Madrid Gazette*, January 14, 1932.

mean that the matter constituting its object may be optionally, truth or falsehood, submission to the law or sedition, patriotism or negation of fatherland, religion or disbelief; but merely and simply that education as a function belongs fundamentally to society and not to the State. Neither does it embrace all men in relation to all subjects that can be taught, but those who have knowledge of them, for an essential condition of teaching is a previous knowledge of what is to be taught. To claim that "liberty of education" should protect the propagation and communication of untruth against the duty of *veracity* natural to every man,[1] and that it should give teaching authority to one who himself needs instruction, implies such monstrous aberrations that enunciation alone constitutes refutation.

At this point a remark suggests itself in favour of the supposed right of the State to education, founded upon its specific mission. The State, it is said, must direct men to the common good as the recognized organ of authority, and in consequence, its duty is to teach those who are directed all they should know in relation to their end. The sophism that has introduced itself into this observation is not so deep as not to be easily pointed out. It is true that social authority directs men to their temporal destiny, yet not independently of society but as its organ.[2] If authority knows the *common good*, it is not because its discovery was made in spite of society, but because authority received that knowledge from society just as it receives the necessary power for its authoritative mission.[3] It should be added that if authority directs the associated to the attainment of the common good, it does not do so as the substitute of society. It has been

---

[1] Part II, Ch. I.   [2] Part II, Ch. VI.   [3] Part III, Ch. I.

seen[1] that the matter of the *common good* was supplied
by society itself and that the specific work of the
State consisted in consecrating rights, in giving satisfaction to needs socially felt, and in avoiding the
clashes that might be produced in the exercise of
activities of a social nature.

All this is under the supposition that man only
belongs to one society: civil society with its natural
components. But it has been said[2] that beside the
civil society there existed the religious society of which
the State is not an organ. Moreover, it is clear that
the latter would be without even the motive of its
temporal mission brought forward to justify "State
education," in everything concerning the religious
order, even in the natural category. August words
confirm this conclusion with their supreme authority.
"In this proper object of her educational mission,"
Pius XI has said in his Encyclical on Christian education, "that is, in faith and morals, God himself has
made the Church sharer in the divine magisterium
and, by a special privilege, granted her immunity
from error; hence she is the mistress of men, supreme
and absolutely sure, and she has inherent in herself
an inviolable right to freedom in teaching." By necessary consequence, the Church is independent of any
sort of earthly power as well in the origin as in the
exercise of her mission as educator; not merely in
regard to her proper end and object, but also in
regard to the means necessary and suitable to attain
that end. . . . And this must be so because the Church,
as a perfect society, has an independent right to the
means conducive to its end, and because every form
of instruction, no less than every human action, has a
necessary connection with man's last end, and there-

¹ Part III, Ch. VII.   ² Part II, Ch. II.

fore cannot be withdrawn from the dictates of the
divine law of which the Church is guardian, interpreter and infallible mistress. This truth is clearly
set forth by Pius X of saintly memory: "Whatever a
Christian does, even in the order of things of earth,
he may not overlook the supernatural; indeed he
must, according to the teaching of Christian wisdom,
direct all things to the supreme good as to his last end;
all his actions besides, in so far as good or evil in the
order of morality, that is, in keeping or not with
natural and divine law, fall under the judgment and
jurisdiction of the Church."

It is the family society that gives life to man, and
when he is born, takes him to its bosom. Still more,
when he emerges to life man would perish without
the cares which the family naturally affords him. If
he is deprived of them, they must be supplied to him
although, within their nature, no improvement or
substitution by others of a different lineage, can be
feasible. One cannot entertain the slightest doubt
about this universal fact: the family is primarily constituted for the training of the child.

But this by no means signifies that the family is not
to avail itself of means not within its own powers in
order to procure that formation in a normal and
regular way. In formation, the idea of preservation
is implicitly understood, and it would be nonsense to
maintain that parents should themselves medically
attend their children in the diseases from which they
may suffer. To train a child means, fundamentally,
the responsibility of the accomplishment of the
attempt; nowise does it imply the necessity of having
within oneself every means required for its realization.
Let us dismiss once for all the stolid allegation, so
fully broadcast, that the function of education cor-

responds to the State because the family has no knowledge of the matter it must contain. Does the State,
perchance, possess the knowledge? In order to educate,
does it not have recourse to the same teachers as those
called upon by the family?

Moreover, that responsibility for the training of the
child is firstly ascribed to the parents because, without the cares of the family or the analogous ones
supplied in its default, the rational nature of the
child upon which the instruction to be received is
indispensably conditional, could not possibly be
awakened. With unparalleled impassibility, those
who sustain the absurd thesis mentioned above,
entirely disregard what constitutes the inevitable
antecedent of the procedure of the teacher. What
would the latter make of a mass of flesh with a purely
animal life? This transformation of a being, intelligent by the exercise of its spirit, is slowly brought
about every day, every hour and every moment by
the action of the family. "The child," it has been
said with singular relevancy, "thinks *essentially* in its
early years as an instrument of paternal intelligence.
Now, being incapable of thought without metaphysical and moral ideas, unable to possess these
without language, or to make use of language without
paternal society, whence could the child set out into
the paths of the intelligible world, if the understanding of the father had not infused into it the first
thoughts, thus quickening an intelligence that lay
inert? That the child should begin to think with the
thought of the father is, therefore, a law of Nature."[1]

Eminent confirmations of this doctrine are found
in the Encyclicals of Leo XIII and Pius XI. "The
children are something of the father," says the former

[1] Taparelli: *Critical Examination of Representative Government*, Part I, Ch. VII.

in *Rerum Novarum,* "and, as it were, an extension of the person of the father; and to be perfectly accurate, they enter into and become part of civil society, not directly by themselves, but through the family in which they were born. Therefore, the father's power is of such a nature that it cannot be destroyed or absorbed by the State, for it has the same origin as human life itself." "By nature," Pope Leo defines in *Sapientiae Christianae,* "parents have a right to the training of their children but with this added duty: that the education and instruction of the child be in accord with the end for which, by God's blessing, it was begotten." "We have," declares Pius XI, in *Christian Education,* "two facts of supreme importance: the Church placing at the disposal of families her office of mistress and educator, and the families eager to profit by the offer and entrusting their children to the Church in hundreds and thousands. These two facts recall and proclaim a striking truth of the greatest significance in the moral and social order. They declare that the mission of education regards before all, above all, primarily the Church and the family, and this by natural and divine law, and that therefore, it cannot be slighted, cannot be evaded, cannot be supplanted."

The complement of the family and the product of its natural evolution, as previously laid down,[1] is civil society. Within it, therefore, must reside the complement of the educational action of the parents and the deposit of the means they need for its consummation. The character of the formula of social contribution in the matter of education is shown to us by Spanish tradition in those immortal precepts devoted to it in the second *Partida.* "Study," reads

[1] Part II, Ch. II.

the first law, title XXXI of the said *Partida*, "is the union of teachers and learners set up in some place with the will and understanding to acquire knowledge." In the sixth law of the same title the concept is extended in the following terms: "The wise men of old forbade councils or brotherhoods of many men to be set up in the towns and kingdoms because more evil than good issues from them. But we hold just that teachers and learners may do so in general study because they meet with the intention of doing good, and they are strangers to the places of parties."

Nothing could be plainer. Society participated in the educational work complementary to the family community, not through State institutions pertaining to authority in office, but under the form of corporations created by the application of the general principle of sociability to a particular end. The Spanish university with all its exuberant growth of complementary foundations, sprang from social initiative, not from State imposition, and although the State regulated it in the juridical order, like everything else coming under its action, it respected scrupulously the autarchic life evolved within the proper orbit of that institution.

To affirm that education is a social and not a State function by no means implies that the State has no rights in the matter. It has been remarked before that in the attainment of the *common good* the State had a definite task to fulfil: the consecration of rights, legal satisfaction of needs, co-ordination of activities. Social action would be futile in the matter of education, were it not the object of juridical consecrations, of legal provisions for the remedy of needs, of measures for the furtherance of peace and security, and for the proscription of sedition and disorder. A most extensive field is opened to the zeal of authority without need of trespassing upon the territory assigned to society in the matter of education. Furthermore, it is entitled to exercise the suppletory function which has repeatedly been alluded to during the development of this subject. "It also belongs to the State," proclaims Pius XI in the Encyclical quoted, "to protect the rights of the child itself when the parents are found wanting either physically or morally in this respect whether by default, incapacity or misconduct." Nothing need be said—so clear is the right of the State in this aspect of education— of the educational process exclusively affecting the *civic* order. Without contradicting the higher standards of the formation of *man*, the State regulates, by its own right, the education required by the relations the citizen must bear to it.

Liberty of education, so understood, is vital to man. If oral education—that of school and university— is the function of the State, and therefore, its monopoly, there is no reason why the same should not apply to written education which is constituted by the Press and by books. It is useless to protest against the conclusion. It is useless for revolutionaries to attempt to denaturalize it when placed before them. It is seen in the antecedent like the image in a mirror.

CHAPTER XI

NATIONAL ECONOMY

THE Treasury, the third instrument of empire, already examined in its relation to the executive organ of the State, has a fundamental aspect that cannot be passed over in silence. Its origin lies in national economy, and only with proper knowledge of this, can it be adequately constituted. It is therefore expedient to give a clear idea of the economic order as the foundation of public finance.

The most elementary observation reveals in the human being privations creating needs for the satisfaction of which the exterior world must be sought. Yet Nature does not offer the means of appeasing them in the same way. Some, like the oxygen of the air, water, and certain matter of a spontaneous vegetable kind, are given without any resistance, and man makes them his own with no appreciable effort. Others, like the basic elements of food, habitation and clothing are wrested from Nature by a more or less onerous application of human activity. This being of a rational character, even the functions of the animal order wherewith it is exercised, will be distinguished by the same note which may be defined in the one word *producer*. This is equivalent to saying that man not only provides satisfaction for his needs with the means afforded to him by Nature, in the state in which they are found, but also by

modifying them, combining them, and transforming
them by his labour.

Nature and labour are, then, the two factors of
production; they are completed by a third. It has
been said before that society is a natural condition of
man. If he is naturally sociable, the function of
production must be fulfilled in society. Marx was
right when, accepting—perhaps unknowingly—the
dictates of Catholic philosophy, he wrote that "the
individual, isolated hunter and fisherman with whom
they begin"—referring to the economic investigations
of Adam Smith and Ricardo—"belong to the undiscerning imaginations of the eighteenth century."[1]
With law and labour as active factors, and with society
as an atmosphere and natural multiplier of his efforts,
man produces the objects that give satisfaction to his
needs.

But as he is a rational being, his labour will be
influenced, on one side, by the knowledge he pro-
gressively acquires of the principles and laws of
Nature, and on the other, by the professional habit.
As he is sociable, the result of his endeavour will be
affected by the division of labour, the co-operation of
activities, the concerted direction towards the end
sought, and the locality. Finally, as he possesses the
sense of the relation of a means to an end, and in
Nature, besides the material of production there exist
forces applicable to the same, he may dispose of natural
energies which, by means of appropriate artifices,
exceed human potency in a fabulous proportion. So
the productive process is completed. Land, labour
and society are its essential factors. Habit, division
of labour, co-operation, the directive function,
locality, machinery and capital are the means and

[1] Charles Marx: *Criticism of Political Economy*, p. 306.

conditions of the application of human industry to Nature and of increasing the output of production. Whence it is inferred that all economy excluding any of the factors, conditions and means just stated will be at least deficient. It is not surprising, after what has been said, that neither the physiocratic system of Quesnay, nor the Liberal and Socialist economies of Adam Smith and Marx respectively, have given satisfactory results. Quesnay held that wealth is produced by the land alone; Smith attributed this power to labour, while Marx made this factor supreme. The traditional school teaches that wealth is the social result of the application of the industry of man to Nature in the conditions and with the means enumerated, for the satisfaction of human needs. This quality of things is termed *utility*, which springs from its *relation* to man and not simply to Nature or to labour.

From the foregoing it is inferred that the wealth obtained may not belong to one alone of the factors or means taking part in production. "What is the first consequence?"—asks Mella.[1] "That of the harmony of classes and not of place; reciprocal dependence; solidarity amongst them." Again he inquires: "What is the second? There is no right *to the whole product of labour*, because all categories of labour, all classes are collaborators in any work, all have a share in that work. . . . Imagine, gentlemen, a worker who, after much sacrifice and thrift, succeeds with his small capital in acquiring a piece of land that is a wilderness. He purchases a few machines and some seeds, and transforms and cultivates the soil. That man, feeling satisfied, says: 'The savings from my personal labour have enabled me to buy a piece of barren land. I

[1] Juan Vázquez de Mella: *Complete Works*, Vol. XII, p. 327.

have contrived to buy the necessary tools and seeds, and, thanks solely to my own efforts, I have transformed this unfruitful ground into fertile land. It is all the exclusive result of my work. I alone have done it.' But several persons who have not cultivated the land can challenge that statement. The priest, in the name of ethics may say: 'I have encompassed your land with a barrier of respect and duty. I have inculcated in your own mind and in that of your family the true spirit of the precepts of the Decalogue which lives in your neighbours. Without that wall of moral duties, the fences of your farmstead would have fallen to the ground.' The representative of public health might say: 'I have saved you from an epidemic, from sickness. To this immunity I have afforded you is due your continued ability to cultivate the land.' Those responsible for the protection of labour might urge: 'We have prevented litigation by which greed sought to ruin you.' The delegates of material authority, of constraint, might add: 'Without the uniform of the civil guard, without the rifle which marks the radius of action ensuring your rights, your fruits would not be safe even in your granary.' 'We have all worked for you, though you may have worked for us. You give us food with your labour; but we have given you protection and perfection with ours. Without it, your efforts would have been vain, because before you cultivated, before you laboured, there was a close solidarity, a bond of brotherhood between these hierarchies of labour which, together and in agreement, have collaborated in that work which you considered exclusively yours.' "

The subordination of economy to government, to ethics and to religion is fully apparent.

As man labours in society, of which authority is the

essential attribute, the temporal human destiny being attained in the nation whose authoritative organ is the State, there can be no doubt about the evidence of the subordination of economy to government. Without peace and without justice, nobody can work, and peace and justice do not spontaneously arise in the world. Their establishment is the exclusive mission of the State, and they will not be established unless the State adjusts its constitution to the natural laws of the political order, which were not born of the good-will of those who govern and those who are governed. When the essential conditions of labour are absent, there can be no return for two reasons. In badly governed countries, it is indeed notorious that unrest robs industry of its fruits, because there is no proper organization, and because the worker finds himself obliged to be his own policeman.

The coherent and stable political constitution determines and demands the moral law as the law of labour. It is so determined because the administration of justice is the exclusive mission of every State, and justice is part of the moral law. It is so demanded because man is a moral being, and his activity, which is unique, cannot be dissociated from ethical considerations in the economic or in any other order. It is possible to conceive a perfect organization of production, from a technical point of view, based on slavery. Nevertheless, sooner or later, an economy so established would give way in all its parts and the social catastrophes would sweep away every economic advance that had been secured. Nor must it be forgotten that the wealth acquired must be the object of distribution among those who in social solidarity produced it; and that it is perforce regulated by principles of morality.

Man being, as it was said, naturally religious, his activity in the economic aspect will be likewise subordinated to the religious law, which exercises an eminently positive influence in economy. Applying economic activity to Nature, the work of God, it will, of necessity, be subject to the ordinances laid down by the Creator for that application. Man, in consequence, must not take a single step in the economic order without first interpreting the divine commands; and once interpreted, humbly and submissively, they must be strictly adhered to. All protest and evasion are useless; indeed they are distinctly inconvenient to national economy.

This subordination of economy to government, to ethics and to religion does not ignore the self-existent character of economy as a science. It contradicts at once its absolute independence and its hegemony over the others. The material needs of man, distinct from the other needs affecting his life, are the proper object of economy. That this is regulated by permanent laws is certain, since whatever the circumstances may be, those needs have always a common substance and are satisfied by means fundamentally identical. Neither the individual nor his essence varies; neither does the nature of needs nor that of the means of satisfaction undergo change. Without food, without habitation and without clothing, man would not live. The sum of these laws determines the proper orbit of economy and, therefore, fixes its substantiality.

The existence of natural economic laws does not assume their identity with physical laws. The latter are independent of man and act irrevocably; the former have man as agent, and he may infringe them although subject to stern sanctions. Neither Quesnay's physiocrats nor Adam Smith and his school held this view. "It is the essence of order," Mercier de la Rivière has said, "that individual interest be not separated from the common interest of all, and this is attained under the régime of liberty. The world then moves of itself." "In the body politic," wrote Adam Smith, "the wisdom of Nature has happily adopted ample precautions for remedying many of the ill effects of the insanity and injustice of man in the same way as it has taken others in the body physical for repairing the injuries caused by indolence and intemperance." "I believe," affirmed Bastiat, "that evil is limited by good and provokes good, while good cannot be converted into evil, whence it follows good must finally predominate." "*Laissez faire*" was the practical conclusion of these doctrines which, in concert with Socialism, have dragged the world into the abyss where it labours to-day.

If economic Liberalism made economy independent of man, Socialism made it superior to him. Both fallacies were to coincide in what is the end of every error in the social order: complete social derangement. "My investigations," wrote Charles Marx, "obtained this result. . . . In the social production of their existence, men enter into certain necessary relations independent of their will. These relations of production correspond to a given degree of development of their material productive forces. The sum of these relations of production constitutes the economic structure of society, the real basis upon which a juridical and political superstructure is raised, and to which determined social forms of conscience correspond. The manner of production of material life governs the process of social, political and intellectual life in general. It is not the conscience of men that determines the reality. On the contrary, it is social reality that determines conscience. At a certain stage in its development, the productive forces of society become contradictory to the existent relations of production. . . . An era of social revolution then opens. The change brought about in the economic foundation, more or less slowly or rapidly, subverts the entire colossal superstructure."[1] Here is dogmatism upon facts and things of the natural order, fatalism that is contradicted by the appeal to force for the purpose of attaining objects,[2] and the sombre slavery of man to economy. How could they fail to be other than the most efficient co-operators of the dogmatism, the fatalism and the serfdom which under apparently contrary forms had been heralded by economic Liberalism?

It should be remarked that the accordant conclusion which, while maintaining the substantiveness of economy, subordinates it to superior orders of truths, is due to Catholic philosophy. The defence of Catholicism, therefore, is not only an undertaking required for the salvation of our own souls; our rights of citizenship equally demand it. In this mind, we shall study the third factor of production: labour. The other two were opportunely investigated.

Human perfection is not that offered to our observation under muscular tension. It is something higher. In any of its forms, the domination of man by matter is manifest. There is no toil without pain or sorrow. Yet, notwithstanding that mark of bondage weighing upon humanity, there is nothing in the world that can so elevate and ennoble man, because its end is the

[1] Charles Marx: *Criticism of Political Economy.* Preface.
[2] "Communists do not descend to disguising their opinions and their schemes. They openly proclaim that their purposes cannot be attained except by the violent overthrow of the whole traditional social order. The directing classes must be made to tremble at the thought of a Communist revolution." (*Communist Manifesto.*)

domination of matter by him. What is, then, labour
in reality? Is it a badge of servitude or is it a means
of human dignification? For the purpose of unravelling
the mysteries of property, we were obliged to turn to
Revelation. We are now indebted to it for the key
to the contradiction that labour seems to offer. If
property differs through the manner in which it is
exercised in the two states, before the Fall and after,
in which mankind has lived, it must be attributed—as
we have seen—to the fact that human activity in the
latter state was characterized by weariness and pain
which were absent from the former state. This
explains how labour, in itself, ennobles, but in the
pain it gives, is obnoxious; in its exercise, man appears
subject to matter, and in its end he finds his own
dignification.

It follows immediately from this that in labour there
is something more than a purely economic aspect.
Being a means by which man makes himself perfect,
it implies, evidently, a moral duty, for everything
helping him towards his destiny is such. The influence
of this aspect of labour in production cannot be more
exalted. When he who works feels the ethical
emotion, he yields fruits utterly different from those
of the worker who, in his task, seeks exclusively the
acquirement of what is needful for his subsistence or
for morbose satisfactions. If he not only does not see
the moral aspect of his work but associates with it
sentiments of hatred, the disastrous effects of this state
of mind in the economic order are better not related.

Besides a moral obligation, work is a social duty.
It is so in a double sense, because in production—
social in character, as already stated—man must
avoid being a burden to his fellows, and because that
character seals and qualifies the economic relations

generating mutual duties. There is, therefore, no cruelty in the vehement words of Saint Paul which audacious irreverence has modified, giving them a Socialist flavour: " . . . if any man will not work, neither let him eat."[1] Work, in its aspect of social duty, leads to the doctrine Mella called "integral labour." It is obvious from previous remarks about the production of wealth that types of labour, very different from the purely economic, co-operate in the result, which will not be achieved without the exercise of activity of a moral order, of protection of health, of legal protection and of coactive protection. But apart from this, within each of these forms of human activity, there is another gradation of labour. "While it is true that the kind in which muscle has a more decisive participation does not cease to be influenced by reason, it is termed *muscular* or *manual* because there is nothing spiritual in it except that which is necessary for it to be described as human. Moreover, as man creates organs of labour through his knowledge of the relation of means to an end, there must exist also a *mechanical* form which assumes another anterior and superior, the *technical;* and this implies another, even higher in the scale, which is that of *scientific application* which, in turn, required *instruction,* which took its principles from *invention.* So, from that lowest form of work where least intelligence abides, another is reached resplendent with the light of genius in the great inventions that attend the birth of every industry. . . . All these categories of labour have an intimate link of interdependence . . . which shows that there can be no intellectual work without material work, and no material work without intellectual work. Withal, neither could endure if the work of protection

[1] St. Paul: 2nd Epistle to the Thessalonians, II-III, v. 10.

and perfection did not exist."[1] So labour has a *social function* forgotten by many who with unreasonable zeal exaggerate that of property.

Adam Smith did not detect this link of interdependence in the various categories of labour. A prey to the purely material aspect of production, he sundered them in barbarous fashion, striving to isolate economic activity from all other forms of human exertion. "The sovereign, for example," he wrote, "with all the officers both judicial and military who serve under him, the whole army and navy, are so many unproductive labourers. They are simply the servants of the public, and are maintained by a part of the annual produce of the industry of the people. Their service, however honourable, however useful or necessary it may be, produces nothing for which an equal amount of service can afterwards be procured. The protection, security and defence of the commonwealth, the effect of their labour in one year will not purchase its protection, security and defence for the year to come. In the same class must be ranked some of the gravest and most important and some of the most frivolous professions: churchmen, lawyers, physicians, men of letters of all kinds; players, buffoons, musicians, opera singers, dancers, etc."[2] Actually, those sentences contain such aberrations against human nature as the inexistence of solidarity among men, the parasitism of those who do not work manually, and the insignificance in the economic order of every kind of brain work. Can it be wondered at that Socialism should condemn the *bourgeoisie* out of its own texts? What authority is left for lamenting that value is placed upon the sweat of the workman in produc-

[1] Juan Vázquez de Mella: *Complete Works*, Ch. XXII, p. 327.
[2] Adam Smith: *Wealth of Nations*, Bk. II, Ch. III.

tion, and not upon the *utility* discovered by intelligence through the medium of its spiritual labour of invention?

But the opposite error to which Proudhon, among others, gave form, must also be avoided. What in Vázquez de Mella contained an orthodox import that could only be the exact meaning is, in Proudhon, a misconception. He also asked himself: "Who would be bold enough to say: 'I produce all I consume, I need nobody'." But instead of answering his own question like the traditionalist master, saying: "there is no right to the *integral product* of labour because all classes participate in it," the great deceiver proclaimed that "this undisputed and indisputable fact of the general *participation* in each species of products *causes all private productions to become common property*."¹ With these identifications of different and even contrary concepts has Revolution shaken the world!

Man's conduct in production must not be confused with the part played by him in society. What was called forth by another motive should be recalled here. In man there is a principle of operation upon which depend all his powers, and so, the work accomplished directly by these is the work of an individual person. But society, which does not constitute a physical being but a moral one, has no proper operative principle. For this reason, what is the work of man cannot be attributed to society although by supplying conditions for production, in one form or other, it may *participate in the product*. This can never become *common* in the sense of possession although it may be *shared* by several. In regard to the product, there is collaboration, joint participation, solidarity. There is no identification in the operative principle nor the absorption of it by society.

¹ P. J. Proudhon: *What is Property?*

One may now proceed to examine human labour under the same aspect as it was exclusively considered by the Socialist and Liberal schools, namely, the economic aspect. The products obtained with the application of human exertion contain materially a part of physical nature but not a part of the activity of the worker. In a piece of moulded clay, the brute matter of which it was formed will always be found, but never the effort spent in moulding it. This did not enclose itself in the product like matter; it left an impression, "a trace of the person." The fruits of economic human activity are therefore outside personality. They do not contain it nor do they exhaust it. Production evolves its products entirely separated from economic activity, while the latter is united with the human personality.

Hence are derived two far-reaching consequences. The first—a confirmation of what was said above—is that prior to all economic relation, to every economic fact, the concept of human personality is discovered, to which modes of production and economic relations must be subordinated, for the laws of labour are principles of that same personality. The second is that what is said of the fruits of production cannot be said of the energy of labour. This, in fine, IS NOT A COMMODITY, as the Liberal and Socialist schools jointly maintained; the former by submitting it to offer and demand, the latter by assessing its worth coequally with "the value *of the beasts of burden* by the food necessary for their upkeep."[1]   No words can describe such brutality!

[1] Charles Marx: *Capital*, Vol. III, p. 427.

CHAPTER XII

THE NEW STATE

No fundamental point seems to have been omitted in the investigation of the State which should supersede that brought into being by the Revolution, and when approaching its completion, our feelings are similar to those of Chesterton, the great English paradoxist. He tells us in his discerning and joyous *Orthodoxy* that although saturated in his first period by all the anti-Christian lies of sceptic literature, such profound doubts had arisen in his mind that he decided carefully to analyse the arguments of a rational order with which sectarianism opposed Christian dogma, and that having done so, he succeeded in creating a philosophy of life for his own private use. He then experienced a keen desire to compare the principles which had brought peace to his soul with those others that are the rational basis of Christianity, perfected and illuminated by the supernatural. With emotion he observed that all he had discovered, as something new, had been preached to mankind by the Christian religion for nineteen centuries. So Chesterton becomingly compares himself to a pilot who, having wrongly set his course, might imagine that during the night he had discovered a new land in the Southern seas. The coming of dawn, exposing the error, reveals old England, discovered many centuries before in the waters of the North.

In this study of the New State, our experience has been exactly the same as that of the English paradoxist: we have discovered that the New State is no other than the Spanish State of the *Reyes Católicos*.[1]

[1] Ferdinand and Isabella.